Counter-dependency:

THE
FLIGHT
FROM
INTIMACY

JANAE B. WEINHOLD, Ph. D.
BARRY K. WEINHOLD, Ph. D.

CICRCL Press

CICRCL PRESS
A Division of the Colorado Institute for Conflict
Resolution and Creative Leadership,
A Colorado, non-profit, tax-exempt corporation

**For information about the Weinholds' workshops and
programs or for ordering information about this book,
write to: Janae and Barry Weinhold
330 West Uintah St., Suite 171
Colorado Springs, CO 80905**

Names and identifying circumstances used in the case examples in this
book have been changed to insure confidentiality of client case material.

This book is manufactured in the United States of America.
Typing: Shea Richland
Cover design: Ann Kircher.
Editing: Edward Kenesky and Jack Fine.
Printing and binding: Johnson Printing, Boulder, Colorado.

This book is printed on acid free, recycled paper with soy-based ink.

Published by CICRCL Press, a division of the Colorado Institute for
Conflict Resolution and Creative Leadership, 330 West Uintah, Suite
171, Colorado Springs, CO 80905.

Weinhold, Janae B. and Barry K.
Counter-dependency: The Flight From Intimacy.

ISBN 1-882056--00-0

Foreword

Counter-dependency is the untalked about polarity of co-dependency. One reason many severely co-dependent people go without treatment is the failure to focus on counter-dependency. Many lonely, agoraphobic, rebellious, sexually-addicted people are counter-dependent. Most of us who define ourselves as co-dependent, exhibit some counter-dependent behaviors.

We need this book to fill a gap in our understanding of co-dependency. The Weinholds are experts in this field. I recommend their work as having the highest integrity. This is a crucial addition to the literature on co-dependency.

John Bradshaw, Author of
*Homecoming: Championing
and Reclaiming Your Inner Child*
and host of nationally televised
PBS series

Contents

INTRODUCTION

"I have never known a patient to portray his parents more negatively
than he actually experienced them in childhood, but always more positively—
because idealization of his parents was essential for survival."

Alice Miller
For Your Own Good

It has been a long day. I have been struggling with the
organization of my doctoral program, with orienting myself in a
new life in a strange city and with worrying about how I am going
to support myself financially during the next two or three years.
Ordinarily I can talk myself out of my fears by using my well-
practiced "be strong and act tough" program. Tonight, however,
I am feeling overwhelmed as I realize the magnitude of the
commitments I have made by marrying Barry and agreeing to
become a full partner with him. I am afraid I will fail. I feel little
and vulnerable. I go downstairs to find Barry.

He is watching the sports news on television. When I sit down
beside him he barely notices that I am there. I sit quietly for a few
moments, hoping he will notice my fragility. When he doesn't, I
tell him how tired I am and ask if he is ready to go to bed. He says
he will be there in a few minutes, if I want to go ahead.

I go upstairs and get into bed, waiting for him to come. In the
dark my wall of toughness crumbles and my unspoken fears begin
to consume me. I curl up in a little ball and start to cry. It is a half
hour before Barry comes to bed. By that time I have gone deep
inside myself, feeling abandoned and hurt by his delay. When
Barry gets into bed I move over onto my side and pull away from
him. He immediately knows that something is wrong and comes
toward me. He asks empathically what is wrong.

By this time I have converted my unspoken fears into anger at
Barry for not noticing my needs and for not hurrying to bed to take
care of me. I try to make him "bad" by telling him he is

unsympathetic, insensitive and unavailable when I need him. I begin to lash out at him about how awful he is and forget all about what I originally wanted from him. He continues to talk softly to me, trying to get to the bottom of my anger.

My anger now has totally lifted me out of my fears and my vulnerability. In the strength of my anger I hurl one last insult toward him and leap out of bed. I put on my robe and slippers and find a blanket as I head into the living room to sleep on the couch. I lay down and pull the cover over me in righteous indignation and try to sleep.

The solitude feels familiar. It reminds me that I am the only one I can count on in my life. No one has ever been there for me when I really needed him or her. For several minutes I go through my list of lifelong hurts. The steam of my anger and resentments finally cools and all I feel is the pain of isolation.

I begin to realize that even though my behavior feels familiar and justified, it doesn't get me what I want. What I really want is to be close to Barry and to be comforted by him. The next moments are some of the most difficult of my life, for in them I understand that I have choice. I can choose to let down my wall of resentment and bravado and let him see who I really am underneath it. Or I can keep up my wall and set in motion another doomed relationship. It is difficult to acknowledge my pattern of isolation and abandonment, and the difficulty I have in revealing my wounds and vulnerability.

In my first marriage, my husband seemed distant and unavailable. I was usually the one who pursued him and played out the part of the co-dependent partner. Barry, however, is very available. I see now that his desire for closeness and his availability as a partner is forcing me to look at my own fears and resistances to intimacy. The realization that I am now behaving like my ex-husband in my relationship with Barry shatters some illusion I have about myself. I feel ashamed and vulnerable.

From some deep part of myself I feel a push toward wholeness and hope for a new life. This helps me gather my blanket and return to the bedroom. Barry is still awake. I ask him if he will help me sort through this episode. He is still hurt about the way I yelled at him and made him bad, but he, too, says he wants to be close. Out of our mutual commitment to make this relationship work, we begin to unravel the pieces of the conflict.

What I have come to understand is my lifelong pattern of looking good and appearing strong in the midst of crisis and traumas: the emotional abuse and abrupt abandonment at eleven months by my mother; her suicide when I was twelve; her homicide of my brother when she committed suicide; my abusive first marriage; my divorce; and my decision to venture out into the world of work at the age of forty with fears of being single.

The decision to finally reveal my counter-dependent side to Barry on this evening in 1985 was the first time that I ever opened myself up to the fears and rewards of intimacy. No longer could I play the suave, cool, capable person so many people saw as me. Breaking free of my counter-dependent patterns has been one of the most difficult tasks of my life. It has brought me to the depths of my psyche through two breakdowns, which have allowed me to remove the barriers to a full, intimate partnership with Barry.

WHAT IS COUNTER-DEPENDENCY?

People with counter-dependent behaviors appear strong, secure, hard-working and successful on the outside. On the inside they are weak, insecure, fearful and needy. They may function quite well in the world of business, but they are often failures in the world of relationship. Frequently they have poor relationship skills, are afraid to get close to others and avoid intimate situations as much as possible. They also are very well defended against anyone seeing their secret weaknesses and vulnerability. In short, they keep very busy trying to show other people that they are okay and that they do not need anything from anyone.

Counter-dependent behaviors in adults often control and restrict the amount of love, intimacy and closeness they can give and receive in their lives. These behaviors can create feelings of loneliness, alienation and a sense of "quiet desperation." Some of these behaviors include:

- an attempt to hide normal fears, anxieties or insecurities from others
- an inability to identify and/or express important feelings
- an attempt to always "look good" and always be "right"
- a lack of trust of other people's motives
- anxiousness in close, intimate relationships
- a reluctance to ask for help from others when needed
- a preference to work alone
- a constant fear of making a mistake
- a low frustration tolerance, marked by temper tantrums or fits of anger when frustrated
- an inability to relax and a constant need to be engaged in work or activity
- a fear of being smothered or controlled by the needs of others
- a low awareness of the needs or feelings of others
- a tendency to sexualize all nurturing touch
- addictions to work, sex, activity or exercise

HOW DOES IT DIFFER FROM CO-DEPENDENCY?

It is important to understand how counter-dependent behaviors differ from co-dependent behaviors. They are distinctly different behaviors that are caused by very different experiences in early childhood. The chart below shows the main differences between these two sets of behaviors.

Behavioral Differences

co-dependent behaviors	*counter-dependent behaviors*
• cling to others	• push others away
• act weak and vulnerable	• act strong and invulnerable
• are overwhelmed by their feelings	• are cut off from their feelings
• are other-centered	• are self-centered
• are addicted to people	• are addicted to activities, substances
• are easily invaded by others	• are "armored" against others' attempts to get close
• have low self-esteem	• have inflated self-esteem
• act incompetent	• try to "look good"
• have depressed energy	• have manic energy
• act insecure	• act secure
• act dependently	• act independently
• feel guilty	• blame others
• crave intimacy and closeness	• avoid intimacy and closeness
• are self-effacing	• are grandiose
• have victim behaviors	• have persecutor behaviors
• are people-pleasers	• are people-controllers
• suffered from neglect as a child	• suffered from abuse as a child

In addition, people with predominantly co-dependent behaviors will often end up in relationship with people who have more counter-dependent behaviors. This can lead to many conflicts and misunderstandings. Adults with counter-dependent patterns often have a series of relationship failures. They often form very superficial relationships which they cannot sustain or which they never allow to become very intimate. The following examples illustrate some of the kinds of difficulties adults with counter-dependent behavior patterns encounter.

John is a very hard worker who pushes himself and his co-workers extremely hard. However, he has frequent "rage attacks" whenever the smallest thing goes wrong. Despite his high job performance, he is passed over for promotion because of his poor relationship skills.

Sam is very bright and seems to handle life rather easily. He is a sharp dresser and very likeable person, but inside he feels very insecure and has low self-esteem. When he is asked to give a presentation at the monthly sales meeting, he has to snort some cocaine to get himself "up" for the presentation.

Joan always looks as if she stepped off the pages of a fashion magazine. She is witty and fun-loving, but is very hard to get close to. Nobody knows her secret fear of sexual intimacy.

Susan always seems to be on the go, caring for her children, cooking for her husband and family, working for local charities, playing tennis or exercising at the club. At home, after all the work is done, she has trouble just sitting and relaxing. She has frequent migraine headaches that can send her to bed for days. Her husband complains that he never gets enough time with her and finally, in desperation, has an affair with someone at the office.

WHAT ARE THE CAUSES OF COUNTER-DEPENDENT BEHAVIORS IN ADULTS?

Counter-dependent behaviors are caused by a failure to fully complete the two most important developmental tasks of early childhood: bonding and separation. When these tasks are not completely mastered at the appropriate age, they are carried along as excess baggage and affect each subsequent stage of development. If these tasks are not completed later during childhood and adolescence, people then carry these unmet needs with them into their adult lives and eventually develop problems in their relationships. They end up with addictions, serious conflicts, problems with closeness and intimacy, and experience unfulfilling and unsuccessful relationships.

From birth to three years of age, children need to complete these two important developmental tasks of bonding and separation. Bonding with parents and others, which usually starts at birth, allows children to develop a sense of basic trust and safety. It requires lots of physical contact, holding and nurturing touch and pleasant reassuring messages to the child. Children need to know they are loved for who they are and that they are wanted by their parents. Bonding provides a solid foundation for children to gradually separate physically and emotionally, gradually move away from mother and father, so that they can explore their world safely and securely and learn to become emotionally autonomous human beings. Children also need supervision and support to become emotionally separate from their parents. If their bonding is strong and the necessary support is provided, children will achieve emotional separateness from their parents and complete the separation process by about age three.

When children become emotionally separate, they have the self-confidence to rely on their own internal signals in decision-making. No longer will they need to rely solely on others to direct their lives. By the time they complete this important step known as "psychological birth," they will have developed a healthy sense of self that enables them to accept responsibility for their actions, to share and cooperate, to handle frustration in appropriate ways, to respond effectively to the authority of others and to express feelings in healthy ways. When the developmental needs surrounding bonding and separation are not met, people remain stuck in co-dependent or counter-dependent behavior patterns that recycle over and over in their lives.

What happens during early childhood that interferes with the successful completion of these developmental tasks? Usually it is some form of emotional, physical, spiritual or sexual abuse. It may also be neglect or some form of physical or emotional abandonment. These kinds of early traumas, if they are not recognized and resolved, can seriously affect an adult's ability to get close to other people. Adults, who experienced abuse from people they trusted as small children, may continue to be afraid of similar abuse or abandonment when they try to get close to other adults. As a result, these people construct physical and psychological walls around themselves to try to protect themselves from getting hurt.

Although people often don't remember many of these early childhood traumas at first, they have been carrying the effects of them all of their lives. Another factor that often contributes to the denial of these events is the belief that whatever abuse they may have suffered as a child was done by well-meaning parents for their own good. Children are often led to believe that they were the cause of any abuse they may have suffered.

Emotional abuse of a child by a parent or other adult can involve the withdrawal of love, verbal abuse, a lack of understanding or respect for the needs of the child, and the attempt to over-control the activities of the child. Evidence of these traumas can be found by looking at what is currently happening in an adult's life. Symptoms such as fractured relationships, abuse, divorce or addictions are strong indicators of childhood traumas. Physical abuse can cover a wide range of physical punishment for "wrongdoings," including being slapped, punched, hit with a stick and spanked or hit on the bare skin that leaves marks or bruises. Sexual abuse of children by parents or adults also can cover a wide range of both intentional and unintentional activities from actual incest to giving a child incorrect or no information about sex. Adults who were physically or sexually abused as children have difficulty being close and intimate with others.

Abandonment may be physical, emotional or spiritual. The wounds of physical abandonment, the absence of relationship, is sometimes easier to break free of than emotional or spiritual abandonment. In physical abandonment, a person has an experience or obvious deficit that makes their loss concrete. Emotional and spiritual abandonment can happen when a parent is physically present in the family but is emotionally absent or neglects to support the inner life of the child. These types of abandonment are less concrete, more difficult to identify and leave scars that are less tangible.

IS IT POSSIBLE TO BREAK FREE FROM COUNTER-DEPENDENT BEHAVIORS?

Fortunately, by reading books on the subject, doing various written exercises, talking to other people who had similar experiences and through therapy, people can break through their denial. They begin to remember the actual abusive incidents, to understand that *they* were not the cause of that abuse and to learn ways to overcome the effects of these traumas. Breaking free from the effects of these traumas in adults is both possible and likely once people understand the actual causes and have developed the specific tools needed to achieve wholeness.

The application of research from developmental psychology to the treatment of problems such as counter-dependent behaviors is relatively new. Only a few people have approached relationship addictions using a developmental model. In addition to ourselves, only John Bradshaw, Pam Levin, Jean Clarke and Jon and Laurie Weiss have written about the application of this research to the addictions field. Developmental psychologists Stephen Johnson, Erik Erikson, Robert Havinghurst, Jean Piaget and Margaret Mahler and James Masterson contributed much to our understanding of how human development evolves. Our developmental approach offers much hope for helping people change these dysfunctional patterns of behavior, because it provides a step-by-step program that does not require medication or long-term psycho-therapy.

We believe that the incomplete developmental tasks of bonding and separation create predictable problems in adult relationships. By locating the specific breaks in the early developmental process, and then repairing these breaks through a series of corrective parenting activities, people can finally complete their developmental tasks and begin to live more functional and effective lives.

While co-dependent behaviors are mainly caused by severe neglect and abandonment, counter-dependent behaviors are mainly caused by emotional, physical or sexual abuse. People who experienced all of these traumas will alternate between co-dependent and counter-dependent behaviors as adults. Therefore, even those who appear to have more co-dependent behaviors may also have latent counter-dependent symptoms which appear only in certain intimate relationships. A large portion of the adults in our society have relationship problems directly caused by counter-dependent behaviors, co-dependent behaviors or a combination of the two. At present, only the co-dependent issues have been identified, leaving the causes of counter-dependent issues and co-dependent/counter-dependent combinations unidentified and unexplored.

Because counter-dependent characteristics are so pervasive in the U. S. culture, they often go unnoticed. They are so woven into the fabric of our lives that they cannot be seen. This book will show you how to easily and quickly identify the sources of their counter-dependent issues and helps you identify the specific unmet developmental needs that keep them behaving in the same dysfunctional ways. It also shows you effective ways to finally get these needs met. Once these needs are met, your counter-dependent behaviors will be changed and you can have more functional and intimate relationships.

Estimates are that 96 to 98 percent of the adult population of the U. S. experience some level of dysfunction in their relationships, caused by unmet needs from their early childhood. There is a continuum from mild dysfunctions, such as not being able to ask directly to get needs met, to severe dysfunctions, such as eating disorders, that prevent people from being able to have successful long-term relationships. We estimate that about 75 percent of the adult population may have moderate dysfunctions that lead to long-standing conflicts or a lack of intimacy.

With statistics of this nature, it is evident that dysfunctions involving counter-dependent and co-dependent behaviors have a broader source than the experiences from our family of origin. We believe that most of the institutions in our society unwittingly support counter-dependent and co-dependent behaviors. We also believe, however, that these personal/social/cultural symptoms are a reflection of where we are in our evolution as a species, and not just the result of having bad parents or being sick people. Only in the last five to ten years has new information regarding optimal parenting, birthing and human development been available. With this new information, we can now see that some of the methods our parents used to raise us and the methods we used to raise our children were dysfunctional. From this perspective, there is no need to finger-point, judge, blame or feel ashamed. It is just where we are in our growth as humans. We believe all humans are hungry for a message of hope, for being seen as okay and for finding ways to improve their lives in ways that let them feel empowered. That is what this book is about.

WHAT IS UNIQUE ABOUT THIS BOOK?

This book is the result of over seven years of intensive research. While many of its ideas may seem radical, we know they are valid and that the tools which we offer are effective. We believe that there are many elements which make this book unique.

It is highly personal. In our journey together as a couple, as professors and therapists and as parents, we are committed to "walk our talk." Our relationship, which has served as our laboratory, has been a primary source for learning about dysfunctional family patterns and for breaking free of them. In most instances, our personal issues have been catalysts for understanding deeper and more complex levels of human development. We have taken the "gems" we have drawn from our individual work and our work as a couple into breaking free in our relationship with our parents, children and grandchild. We have used these learnings with our clients and students in our psychotherapy, and in our classes and with many participants in our workshops, seminars and other public appearances. When the material became solid enough through applying it in these many areas, we wrote about it. What we share here with you in this book comes from our own journey. In fact, you will find our own stories in the final chapter.

We reveal counter-dependency as the missing piece of co-dependency. This book is the first known published work on the subject of counter-dependency, a term which may be unfamiliar to you. There are over 350 books about co-dependency as well as countless magazine articles and talk show interviews on the subject, while the equally serious problem of counter-dependency has been virtually ignored.

We recommend committed relationships as a source for healing. Our approach is particularly unique because we recommend using committed relationships to transform developmental deficits such as counter-dependent and co-dependent behaviors when possible. It is our belief that our wounds occurred in intimate relationships and that they must also be mended there. We have found that using relationships as a primary source of freeing ourselves offers individuals, couples and families an opportunity for creating intimacy in a way that most are unable to even imagine in the beginning of their discovery work. As you develop the skills you need to create more intimacy, you will develop new levels of closeness and a sense of spiritual connection.

We offer an expanded definition of intimacy. Our approach to intimacy is also unique, as we redefine intimacy to include *all* experiences of feeling connected. We believe that people who help each other heal the wounds from childhood experience what we describe as *depth intimacy*. In depth intimacy there is often a feeling of "touching souls." It usually happens only when each person strips away the facade of looking good and acting strong, revealing both the vulnerable core being and the essence of the Self. By helping each other, the wounds from childhood of both partners are able to move forward developmentally and become more individuated and psychologically separate.

This kind of intimacy is different than *pseudo-intimacy,* in which there is an emphasis on happiness and good times or in trying to rise above the differences and conflicts. It has been our experience that people who try to use this approach often bury their problems and pretend they are not there, until some small incident touches the hidden issues and creates a huge conflict.

A third kind of intimacy we define as *transcendent intimacy.* This form of intimacy requires individuals who are psychologically evolved and are able to experience a high level of spiritual oneness without losing the awareness of their separateness. Advanced sexual practices such as Tantra Yoga involve moving into these states of ecstatic beingness by directing and controlling the flow of sexual energy.

A balanced relationship, we believe, involves both *transcendent* and *depth intimacy.* It uses the conflicts of daily life as doorways for discovering and healing each paerson's brokenness. Here in the depths, you can experience your "soul" connection. After breaking free from a deep wound, there is often space for transcendent experiences where you can experience your "spirit" connection. These two kinds of contrasting intimacy can create an energetic thrust that actually moves both partners forward in evolution. It is our belief that couples who develop skill in both kinds of intimacy can use their relationship as an opportunity for "soul evolution."

We believe breaking free requires a holistic approach. We also believe breaking free of counter-dependent behaviors involves transformation at the physical, mental, emotional and spiritual levels. People addicted to substances must first address their physical dependency and then begin to address the other issues behind their substance abuse. The holistic program we use for breaking free involves therapies for each of these levels.

We present a broad approach for helping you identify counter-dependent patterns that may be causing problems in your lives and in your relationships.

We "disease" no one. We offer a nonmedical, developmental understanding of the causes of counter-dependent behaviors and present a hopeful, developmental approach to help you acheive full wellness. We identify the social and cultural roots of counter-dependency, indicating its role in social and cultural evolution.

Unfortunately, many people felt diagnosed as "sick" by the co-dependency movement. Its diseasing orientation was judging and shaming in many ways. People were diagnosed as "co-dependent" and left with feelings of shame and low self-esteem. This diseasing approach caused many people with co-dependent behaviors to deny their unmet needs. Their deep sense of shame often kept them from doing the deep transformational work necessary to get these needs met. Instead, they quickly erected protective defenses and jumped into acting counter-dependent. This diseasing orientation and people's reaction to it were responsible for the sudden collapse of the self-help movement and for the erection of defenses against intimacy.

In this book, rather than being diagnosed as sick, you will be able to identify your own journey to wellness. If you are interested in breaking out of the cultural trance and achieving higher levels of functioning, then this book will interest you. Our belief is that every individual, every couple, every family and every culture is working as hard as possible to become whole.

In addition to looking at "what is right" about counter-dependency, you will also find many self-help tools designed to put you in charge of changing old, unhealthy patterns of thinking and behaving. By chnging these patterns you can develop healthier and more intimate ways of relating. We believe that people can eliminate these counter-dependent behaviors without extensive therapy, if they make themselves aware of their problems through reading, participating in support groups and though cooperative efforts in their intimate relationships. Chapter Five, "The Counter-dependent Culture," shows how millions of Americans have accepted a lower quality of life because they have passively accepted the judgmental and diseasing approach as the truth about addictive relationships.

We stress self-sufficiency and personal empowerment. We provide the reader with essential skills needed for breaking free from the effects of counter-dependent patterns. We show couples how they can work together to help each other break free of counter-dependent behavior patterns. We provide practical written exercises to help the reader learn more about how to identify counter-dependent patterns and how to move toward wholeness.

We offer a vision of life beyond dysfunction. We help the reader develop a vision of life beyond counter-dependency and other kinds of dysfunctional behaviors. Many self-help programs have not provided people with clear visions of what it means to be whole. We know that without a vision, people cannot move forward in their growth.

NOTE: If you are currently in therapy, please get your therapist's permission before doing the exercises included in this book. If you are not in therapy, we recommend doing them with a nurturing and supportive friend or partner or in a support group.

Part One

THE CAUSES OF COUNTER-DEPENDENT BEHAVIORS IN ADULTS

Chapter One

Counter-dependency: The Other Side of Co-dependency

"But he's a human being, and a terrible thing is happening to him.
So attention must be paid. He is not to be allowed to fall into his grave
like an old dog. Attention must be finally paid to such a person."
Arthur Miller
Death of a Salesman

AN OVERVIEW OF THE PROBLEM

In our earlier book, *Breaking Free of the Co-dependency Trap* (1989), we identified the cause of co-dependency as "... a failure to complete one of the most important developmental tasks of early childhood, that of establishing psychological autonomy." We then showed readers how to complete this task and eliminate co-dependency problems from their life. Co-dependent behaviors are rather easy to identify. The major signs of co-dependency include:
- feeling anxious and insecure without knowing why
- constantly worrying that others will reject you
- feeling trapped in an abusive relationship
- not trusting yourself and your own decisions
- taking care of others instead of yourself
- trying to please others
- having few or no personal boundaries
- not knowing what you want or need
- acting like a victim or martyr.

By contrast, hidden away in an office building somewhere is a person working late at night whose counter-dependent behaviors may not be as apparent, but are just as dysfunctional as those of his or her partner or friends who may display the more visible behaviors of co-dependency.

3

How can you tell if someone has counter-dependent behaviors? When you review the following list, you will likely see an unmistakable pattern of behavior that resembles a two-year-old child as much as an adult. We believe that most people did not get their critical developmental needs met when they were between one and one-half and three years of age and that these needs are still present in most adults. Any important developmental need or task that is not completed on schedule gets dragged along as excess baggage and continues to press for completion. Counter-dependency represents a person's attempts to compensate for these unmet needs.

CHARACTRERISTICS OF COUNTER-DEPENDENCY

As you read the list, see how many of these behaviors you can recognize in yourself. The first step in eliminating your counter-dependent attempts to get your vital developmental needs met is to begin to identify these behaviors.

Do you...

* have trouble getting close to people?
* have trouble sustaining closeness in intimate relationships?
* tend to make people bad or wrong when you leave them or they leave you?
* have trouble feeling your feelings except "justified" anger or sadness?
* have fears of other people controlling you?
* tend to say "no" to the new ideas of others?
* rebel or move away from people who try to get too close to you?
* get anxious in close, intimate relationships?
* feel constantly afraid you will make a mistake?
* try to be perfect and expect others to be perfect?
* refrain from asking for help even when you need it?
* have a strong need to be "right?"
* have thick layers of muscle or fat across your shoulders, chest or abdomen that create a kind of "body armoring?"
* get afraid of being consumed by the needs of others?
* fear that others will reject you if you show your weaknesses or fears?
* get bored easily and need to seek new thrills?
* make high demands on yourself or others?
* tend to see people as all good or all bad, depending on how they relate to you?
* work long hours, go into work on weekends?
* keep very busy with hobbies, recreation or doing things?
* find it difficult to relax and do nothing?
* have difficulty with free play or unstructured time?

4

- have fits of anger when you don't get your way?
- take outrageous risks in sports or business dealings that you secretly hope will make you rich and famous?
- believe you are entitled to have others treat you in special ways?

Like people with co-dependent behaviors, people with counter-dependent behaviors also feel they are not whole and complete without the help of someone else. However, they try to hide this fact from others so they can appear *as if* they really don't need other people very much. In order to maintain this deception, they often sink an enormous amount of energy into fooling themselves and others regarding the depth and range of their needs. They often do this through an almost compulsive adherence to activities that others will value and reward, such as work, hobbies, recreation or community activities which serve to keep them busy and make them look good. In this way they hope they won't have to feel their deep fears of being rejected, abandoned, abused or smothered by those they were close to while growing up.

CAUSES OF COUNTER-DEPENDENT BEHAVIORS IN ADULTS

There are basically two reasons why people behave this way: (1) they did not get enough effective bonding during the first year of life and (2) they failed to get parental support to help them become emotionally separate from their parents during the second and third years of their lives. We estimate that only one or two percent of the adult population has been able to successfully complete these two important developmental tasks during early childhood. As a result, these unmet developmental needs show up constantly in adult relationships, preventing people from enjoying fully functioning lives.

Counter-dependent behaviors in adults mainly are the result of not successfully completing the psychological and emotional separation from one or both parents during early childhood. Ideally, people should have completed their so-called "psychological birth" by about age three, if they were able to receive proper parental and societal support and guidance. What often interferes with the completion of this very important developmental milestone is the presence of emotional, physical and/or sexual abuse during the first three years of life.

The severity of this abuse often determines the severity of the adult problems that result. We all know individuals who have

5

overcome their abusive childhood experiences to lead seemingly normal or successful adult lives. Unfortunately, this is the clear exception to the rule. Many times we do not become aware of the effects of childhood abuse until an adult crisis or relationship stresses bring them to the surface.

It should not be surprising that abuse is behind this problem. We live in one of the most violent and abusive cultures on earth. The targets for much of that violence and abuse are family members, especially children.

A nationwide study (Stau et. al 1980) indicated that between 3.4 million and 4 million children have been "beaten up" by a parent before they leave home. Their study indicated that as many as 1.8 million children had parents threaten them with a knife or gun. This study covered only those cases of known abuse, and we know that probably only about 10% of abuse in the family ever gets reported. In addition to the intentional child abuse figures quoted above, many parents abuse their children in the name of good parenting. Often in the name of good parenting parents will slap, punch, hit with a stick or belt on the bare skin, bruise, cut, scald, burn, torture, beat, and actually maim their children in the process of disciplining them.

Parents also abuse their children emotionally, which usually doesn't leave visible marks, and may be even more widespread in the family than physical or sexual abuse. Again, this kind of abuse is often done to the child "for his or her own good." Alice Miller (1984) says that most emotional and physical abuse is done by parents who think they are doing it for the good of the child. Parents teach their children "lessons" through their use of lies, subterfuge, manipulation, ridicule, shame, scorn, coercion, humiliation, isolation, abandonment, threats of violence and threats or actual withdrawal of love. Some parents also abuse their children through habitual neglect of their children's basic needs. Physical and emotional neglect actually may turn out to be the most damaging form of childhood abuse.

We can only imagine how much intentional and unintentional sexual abuse is present in families. Susan Forward (Forward & Buck, 1978) writes that the families where incest is present "come from every economic, cultural, social, racial, educational, religious and geographical background." The overall picture of child abuse in the United States is not very pretty. Witness the following facts:

6

The American Humane Association reported that:
- Over 2.4 million children were victims of child abuse in 1989
- One of three adult women was a victim of sexual abuse as a child
- One of six adult men was a victim of sexual abuse as a child
- Over 40% of all children have been physically or sexually abused at least once by their parents (statistics on emotional abuse are not available)
- 80% of all criminals in our jails were abused as children
- 95% of all death row criminals were abused as children
- 95% of all prostitutes were sexually abused as children
- 60% of all children who were abused suffer from serious physical illnesses during infancy and
- 50% of all children who were abused were malnourished or "failure to thrive children" as infants.

In many cases, adults with counter-dependent behaviors have little or no awareness of the abuse they suffered as infants and children. In order to tolerate receiving this level of abuse, many children had to believe that they actually deserved this abuse. We see clients with obvious abuse in their background who report that they had wonderful parents and a very happy childhood. Secretly, however, they suffer from low self-esteem and still inflict some form of abuse on themselves and others. With some therapy, frequently these people begin to remember their childhood abuse.

As the memories return it is possible for them to begin to see some of their seemingly normal childhood incidents as experiences of abuse. When they have support in expressing their feelings and support for remembering their experiences, they can begin to identify their unmet developmental needs. It is common for people who suffered abuse to believe that they didn't deserve to get their needs met. Breaking through these self-limiting beliefs and denials is often a first step to recognizing the abuse and uncovering the deep wounds from childhood that they still carry.

THE FOUR STAGES OF DEVELOPMENT

We divide all of human development into four separate stages: co-dependent, counter-dependent, independent and interdependent. If anything interferes with the completion of one developmental stage, it is difficult to move to the next stage. In our opinion, most people got stuck in the co-dependent and counter-dependent stages and continue to recycle unsuccessful attempts to meet these unmet needs from the first two stages in their current

7

adult relationships. We find most adults are still trying to get their needs met from these two initial stages. Because they believe they should appear grown-up, many adults often deny or ignore their unmet needs from childhood. Below is a brief description of each stage and the primary needs that should have been met.

Co-dependent Stage. The child begins this stage before birth and continues in it for the first six to nine months. We now know that during this period children must receive lots of love and support from others in order to meet their bonding needs. Children need their parents to hold them, to sing to them, to touch them, to speak to them in loving ways, to mirror back to them their essence, to treat their feelings seriously, to respect their needs and give them positive support to explore their world safely and effectively. Children who did not experience enough of these activities grow up still looking for these needs to be met. They often behave in co-dependent ways to try to get these needs met.

Counter-dependent Stage. The counter-dependent stage of development usually starts about the age of nine months and lasts to about age three. During this time children begin to physically and emotionally separate from the safety and security of bonding with their parents and begin to develop a "love affair with the world." Children are naturally curious about the world around them, so they gradually move further and further away from their parents. As they learn to crawl and walk, they venture even further away. Sometimes they have to dart back quickly to see if their mother or another family member is still there, or to get comfort and reassurance if they get hurt or scared. During this important stage of development, when they begin to learn that they are separate human beings rather than part of someone else, there are specific kinds of emotional support they need from each parent. If this emotional support is not available *or* if any emotional, physical or sexual abuse is present, the children will not get these important needs met. Adults who had something interrupt the developmental process will often use counter-dependent behaviors to compensate for not getting these needs met.

Independent Stage. Between the ages of three and five, the child is learning to function autonomously. It is a time of coming back together for the child and the parents after a period of

8

opposition. During the independent stage, the child begins to move into more mature forms of intimacy, to master self-sufficiency skills and to learn parallel play with other children. If the important developmental needs from the previous two stages were not met, the child will have difficulty learning to do things independently, clinging or acting as if they have it made on their own. In the latter case, they start to erect walls around themselves and do not learn good socialization skills.

Interdependent Stage. In this stage, from about age five or six to age eighteen, the child gradually develops compassion, empathy and cooperation. Interdependence is a highly complex stage of development because it requires that the child is able to move fluidly and consciously between the three previous stages. This fluidity is possible only if the child is able to communicate clearly his or her needs to others and successfully negotiate with others if there is a conflict of needs and wants.

The relationship between the bonding needs of the co-dependent stage and the separation needs of the counter-dependent stage is significant. The more complete the child's bonding is, the more effectively he or she will complete the separation stage. If the child's bonding was weak in any way, it usually means that he or she will have to limit his or her exploration. If an adult has not met these needs completely in childhood, it can be frightening for her to be alone or emotionally separate.

COUNTER-DEPENDENT AND CO-DEPENDENT BEHAVIORS

People who were forced out of the co-dependent stage prematurely by abusive or rejecting parents often develop counter-dependent behaviors to push people away and therefore do not learn some of the essential skills for being intimate. These people often associate being close and intimate with hurt and pain. As a result, they have trouble getting close to other people and staying close. They often develop compensating behaviors to help them hide their deficiencies from others and, more importantly, from themselves. They learn to be superficially pleasant, hard working, highly successful men and women. Inside, however, they hide their real fears: they are afraid of intimate situations, feel very insecure when they aren't in control and are unable to form or maintain close relationships.

9

In relationships, opposites usually attract. The typical pattern in our culture is that women with co-dependent behaviors usually attract men with counter-dependent behaviors, although this pattern can be reversed. Frequently, the female who has unmet co-dependent needs and the male with unmet counter-dependent needs have patterns of behavior that intertwine perfectly. Because of this perfect match, it is often very difficult for a couple to recognize the real causes of their problems. In addition, the traditional social stereotypes and expectations of men and women also support this matching process, making it even more difficult for them to recognize the source of their problems or to resolve them. Society often programs men to be strong and independent and expects women to be weak and dependent.

In either combination, the relationship partners often find that their counter-dependent/co-dependent mix leads more to conflict and competition than to intimacy and cooperation. This sets up a virtual war between the sexes—a war that has no winners, only losers.

Drawing Battle Lines in the War Between the Sexes

The following scenario illustrates how people with co-dependent/counter-dependent issues are drawn into relationship with each other and how their patterns interlock. It is a singles' party and Renee notices Mark across the room. Mark is talking to several other men and they seem to be listening intently to what he is saying. To Renee, Mark looks powerful, strong and secure. She waits for the right moment and then approaches him cautiously.

Renee: "Excuse me, I'm looking for the hostess."
(Maybe he'll notice me if I ask him a question.)
Mark: "She just stepped into the kitchen, I believe. Hi, I'm Mark. What's your name?"
(She looks sort of cute.)
Renee: "Ah, I'm Renee."
(He's so good-looking. I probably don't stand a chance with him.)
Renee: "You seem to know a lot of people here. I hardly know anyone."
(Maybe he'll feel sorry for me and talk to me.)
Mark: "Yeah, I do business with a lot of these people."
(She seems to think I'm important. Maybe I can impress her.)

10

Renee: "Really? What is your business?"
(Maybe I can get him to talk about himself so he won't ask anything about me.)

Mark: "I'm in stocks and bonds. In fact, I was just talking to the guys over there about some speculative stocks I thought that they might be interested in."
(Hmmmn. She seems interested in me and she's kind of cute. I can't tell her that I'm about to lose my job. I'll have to play it cool so she doesn't see how nervous and insecure I am.)

Renee: "I don't know much about investing and those things. How did you learn about all that?"
(He seems so sure of himself. I wish I could feel that confident. He seems like he'd be an exciting person to be with. I feel a little flushed. I hope he doesn't notice.)

Mark: "Oh, I've done a lot of things. Maybe I could tell you about it sometime, and give you some stock tips. Let's have dinner some night."
(If she is really interested in me, maybe she will go out with me. And besides, a good lay would get my mind off the problems I have at work.)

Renee: "Gee, that would be great. I get so confused about financial things."
(He wants to help me. I've been so lonely and depressed. I could use someone exciting in my life.)

Mark: "How about dinner this week, say Tuesday evening?"
(She looks easy. Maybe she will invite me back to her place after dinner to talk further.)

Renee: "That sounds like a great idea. I think I'm free that night."
(He must like me and really wants to get to know me.)

Mark: "Fine. I'll come by about seven."
(Hope she doesn't back out now that I've stuck my neck out.")

Renee: "Here's my address and phone number."
(I'll have to call Laurie to reschedule our visit on Tuesday night. I wonder if he is married or has someone special.?

Mark: "You're place isn't far from where I live. I'll ring the bell for you when I get there."
(She turns me on. Maybe she will invite me in for a drink and we can make out some before we leave. I could sure use some good sex right now.)

The next day all Renee can think about is her dinner with Mark. At work she can't concentrate and makes many more mistakes than usual. Mark is also having his problems. He worries that she may not like him and that he might accidentally reveal his insecurities. He begins rehearsing his lines so he can

11

look confident and still be in control. Then he remembers how easy it was to deceive Renee and anticipates that he can let down some of his guard with her. Finally, he begins to obsess about having sex with her, thinking about how she might be in bed, which keeps his mind off his problems at work for the rest of the day.

You can begin to see how the attraction between Mark and Renee is one of opposites. Renee appears weak, insecure, dependent and passive, as she seeks someone important to help structure her life. Meanwhile, Mark tries to project an image of strength, aggressiveness, success, independence, and power. The attraction of opposites is a very common pattern in relationships, one that can help set up a dysfunctional relationship in which two half persons come together to try to make one whole person. These kinds of relationships seldom ever lead to any genuine intimacy. Eventually the passive person, who is being dominated, gets tired of playing that role and wants to change the rules. Men with counter-dependency issues often discard a relationship if they feel their partner is no longer willing to serve them and be dominated. This pattern is changing today, as women in our culture tire of being dominated and demand more equal relationships.

Historically, women have shouldered most of the responsibility for making relationships work and, therefore, have shouldered most of the blame when relationships fail. However, as more women take their power and find their own voice, they are able to speak out more clearly. They often refuse to take full blame for the failure of a relationship. This forces men to look at their own counter-dependent issues that may have contributed to their lack of intimacy or the failure of their relationships.

More and more men are taking courageous first steps, such as entering 12-step programs or therapy. Unfortunately, this still happens too often for men only *after* their wife or partner has left them or has threatened to leave them and they are in a crisis. This puts many men in a reactive position which makes it more difficult for them to grow and change.

We present the following beliefs and assumptions about the causes of and the elimination of counter-dependency issues and problems.

THE ASSUMPTIONS OF OUR APPROACH

• **It is not a hopeless, lifelong illness.** Counter-dependent behaviors are caused by the failure to complete one or more of the

12

important developmental tasks of bonding and separation. We have developed effective ways to help people identify the missing pieces from their early childhood, which we call *unmet developmental needs*. We then teach people easy-to-learn corrective parenting skills that help them get these needs met in their current relationships. We do not see counter-dependency as a hopeless, lifelong illness with no hope of change. We believe that people can change their compulsive and addictive counter-dependent behaviors if they are willing to do the necessary physical, mental, emotional and spiritual work. This includes finding the sources of their problems and developing effective methods for eliminating these behaviors.

• **There is something right about having counter-dependent behaviors.** These counter-dependent behaviors actually can be seen as a transformation in progress. Rather than just being seen as dysfunctional behavior patterns, these symptoms are actually unskilled attempts to break free of or complete the developmental deficiencies of early childhood. This approach prevents people from "diseasing" and shaming themselves. Most people know much more about what is wrong or unhealthy with themselves than they do about what is right or healthy about themselves and their behavior. Therapists can add shame to their clients by using labels and diagnoses that imply clients are flawed in some important ways.

• **Unmet developmental needs recycle in our lives.** There is a natural drive in all of us toward wholeness and completion. As a result, any developmental task we didn't complete on schedule will continue to show up again and again in our lives and press for completion. If we don't pay attention to these needs, they will continue to press us even harder to get our attention. Some people actually get physically ill, get divorced or quit their jobs, in order to avoid dealing with their pressing unmet developmental needs. Because people with counter-dependent behaviors often don't understand where these unmet developmental needs come from, they feel ashamed that they haven't learned the skills to deal with them, and they try to hide their unmet needs from others. As a result, these unmet needs tend to recycle again and again in their lives with no resolution.

• **Changing these patterns requires learning certain skills and developing new understandings.** Frequently, when people try to change, they need help in locating the causes of their counter-dependent behaviors. We provide written exercises to

13

help people learn to identify the causes of their counter-dependent behavior patterns. In addition to understanding the causes of their problems, people often need skills to help them get their unmet needs met and finish the unfinished business that has been recycling in their lives. This book contains many skill-building exercises for teaching people how to meet their unmet needs and change their counter-dependent behaviors.

• **Counter-dependency is also a social and cultural problem.** Any psychological issue as widespread as counter-dependency must also have social and cultural roots. When looking at the primary characteristics of counter-dependency, it is easy to see that the present culture often supports and promotes them as healthy, functional behaviors. For example, many companies require their workers to put in long hours and ignore their family responsibilities. Being strong, hard, manipulative, dominating, self-made and ruggedly independent are all part of the old mythical hero of the American Dream. The throwaway culture says, "If it doesn't work, throw it away and buy a new one." Many Americans in the '70s and '80s applied this rule to their relationships as well. Only the threat of AIDS and a slowly growing awareness of intergenerational family patterns has slowed down this tendency. As a result, people are no longer divorcing in the record numbers of the '70s and '80s. Now we need to change the widespread social and cultural denial and start addressing counter-dependent behaviors.

We are not judgmental about people behaving in counter-dependent ways, and we realize that as a culture this is just as far as we have evolved. We will explain more fully this exciting new way of looking at addictions and provide a broader understanding of the social and cultural causes of the problem, as well as what is needed for change. We believe, given the social and cultural conditions that currently exist in this country, it would be difficult to grow up here and not have counter-dependent behaviors.

• **Counter-dependent issues require a systemic approach to recovery.** The interrelatedness of the different levels of the problem, including the societal levels, indicates that we need to look at counter-dependency issues very broadly, as they contain interactive systems. Individual therapy is limited when it doesn't use a systems approach, which is why we believe that couple, family and group therapy and support networks are necessary elements of changing these behaviors.

14

• **Elimination of these behavior patterns is possible.** The prevalent idea in the addictions field is that it is not possible for people with relationship addictions to change. We don't subscribe to this idea. If people are willing to do their physical, mental, emotional and spiritual work, they can transform their addictions to relationships and learn how to live more functional and effective lives.

RESOURCES FOR BREAKING FREE FROM COUNTER-DEPENDENT PATTERNS

In your journey toward full transformation, there are certain resources that we would like to suggest to you as potentially useful. As you use these resources, it is important to remember that you need physical, emotional, mental and spiritual support in breaking free of any dysfunctional patterns. These kinds of support help you slowly lower your defenses and begin to reveal your wounded inner child. Resources that can assist you in changing your counter-dependent behaviors are as follows.

• Start by *reading books* like this one so that you can begin to understand the dynamics and possible sources of counter-dependent behaviors. You may also want to attend classes and workshops that focus on intimacy and how to change your counter-dependent patterns.

• You may want to *join a support group* where you can begin to share with others who have the same issues. It is very comforting to know that you are not the only person who has counter-dependent behaviors. In a good support group you will get emotional support and encouragement. One caution is that some Co-dependents Anonymous (Co-DA) groups tend to look at co-dependent behaviors as a disease from which you can never recover. If you find this approach restrictive, you can take what you need from these groups and leave the disease model behind for those who seem to need it. Also, shop around for a group that fits your needs. We have found that these groups can vary greatly in the kind of emotional support they provide. Some are very good and some are not.

• *Psychotherapy* is often necessary to help you move through blocked or repressed feelings. We recently heard John Bradshaw tell an audience, "You can't do your feeling work in a 12-step group. They are not set up for that." Individual psychotherapy

15

usually is set up to help people remove emotional blocks and to learn to express repressed feelings. We also recommend couple, group or family therapy because of the systemic nature of the problem of counter-dependency. We frequently work with couples to teach them how to help each other. Therapy is often the only place where you can develop the skills and understanding you need to create successful relationships. We usually work for three to six sessions with a couple on this process and then (if they demonstrate that they can do it) we encourage them to work independently of therapy to see how well they do on their own. They can use us as consultants if they get bogged down. They can also come back for a short series of sessions to refresh or advance their skills if they get stuck.

• *Working in committed relationships* is the most powerful place to work on counter-dependency . A committed relationship is one where both people agree not to leave or to make each other bad when conflicts arise. Because counter-dependent patterns are the result of early childhood relationship deficiencies, intimate relationships that offer safety and security are the ideal place to heal these patterns. You can form committed relationships with anyone: your sister, mother, spouse, best friend, children, neighbors, support group members, therapists, ministers and even co-workers. Counter-dependent patterns can appear in *all* relationships, once people feel safe and secure enough in the relationship to let them show.

AWARENESS ACTIVITY: A Self-Inventory:
How Counter-dependent Are You?

Directions: Place a number before each statement to indicate the degree to which this statement is true in your life.

1 = Never   2 = Occasionally   3 = Frequently   4 = Almost always

_____I feel a kind of free floating anxiety when I have nothing to do.

_____I look to other people, substances or activities to make me feel good.

_____I have a difficult time knowing what I want or need.

_____I feel like I am being smothered when I get intimate with my spouse or a friend.

_____I have difficulty in knowing how I really feel inside.

_____I exaggerate my accomplishments a bit when I meet someone new.

_____I get anxious when my partner wants to be intimate with me.

_____I'm afraid people will find out that I'm not who they think I am.

_____I demand perfection of myself and others.

_____I work long hours and never seem to get finished with my work.

_____I don't like to ask other people for help, even if I need it.

_____I prefer to work alone rather than with others.

_____I feel controlled by what others expect of me.

_____I feel it is really important to have the "right answers."

_____I get afraid of being consumed by the needs of others.

_____I function best in structured situations where I am in charge.

_____I feel important when someone asks me for my opinion.

_____I find it difficult to form and maintain intimate relationships.

_____I have trouble deciding if I want sex or nurturing touch.

_____I have trouble relaxing and have chronic tension in my body.

_____I enjoy being the center of attention at social gatherings.

_____I don't like to admit to a mistake.

_____I reject offers of help from others, even if I need it.

_____I have many thoughts about sex each day.

_____I see myself and others as either all good or all bad.

_____I compare myself to others, feeling either one-up or one-down.

_____I am told that I am not aware of the needs or concerns of others.

_____I feel rebellious and fear being controlled by others.

_____I feel hurt when an accomplishment of mine is not recognized.

_____I deny my problems or discount the importance of my problems.

_____**TOTAL**

Scoring: Add your score. Use the following guidelines to interpret it.

102-120 Very high number of counter-dependent behavior patterns
         (Can have serious effects on your functioning level)

79 - 101 A high number of counter-dependent behavior patterns
         (Can have moderate effects on your functioning level)

56 - 78 Some counter-dependent behavior patterns
         (Few effects on your functioning level)

UNDERSTANDING THE COUNTER-DEPENDENT STAGE OF DEVELOPMENT

"Oh, what a tangled web do parents weave when
they think that their children are naive."

Ogden Nash

EMOTIONAL SEPARATENESS: THE CRITICAL TASK OF THE COUNTER-DEPENDENT STAGE OF DEVELOPMENT

If you have identified any counter-dependent behaviors from the list or the inventory in Chapter One, you may wish to look more closely at what happened to you as a child during your counter-dependent stage of development. This history, combined with information about what needs you should have gotten met, can help you identify what went wrong during this period. This chapter presents a closer look at the counter-dependent stage of child development. It also provides writing exercises to help you identify what needs you might have missed that could cause you to develop counter-dependent behaviors as an adult.

In order to understand adult counter-dependent behaviors, it is necessary to go back into the counter-dependent stage of child development and examine it more closely. This stage actually can be broken down into phases which the child must pass through successfully, if he or she is to move into the independent and interdependent stages of development.

In order to achieve emotional separateness and what Margaret Mahler (1968) called the "psychological birth," children first must have good bonding experiences with their mother and father or other bonded caregivers during their first six to nine months of life.

Mahler, a researcher and child psychologist, did extensive observational research with mothers and their babies to better understand the essential ingredients of this process. She found that holding, singing and talking to the child, "mirroring" the child's essence, patient attention to the child's needs and a nurturing touch were essential ingredients for strong maternal-infant bonding. She described this normal state of bonding and called it "symbiosis." The innate drive for both mother and child to bond helps make symbiosis happen. Mahler and others found that there were degrees of symbiosis, depending on the quality of the relationship between mother and child. She found that the stronger the bonding was, the better the chances were that the child would complete the separation stage successfully. This, she said, begins about five or six months of age and is usually completed by two or three years of age.

According to Mahler, the separation stage begins gradually out of the child's innate drive to explore the world and to become an autonomous person. This creates an internal conflict for the child who also enjoys the comfort and warmth of the oneness with mother and father. When a baby starts to separate, the kind of bonding relationship he or she has with both parents is crucial. If mother is depressed, tired, or not available emotionally because she is frightened by the intimacy or stresses of parenting, or if father is unavailable, the baby will actually delay his or her first moves toward separateness, hoping to still get enough bonding.

If this bonding need is not met completely, the child will eventually have to move on without the security he or she really needs. Development continues forward to the next stage whether or not the child has been able to get all his or her needs met.

In some cases, babies begin to separate unusually early, if the mother or father clings too tightly or is too intrusive in trying to control their baby's first attempts to move out into the world. These babies often prefer strangers and as early as three months and may stiffen against their mother's efforts to hold them. This can cause anxiety in the parents. A mother may wonder, "Does this child no longer like me?" and, depending on the mother's self-esteem, she may see the child's attempts to separate as a threat to her identity as a mother. A father may withdraw even further if the child doesn't want to be held or played with.

In either case, the movement from bonding into separation is a delicate process, requiring that mothers and fathers not only have good information, but also have dealt with some of their own unfinished business regarding bonding and separation. Certainly anything not resolved previously by mothers and fathers will surface for them during the first two to three years of the parenting process.

The interplay of the two seemingly opposing forces of oneness and separateness inside of the infant creates the plot for this struggle toward selfhood. The child is plagued constantly by two seemingly contradictory fears: the fear of separation (abandonment) and the fear of oneness (engulfment).

THE FOUR SUBPHASES OF THE SEPARATION PROCESS

Mahler, and Stephen Johnson (1987), who is also a developmental psychologist, found that the internal conflict between oneness and separateness can be resolved, if the child is able to successfully navigate the four distinct phases in the separation process. As you look more carefully at each of the phases, it may help you better understand what you might not have gotten finished and, therefore, what is causing you to get stuck in the counter-dependent or separation stage of development. If you can locate the specific developmental needs that did not get met in any phase of this process, then it is easier to find ways to get those needs met in present time.

The following descriptions of each phase of the counter-dependent stage of development show some of the important developmental tasks that need to be accomplished at each stage. For each developmental task, there also is a set of developmental needs that have to be met. The writing exercise called **The Sins of Omission and Commission** at the end of the chapter will help you identify the specific unmet needs from the co-dependent and counter-dependent stages of development.

As you read the following descriptions of these four phases of the Separation Process, ask yourself: "Knowing what I know about my parents, how did they probably treat me during each of these phases of development." This might help you begin to remember what actually did happen to you and what you might have missed or what you might have gotten that you didn't want.

The Early Exploration Phase (6 months to 9 months)

During the Early Exploration Phase you began to develop an awareness that there is a world outside of the oneness between

21

your mother and father or other bonded caregivers and yourself. At first you looked at this world from the edge of your mother's lap or over your father's shoulder while being held or burped. You saw your mother smile and you smiled back. Imitation helped you learn new responses that helped you create the awareness of watching and doing. Also, you began to notice others and may have reacted with anxiety at first. However, if the relationships with your mother and father were strong, supportive and nurturing, you eventually grew more curious than scared of strangers. If the relationship was weak or you were not yet ready to separate, then the anxiety may have been stronger and you began clinging to your parents when strangers approached.

In the Early Exploration Phase you had no way of holding onto an image of your mother or father when either one was out of physical sight (validating the adage "out of sight, out of mind"). You may have coped with this fear of loss by keeping your mother or father always in view, and eventually you were able to imagine that your parents were still with you even when they were not present. You could only sustain this for short periods of time at first, but gradually you learned to tolerate longer times of being physically separated from either parent. If your mother of oneness was available, nurturing, warm and secure, you could hold on to these necessary qualities in your imaginary mother. Your mother may have assisted you in developing these qualities by being predictable and reliable. For example, when she had to go out she let you know that she was going to lunch and leaving you with a sitter or with your father. She knew the quickest way to destroy your new-found confidence was to sneak away when you were not looking. Also, she knew any prolonged absence of several days at your young age would have devastating effects on you, causing you to feel totally abandoned.

During the Early Exploration Phase, you darted back and forth many times during a day to confirm that the bond with your mother or father was still intact. You may also have gotten needed pats on the head, a loving smile, a brief snuggle, a bottle or an opportunity to nurse on your mother's lap. Each time, however, you were lured back to exploring the world because your drive to separate grew stronger by the day.

Interestingly, your father's role at this time was to play with you, hold you and maintain a strong bonding connection. Soon you learned that your father wasn't just a part of your mother, but a separate person. You saw these differences and similarities and

22

she let you know that she trusted your father, so that you also could trust him. If your mother tried to keep you from your father, then you may have seen your father as a frightening stranger. You also needed other relatives and friends to bond with. Again, you learned to trust anyone your mother trusted.

The developmental tasks for this phase were for you to develop a specific smile of recognition for your mother or your consistent caregiver. During this period, it was also time for you to learn to discriminate your mother from strangers. If the bonding with your mother was strong, you showed curiosity and wonderment toward strangers. If it was less strong, you might have felt anxiety and distress around strangers, especially around eight months of age.

The Full Exploration Phase (10 months to 15 months)

During this phase of counter-dependency, you ventured out further as soon as you could walk. Walking was a celebration of your ability to master the world. This skill was to lead to the development of your "love affair with the world." Separation and exploration became almost a full-time occupation, coupled with occasional trips back to your mother's lap for comfort and reassurance.

Teething and too many "don'ts" slowed you down, but elation over new discoveries could easily dull your pain. The drive for separateness and wholeness, an inborn urge, was in high gear by the end of this phase. Also, by the end of this phase, you had found some transitional objects like a teddy bear, a pacifier, a doll or blanket that represented the feeling of being with your mother when she was gone. You may have carried these comfort objects everywhere you went. Eventually, you abandoned these objects when you were able to develop an inner mother figure that could soothe or comfort you when you needed it.

During this period you loved the thrill of being mobile. In this expansive period you found you could explore a large area in your home and discover all kinds of new things each day. Your excitement often reached a state of euphoria, often causing you to forget about wanting to be close or even eating, unless something scary happened. Because your mother seemed so big and so powerful, you saw her as omnipotent. Because you were not separate from her, you often you felt omnipotent yourself—able to do grandiose things and entitled to have everything that crossed your path. Life seemed limitless.

23

The developmental tasks for this phase were for you to begin to understand that there were limits to mother's presence, energy, patience, time and resources. Because you needed to learn about her limitations gradually, she gave them to you incrementally. When she had to leave you with another bonded caregiver, she stayed away only as long as you could tolerate it. At first this was just for a matter of minutes. As you grew older she expanded this to hours. She made sure that you had a reliable person to care for you while she was gone who could support your feelings if you were unhappy about her absence. She also helped you learn how to take care of your own needs and to learn how to be self-sufficient while she was gone. She provided you with transitional objects, such as soft animals for comfort, so that you could mother yourself in her absence. She knew that this is how you would develop an internal "nurturing parent" inside yourself.

Other developmental tasks for this phase were for you to understand that mother's absence wasn't personal and that she was a separate person with her own needs and interests. She or your caregiver helped you express your feelings of frustration when you weren't able to have things go your way all the time. You also needed a constant adult presence who could monitor your exploration and make sure it was safe.

If we look at addictive behavior, we see that alcohol, drugs, cigarettes, sex, and food can become transitional objects that provide the person with the comfortable, reassuring feeling that an available mother might provide for a child. The object can be used, set aside and reached for when the fears or anxieties of being out in the world get too great. To eliminate their addictions, these people must mourn the loss of the available mother they desired as an exploring infant. The addictive substitutes that replace their feeling of connection to mother only work for a short while, and they also can create a dependency. This dependency can't be broken until you feel your feelings, and you learn that there is no mother who will always be available, but there are some people who sometimes are available for comfort if asked. Other times you may have to learn to feel your feelings alone and comfort yourself using your inner mother.

The Early Separation Phase (16 months to 24 months)

Near the beginning of this phase, you finally realized that you were a person totally separate from your mother. When you first realized this, you may have felt scared and wanted to be held and

24

cuddled again. It may have looked to others as if you had regressed back to an earlier phase of development, but it was probably short-lived. Again, your innate drive to separate took over and you went back to exploring and mastering your world.

Your mother's and father's role during this phase was to keep encouraging your efforts to separate, while providing you with support and nurturing you when you needed it. You were likely to be angry and frustrated when you were unable to master certain tasks or when any restrictions were placed on you by your parents. Your parents needed to accept this anger and frustration and respond empathetically to you. Your parents may have feared that if they simply forgave your outbursts of anger and frustration that they would inadvertently encourage future tantrums. This wasn't true. A warm hug and some assurance that you were still loved was all that you needed. Humiliation or punishment toward you only set up further cycles of tension which you needed to discharge. Repeated reassurances helped you develop a sense of yourself, a feeling of being loved and accepted and the ability to stay connected with your feelings.

Another important part of this phase is the phenomenon called "splitting." There were times during this phase when you mastered a task or returned to your mother and found a receptive warm reunion. You experienced these times as "good" and everything looked and felt good during these times. However, there were other times when you were unable to master a task or when you needed a warm hug, and you found your mother busy cooking dinner or talking on the telephone. These times you experienced her as "bad" and this feeling was generalized to everything. Mother became "good mother" when she was available and "bad mother" when she was not available. The healthy resolution to this conflict occurred gradually as you learned two important things:

• that mother had good and bad qualities and that she was okay despite this mixture and,

• that you also had good and bad qualities, were separate from mother, and that this mixture of good and bad qualities was also okay.

If this split was not resolved, you tended to continue to see yourself, other people and the world as split into good and evil, black and white, right and wrong. As an adult, when you can only think of two solutions (either/or) or tend to use black or white thinking, you know you are experiencing an aspect of this splitting phenomenon.

The developmental tasks for this phase included learning how to resolve your inner conflict between wanting to be separate and wanting to be close. You had to come to terms with the reality that your parents were not "gods" or perfect parents. And because you were becoming separate, you also had to come to terms with your own humanness. Here is where you learned the limits of your sense of omnipotence, grandiosity, entitlement and euphoria.

If you didn't complete these tasks, it is likely that you became stuck at this phase of your development, leaving your view of the world split into polarities of good/bad, all/nothing, or always/ never. You may have maintained your feelings of grandiosity, entitlement, euphoria and omnipotence. As an adult these may be expressed through behaviors, such as manipulation, pride, self-centeredness, addictions to activities and substances, that help you maintain your euphoria and, if all else fails, you may have rage attacks when you are faced with limitations.

This is the critical point in the completion of your psychological birth. During this time period, you made a decision either to become separate emotionally from your mother or to stay co-dependent. If you chose to return to the safety of oneness, you developed more co-dependent behaviors and decided you could know yourself only if you were in an immediate relationship with another person.

If, because of repeated experiences of emotional, physical or sexual abuse, you decided that oneness was unsafe, scary or unavailable, you might have chosen prematurely to separate from your mother or father, so you had to develop more counter-dependent behaviors. You learned to wall off your feelings of vulnerability and fear and your needs for closeness by creating defensive behaviors that pushed people away and/or showed people how you didn't need them. You began creating a False Self that helped you to look capable and act strong. You also developed an illusion about your inflated importance so that you would never have to let anyone see your vulnerability and wounds. If that happened at this point, you became developmentally stuck.

The Complete Separation Phase (25 months to 36 months)

If your needs for emotional separation *were* supported appropriately by loving parents, by the age of three you were developing an initial sense of separateness and identity. The ability to hold

26

yourself as an object of worth separate from other people is called object constancy. As a three-year-old, you had only enough object constancy to feel safe in the world as a separate person if you had built up enough good-mother and good-self experiences. The struggle to maintain this object constancy will continue for the rest of your life as you encounter new problems and crises. As humans we constantly have to reconcile our longings to return to paradise or the bliss of oneness with our intense longing to be separate, autonomous individuals.

The resolution of this issue between ages two and three involves a complex set of variables. The role of the father is critical in the successful completion of this phase. If there was good bonding between you and your father, he became more and more available at times when your mother was not available (bad mother/good father). When your father was physically or emotionally absent during the first three years, this prevented you from emotionally separating from your mother more than anything else could have done. This was even more important for boys who have to dis-identify from mother in order to develop a healthy male self-image.

When you came to your available father, to whom you were bonded, complaining about your "bad mother," it was necessary for your father to know how to respond effectively. If he used this as an opportunity to also vent his feelings of "bad wife," because she has been so consumed by all the demands of child rearing and was not available enough for him, then you may have learned from your father to devalue women and overvalue men. Also, if your father took the side of your mother and criticized you for complaining, he showed you that there was no emotional support available for you to become emotionally separate from your mother. You may have felt betrayed and defeated if this happened repeatedly. What your father needed to do was *support your feelings* without agreeing or disagreeing with your definition of your mother's "badness." ("I see you are really upset that Mommy's gone and until she comes back I am here to play with you.") This response does not blame anyone and acknowledges your feelings.

This is a difficult response for many men who were never taught to respond to feelings in this way. Some fathers get so scared and angry at having to be in the middle of this intense struggle for separation between mother and child that they make excuses to work longer hours or have an affair or even leave the

27

caregiver in that role, supporting both your mother and you, it would have been impossible for you to complete your psychological birth on schedule between the ages of two and three. So what about single-parenting families? No research has been done, but it would seem possible for another bonded caregiver such as a babysitter or relative to help fill that role. However, if this person is a woman, a male child would not likely be able to dis-identify with his mother, causing gender identity problems later. This area certainly needs much more research and study.

The following chart, *"The Tasks of Children and Adults,"* shows the important developmental tasks that need to be completed in each stage of your life. As you read these lists of early childhood tasks, ask yourself, "Did I complete each one of these successfully?" If you are not sure about some of the tasks, you can do further research. You can ask your parents or other relatives about your early life. At the end of this chapter, complete the writing exercises on "The Sins of Omission and Commission." You can also check the chart at the end of Chapter Six, "How to Identify Unmet Developmental Needs and What To Do About It."

THE TASKS OF CHILDREN AND ADULTS

Developmental Stage/Age	Important Developmental Tasks to be Completed
Co-dependent (0 - 6 months)	Develop strong symbiosis with your mother Develop strong bonding with your mother/father Seek stimulation through your senses Decide to live Begin to develop a sense of body definition
Counter-dependent *Early Exploration and Full Exploration Phase* (7 - 15 months)	Learn to discriminate between yourself and others Learn to actively explore your environment, and begin to test separateness Develop autonomy in self feeding and movement (creeping, crawling, walking, climbing) Develop cause and effect thinking Learn to recognize and trust others in addition to mother
Early Separation and Complete Separation Phase (16 months - 3 years)	Develop healthy narcissism or sense of self Complete your psychological birth Decide to think and to solve problems for yourself Give up your illusion of control over others

29

Independent
(3 years to 6 years)

Learn appropriate sex-role identification
Learn appropriate ways to handle your frustration
Develop object constancy

Ask directly for what you want
Develop emotional autonomy
Incorporate the culture by learning the social rules and roles
Distinguish fantasy from reality
Learn to control your impulses
Refine your reflective thinking (think about your actions, figure out how to get your needs met)
Refine your sex-role identification

Interdependent
(6 years to 12 years)

Learn to cooperate with others as partners
Use concrete thinking (abstract thinking not yet developed)
Learn reasons for rules
Learn to argue, negotiate, or debate other points of view
Develop your own way of testing out parental values and beliefs
Develop an activity orientation; learn to do things to get strokes from others

Adolescence
(12 years to 18 years)

Develop your abstract thinking ability
Develop your physical autonomy
Resolve any recycling or leftover problems from childhood

Young Adult
(18 years to 25 years)

Develop a value structure, rather than a rule structure

Engage in dating and sexual experimentation

Achieve emancipation from your parents

Establish effective ways to get your nurturing needs met

Establish long-term relationships

Develop economic autonomy

Develop your own life style

Adulthood--Creation
(25 years to 40 years)

Learn to keep your social commitments

Learn to be productive in your life's work

Complete any resolved problems from your childhood when you have children

Adulthood--Re-evaluation
(40 years to 60 years)

Reassess your life style and life goals

Try out any experiences you missed earlier

Resolve any unresolved problems recycling from your childhood

Adulthood--Resolution
(60 years +)

Accept your self and your accomplishments

Resolve any recycling dependency issues and control issues from your childhood his or her process. Since most parents are not taught these skills before they become parents, they often fall short of this goal and, therefore, leave the child to finish this task later in life.

Again, we want to stress two things. The first is that most parents do the best they can with what they have. The second is that this developmental approach, with its implications for parenting young children and for reparenting Adult Children, is so new that it is just now entering mainstream literature. It is now possible, for the first time in the evolution of humans, to present a perspective to parents that supports the creation of functional humans living in functional families.

THE DEVELOPMENT OF HEALTHY NARCISSISM

As a child you had legitimate rights to be seen, to be understood, to express your feelings and needs, to be taken seriously and to have your feelings and needs respected by your mother and father. These are normal narcissistic needs. Fulfilling these narcissistic needs during the first two to three years was essential if you were to develop healthy self-esteem. In the bonding process, one of the initial ways that you could get your narcissistic needs gets met was through your mother's accurate mirroring of you. While being held or fed, you gazed up at your mother's face, hoping to see a reflection of your essence in her face. This is how infants learn who they really are. If your mother mirrored back her desires for you to be a certain way, perhaps to take care of her own unmet narcissistic needs, then your self-image eventually got distorted. You may have believed it was necessary to take care of your mother's needs in order to be loved or cared for. Mothers must be able to put aside their own needs at times and allow themselves to be used by their children. Children who are mirrored correctly during this bonding stage are able to develop healthy narcissism, which is essential for the completion of the counter-dependent exploration stage of development (Weinhold 1988).

Alice Miller (1981) lists the ways that parents can help their children develop healthy narcissism. As you read this list ask yourself, "Can I imagine my parents doing these things for me when I was a child?" I needed my parents need to:

- React calmly and reassuringly to any of my aggressive impulses.
- Support my attempts to become separate and autonomous instead of

32

being threatened by them.
* Allow me to experience and express my natural feelings and urges such as rage, jealousy or defiance.
* Allow me to develop and follow my natural curiosity during each developmental stage, rather than requiring me to do things to please them.
* Allow me to use them by being at my disposal when I needed them.
* Permit me to express conflicting or ambivalent feelings and treat those feelings seriously and with respect.
* See me as separate from them, as someone with my own needs, wishes, fears, dreams and accomplishments.

With these kinds of parental support the child develops a healthy sense of narcissism and will grow up without unfinished narcissistic counter-dependent needs. The only truly unselfish, genuine people in the world are those who were able to get these healthy narcissistic needs met in early childhood. Alice Miller (1984) describes these people this way: "Children who are respected learn respect. Children who are cared for learn to care for those weaker than themselves. Children who are loved for what they are cannot learn intolerance. In an environment such as this they will develop their own ideals, which can be nothing other than humane, since they grew out of the experience of love" (p.97).

THE PSYCHOLOGICAL BIRTH

The resolution of the conflicting drives for oneness and separateness occurs between the age two to three, *if* the normal, healthy, developmental needs of the child are expressed and met by caring, self-assured, aware and psychologically whole parents. This resolution involves the psychological birth of the individual and is the single-most important developmental task for a person to complete. Without this important completion, people are unable to truly listen to their own rhythms. We estimate that currently only about one per cent of the world's population complete this milestone in their lifetime.

If you did not have parents who were able to help you complete this successfully, what you had to do was develop a False Self, one that looked strong and independent. You hoped this self was more to their liking than the True Self you really are. By adopting this False Self, you helped insure your survival from childhood. You may, however, have retained aspects of your False Self that now interfere with intimacy in your adult relationships that you now want to change.

People with co-dependent behaviors generally retained a deflated False Self, one that looks weak and helpless, while people with counter-dependent behaviors generally have an inflated False Self. The person with co-dependent behaviors is prone to depression, while the person with counter-dependent behaviors is prone to grandiosity to avoid feeling depressed. To complete your psychological birth in early childhood or later in life, it is necessary for you to go through an intense struggle between two seemingly opposite forces: the natural drive toward oneness and closeness, and the equally powerful drive to be an emotionally separate, self-determining individual. When you have not completed your psychological birth, the drive toward oneness can bring up intense feelings of being swallowed up, engulfed or consumed. This experience can feel like death and dismemberment to you. The counterforce of separation can produce intense fears of existential alienation, aloneness and struggle.

To navigate these intense experiences requires spiritual courage. Carl Jung said that such experiences are necessary before the individual is ready to complete the process he called *individuation*. Jung saw this as both a psychological and spiritual process. He said it was sometimes necessary to rise above the conventional wisdom in order to discover "gnosis," the knowledge of the heart that renders human beings free. Jung realized that humans cannot fulfill the promise of their potential if they become to attached to the external world. He urged people to find their spiritual truths inside themselves and not in established religions. This spiritual rebirth Jung saw as a necessary prerequisite to the completion of the individuation process.

In either case, by understanding what happened in your childhood and by developing new skills, you will be able to complete this developmental task now and experience the completion of your psychological birth. You may ask, "How will I know if I have completed my psychological birth?" Basically, you will have regained a sense of who you really are and will be able to handle life's challenges and conflicts, feeling okay about yourself and okay about others. You will be able to be close and intimate when you want to and be separate and alone when you want to as well. Only the person who has prepared him or herself psychologically and spiritually can expect to complete this process successfully.

34

AWARENESS ACTIVITY:
The Sins of Omission and Commission

The following exercise, which involves writing two lists, will help you discover where to begin your search to break free from your counter-dependent patterns. Get a large sheet of paper and divide it into two halves, one on top and the other on the bottom. The top list describes all the things that you wished your parents had said or done for you that they didn't when you were growing up. (Examples: I wish they had told me they loved me or I wish they had given me birthday parties.) The bottom list describes all the things that your parents said to you or did to you that you wish they hadn't, and were in fact hurtful and harmful to you. (Examples: I wish they hadn't humiliated me when I got pregnant in high school; I wish they hadn't punished me by calling me names and hitting me.)

Make your lists as long as you like. If you had parent substitutes, such as older siblings or step-parents in your childhood, you may include them, as well as teachers, scout leaders or any other significant adults.

What do the lists mean? The top half, *The Sins of Omission*, identifies those things that help set up behavior patterns for co-dependent relationships that continue through childhood and into adulthood. These are the things that the small child in you is still waiting for: the perfect parent, the princess or the knight in shining armor, someone to come along who knows what you need and will provide it for you. The resolution of the items on this list will come when you take charge of finding ways to get these needs met in current time. The most important skill to use these it is to learn to ask directly to get your needs met.

The bottom list, *The Sins of Commission,* identifies those things that help set you up to develop counter-dependent behavior as an adult. These items indicate some of the things that the small child in you still experiences as invasive, hurtful or abusive. You may experience these things in your adult relationships as anger and/or old resentments. The skills needed to change the items on these lists involves the release of unexpressed feelings related to these early experiences and giving back the things you took on that you no longer want or need.

The approach described in this book will show you how to complete what is still unfinished about these experiences for you. Generally, all the experiences from both lists can be linked to your

35

to identify what needs were not met and serve as guide for getting these needs met in your current relationships.

Chapter Three

GETTING STUCK IN COUNTER-DEPENDENCY

*"(Hu)man(s are) condemned to be free;
because once thrown into the world,
(t)he(y) are responsible for everything (t)he(y) do."*
Jean Paul Sartre

There is almost always a series of events or core traumas in the first year or two of a child's life that interrupts the developmental process. It may be a difficult birth, an early illness on the part of either the child or the mother, the birth of another child or a series of events that cause a rupture in the bond between mother and child. The nature and timing of these developmental breaks becomes critical for the child, for they often determine how his or her life will unfold. The circumstances of these breaks, along with the child's feelings, memories and perceptions about them, create a pattern of unfinished business that will likely recycle throughout the rest of the person's life. These core traumas often become the source of the most persistent counter-dependent symptoms. Where in the developmental process the traumatic breaks occurs, determines the set of symptoms the child will develop. If they occur before nine months, the child will often develop more co-dependent behaviors as an adult. If they occur between eighteen and twenty-four months, the child is likely to develop counter-dependent behaviors that carry into adulthood. If they occur between nine and eighteen months, the child will probably exhibit both co-dependent and counter-dependent behaviors as adults.

IDENTIFYING THE CORE TRAUMAS

In reviewing the stages of early childhood development, it is possible to see how the period of gestation is like paradise. Life in the womb was simple, uncomplicated, peaceful and harmonious.

37

Everything you needed came without effort. You were imprinted during that time with beliefs and expectations about your life here on Earth.

Then came the birth process. Just being born was very traumatic. You traveled slowly for hours down a narrow canal that put your body (particularly your head) under tremendous pressure. If you were born via Caesarean birth, you may have experienced the trauma of being jerked too quickly out of paradise. If there were drugs administered to your mother or if forceps were used on you, or if there were difficulties with the delivery, you may have been even more traumatized. The birth process may have put an abrupt end to your blissful existence in paradise.

If your birth was easy and you were born in an warm atmosphere with soft lights and soft music, *if* you were laid immediately on your mother's belly, *if* your umbilical cord was cut only after it quit pulsating, *if* you were allowed to nurse soon after your birth, *if* you were placed in warm water and provided gentle massage to heal any birth trauma, and *if* you were kept constantly with your mother, then there was only a brief disruption of your paradise state. The first few moments of your life helped you resume the intrauterine state of bliss between you and your mother. If your birth was difficult and you were born in a cold, sterile hospital room with harsh lights, held upside down and slapped on the bottom, laid on a cold scale to be weighed, medicated in your eyes with harsh chemicals, circumcised, wrapped tightly in clothes that shut you off from tactile contact with people, hurried down the hall to a nursery away from your mother and left there for many hours, then you probably experienced a traumatic disruption of your paradise state and left with severe bonding deficiencies.

Birth trauma, or any abrupt changes in caretaking during these early years, fractures the delicate process of development. If you suffered unintentional abandonment and/or abuse during either your birth or afterwards, by being left with strange caretakers for extended periods of time during the first three years of your life, then you are likely as an adult to have unfinished business from this period.

Only in the last ten or so years has it been known that newborn infants see, hear, feel and thus are acutely aware of everything going on around them. In fact, if you were not drugged, you were born in a heightened state of sensitivity (Verny, 1981; Grof, 1976). Because of human ignorance about this, you may have been treated as though you were an undeveloped lump of clay. It has been commonplace for newborns to have surgery and circumcision without anesthesia, to have needles stuck in them for tests, and to be isolated in incubators and nurseries. Until recently, parents believed it was all right to leave infants in the care of nurses, nannies, grannies and babysitters for extended periods of time during the first two or three years of life, thinking that the child was not aware enough to know the difference in caretaking. Our work with clients indicates that a child remembers everything and carries the scars from these kinds of traumas the rest of his or her lives.

Abandonment between the age of 10 to 25 months is particularly damaging to a child, as it can arrest development and leave the child with many co-dependent and counter-dependent behaviors. A child stuck at this stage will grow up seeing the world as split into good/bad or either/or. Both/and solutions will not be available as options in problem-solving. As a way of compensating for this split, a complex set of dysfunctional adaptive behavioral patterns gradually emerges in the child. For example, intense anxiety and abandonment fears may surface whenever someone leaves, even for a short time. Many adults start fights with their loved ones when they are involved in some kind of separation, such as going out of town on a business trip for several days.

CORE TRAUMAS BECOME A LIFE PATTERN

The points where the bonding process was interrupted and the ways in which it was interrupted are critical, whether it is during the birth process or during the first two years of life. At these breaks, it is almost as though the world stops. Like pausing the tape in a videotape player, life freezes. When this happens, the child takes stock of the situation and identifies it as a personal reality. In these frozen moments, the child creates basic beliefs, values, assumptions and expectations about how life is here on earth and about what kind of experiences life brings him or her. Such experiences are a kind of imprinting or patterning process.

As we have worked with our clients to help them get to the source of their early childhood issues, we have come to understand that the experience of people lives is created in much the same way an onion is created. In the center of the onion are the traumatic core experiences, most frequently the trauma of birth. A common scenario created by someone with a traumatic birth is, "There must be something wrong with me" (belief). "It's okay for people to hurt me because I'm not very important or valuable" (value). "Adults are people who hurt you and can't be trusted" (assumption). "Starting new things in life will be painful for me" (expectation). These beliefs, values, assumptions and expectations form the matrix for the life experiences.

Sometimes complex family dynamics help to set up the original traumas before the child is even born. For instance, if the parents had a lot of conflict in their relationship, they may have become afraid that their relationship wouldn't last. At this point they had three choices: to try to get closer and work through the conflict (which few people have the skills to do); to agree to stay distant and hope to avoid the conflict; or (more commonly) they decide to have a child. The child may actually have been conceived into the family to serve as a buffer in the conflict between the parents.

If you were born into this kind of family situation, you may have made an unconscious agreement with both your parents either to become the dumping ground for all their unexpressed feelings or to play "peacemaker." The family drama frequently looks something like this:

You then served as the fulcrum in the family to help to preserve your parents' relationship. You may also have become the target of your parents' conflicts (so that they didn't have to get mad at each other) or you may have served as a surrogate partner for one or both of your parents to meet the needs that they couldn't get met with each other.

Eventually the trauma becomes a life pattern, replayed over and over again with many variations. Each time it is replayed, the trauma ends the same way that it did in the earliest experiences of it. Each time the experience confirms the early beliefs, values, assumptions and expectations and adds another layer around the core of the onion. With each new layer, new players are drawn into what has now become a life drama based on the original trauma. The "trauma drama" often becomes a self-fulfilling prophecy.

THE LIFE PATTERN BECOMES A SELF-FULFILLING PROPHECY

As you entered adult life, you likely drew new people into your life to play out the circumstances of your early traumas. (Remember, the way human beings learn is by repeating an event that is confusing until its meaning is finally understood.) These people are drawn into your life to help you learn your lessons and become a whole person. If you were birthed by forceps, you may draw people to you who jerk you around or physically abuse you, as the delivering physician did. If your mother was drugged during birth, you may be attracted to drug use. If your mother died or was killed during your early childhood, you may find yourself in relationships where you get close to someone who then abruptly leaves you. If no one shows up from "central casting" to play in your drama, you learn you can take over and play the the roles yourself. You can set up the whole play and then act out all the necessary parts.

If life gets too sweet and too comfortable or if your capacity to receive good things gets stretched too far, you can interrupt the flow of good things yourself. You may find times when it seems as though life is going too well and you begin to anticipate that something bad must be about to happen (as it happened at your birth). The expectation that something bad is about to happen when everything is going well, we believe, is also part of the life drama.

The moments when you experienced the original traumas were also points where you probably made unconscious psychic agreements with your parents. The creation of the traumatic events are often due to a crisis between your parents or your siblings. If you are the oldest or an older child, your traumas may be related to the birth of the next sibling. Your parents, especially your mother, may have had to leave you for several days or a week. Such family circumstances may have created a situation in which you felt abandoned. Or, if you were left with relatives because of a crisis in your parents' relationship or in the family, you may have experienced an abandonment that elicits a survival fear. Out of this fear, then, comes the need for an unhealthy psychic agreement with the parents.

You may have unconsciously agreed to take care of one or both of your parents. This required you to fulfill some behavioral expectation that your parents had for you as a way for the family to maintain its balance. By unconsciously agreeing to this, you may have had to give up some important aspects of your True Self. We have found this kind of psychic agreement to be quite common in the clients we have worked with. Furthermore, this original psychic agreement is acted out in all subsequent relationships where a similar agreement is made again and again.

Psychic agreements are never conscious and never spoken. Some common psychic parent/child agreements that we find in our clients are, "I will take care of your feelings and be responsible for them if you agree to pay attention to me," and, "I will take your abuse if you will let me live in this family." To openly acknowledge such agreements is absolutely taboo in most families. Most people have no awareness of the kinds of agreements they have made as infants, until they begin to do completion and separation work with their parents or parent substitutes in therapy.

As you moved through life creating layers on your onion and attracting players for your life drama, you drew people to play the roles created in the original trauma to help you complete it in a functional way. If, for instance, a male child made an unconscious agreement with his mother to take care of her feelings and another unconscious agreement with his father to be quiet and passive and not threaten his father's superior masculinity, then this child will almost certainly transfer these agreements to significant relationships with other adults. He will probably choose a partner who can play out both his mother's and father's parts. Once a person identifies the agreements of the original trauma drama, those same agreements can be traced through each layer of the onion. When our clients do this, they often see their whole life flash before them and they can actually trace the overlaying pattern from infancy as it is repeated again and again in all their relationships.

Part of what keeps the life drama recycling in adult relationships is that as a small child you were not able to process or heal these original traumas when they happened. Usually you were so small that you were not able to even verbalize your pain or abandonment. Your adult caretakers probably were not even aware that you experienced a trauma, and, therefore, did not know they needed to provide you with nurturing support. You may have unintentionally been left alone to deal with the trauma, which made it even worse.

Each time the life drama is replayed with the same kind of traumatic ending, another layer is added to your onion and more unexpressed feelings are added to those of the previous layers.

42

These unexpressed feelings act as a magnet and help to draw the next act of your trauma drama. Each time the drama replays, we believe that people unconsciously hope that this time the drama will get them what they really wanted in the first place: that their unmet needs will finally be met.

There are several things you will need to do to complete the unfinished business in your core trauma. You must identify your core traumas, to express the feelings connected to them, to receive support for the feelings and have the experiences validated. Once this happens, the "charge" is taken out of the traumas and they can be understood and healed. Frequently, we have clients role play their trauma in a psychodrama, allowing them for the first time to speak the truth about what really happened to them, to have caring people witness this original wound and help support and validate their feelings and their experiences.

THE DRAMA TRIANGLE

The family dynamic known as the Drama Triangle (Karpman, 1968), which involves a a Persecutor, a Rescuer and a Victim, is a common form of life drama. In Karpman's Drama Triangle, the game serves to keep the Persecutor and the Rescuer from communicating directly. You can see in the Drama Triangle diagram below that there is no direct communication link between the Persecutor and the Rescuer.

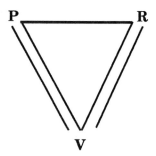

We believe that the dynamics of the Drama Triangle are actually dysfunctional attempts to complete the separation process in the counter-dependent stage of development. The resolutions to the Drama Triangle are simple. First, there must be a commitment as an individual to stop getting your needs met by being a victim and begin to ask directly for what you want and need. Second, you must connect the missing communication link between the Persecutor and the Rescuer on the triangle . When these things are done, it becomes possible to successfully complete the separation process in the counter-dependent stage of development.

GUIDELINES FOR COMPLETING THE SEPARATION PROCESS

As you remember from Chapter Two, the successful completion of the psychological birth requires the support of two bonded caregivers who can help the child become emotionally and psychologically separate from each of them.

There are some very specific guidelines to follow in successfully completing the separation process.

1. When one bonded caregiver is not available to meet the child's needs and the child complains or gets upset, the available caregiver should do the following:
- Support the child's feelings. ("I can see that you are upset because your daddy left.")
- Not agree or disagree with the judgment the child has about the "badness" of the unavailable parent, but offer empathy to the child. ("It's hard when you don't see your daddy all day. You'd like him to stay here with you.")
- Reassure the child that his or her needs will be met. ("I'm here to take care of you while your daddy is at work today.")
- Inform the child that the missing caregiver will return. ("Your daddy will be back at four o'clock to pick you up and take you home.")
- Inform the returning caregiver about the child's reaction to the separation. ("Kevin was sad today when you had to leave. He wished that he could be with you all day today.")

2. The returning caregiver should do the following:
- Ask the child if this is true. ("Were you upset today that I had to leave? Did you want me to stay with you all day?")
- Support the child's feelings and offer closeness. ("You were sad today. Do you need anything from me right now?")
- Express his own feelings about separation to the child. ("I miss being with you too. I feel sad when I have to go to work and leave you.")
- Give the child reasons for the absence. ("Daddy has to go to work to earn money to pay for the things we need.")

3. When the child has a conflict with one caregiver and brings the conflict to the second caregiver, the second caregiver should do the following.
- Support the child's feelings. ("I can see that you are upset with your mother. You look angry. Are you angry?")

44

- Not agree or disagree with the judgment the child has about the first caregivers "badness" but instead offer empathy to the child. ("You are angry because Mother made you clean up your toys. You don't like to pick up your toys just because she told you to.")
- Support the child in dealing directly with the first caregiver to resolve the conflict. ("Are you willing to go to her and tell her how you feel?")
- Provide support for the child in talking to Mother. ("Do you need any help from me when you go to talk to Mother?")
- Let the child know that it is not okay to triangulate and have family secrets. ("If you are not willing to tell her how you feel, I will tell her that you are upset about your conflict with her.")
- Inform the child that you will not resolve the child's conflict with the mother and that you are available to support both the child and the mother when they are ready to resolve it. ("I do not want to get in the middle of this conflict between you and Mother. I will not go to Mother and speak for you. I will only let her know that I am aware you are angry with her. If the two of you want to talk about this, I am available to support both of you.")
- Inform the child that if he or she resolves the conflict without you that you would like to know the outcome. ("When you and Mother talk about feelings about having to pick up your toys, please let me know what happens.")

You may feel awkward and unfamiliar at first using the kind of responses modeled in the examples above. That is because we are just now learning what kind of support a child needs to go through the separation process successfully. None of us probably ever learned this kind of communication in our families or at school. When you do use it, however, you will see how effective it is in helping people feel received and more intimate in their relationships. There are also some guidelines about what *not* to do in either of the above situations.

- Do not contribute to making anyone bad. ("He is never here when you need him.")
- Do not take sides. ("You are right. He doesn't care about you. He doesn't care about anyone.")
- Do not ignore or discount feelings. ("Don't cry. Here, have a cookie.")
- Do not discount the importance of the child's situation. ("I'm busy. Go play in your room.")
- Do not create secrets. ("I won't tell her you are angry at her.")
- Do not rescue. ("I'll talk to your mother and tell her that you don't have to pick up your toys.")

• Do not play "two against one." ("Let's go talk to your mother. We'll tell her that you don't have to pick up your toys.")
Using both sets of the above guidelines is critical for completing the task of separation in the counter-dependent stage of development. If you find yourself using the incorrect responses, you can always go back and change your responses. It is never too late to use the correct responses. Since most of us still have unresolved issues of our own around becoming separate, the communication guidelines identified above are also necessary for resolving conflicts in adult relationships where these same dynamics are present.

THE QUEST TO COMPLETE THE CORE TRAUMA

The person who uses co-dependent behaviors to try to heal the wounds of the early trauma may develop a relationship addiction by seeking one special person who can play "perfect parent" and fulfill all his or her narcissistic needs. In this relationship the person recreates the infantile need for blissful bonding. The intense need to attach to another person and recreate this early experience, i. e., acting co-dependent, is really breaking free in progress. Again, in looking at what is right about this behavior, we understand that people instinctively know that they must return to being dependent if they want to break free of their co-dependent behaviors. When adults learn how to satisfy their need for bonding in healthy ways, they are ready to move on to complete the task of separation in the counter-dependent stage of development. The research is very clear that the more bonded a person is the easier the task of separation will be (Kaplan, 1978).

The person who uses counter-dependent behaviors to attempt to transform the wounds of his or her early trauma may try to satisfy the need for symbiotic bliss in the opposite way. Rather than risk intimacy, a person with counter-dependent needs seeks to return to the bliss of bonding through addictions to activity or substances. He or she may often seek a "high" or transcendent state through the use of work, drugs, alcohol, sex, exercise, religion, meditation or intense emotional states such as rage or high drama. Both sets of behaviors actually alter a person's mood to help him or her avoid the feelings of the early trauma. Through these dysfunctional adaptive behaviors, we believe, people are still trying in the best way they know to break free of their core childhood traumas.

46

TWO DIFFERENT PATHS TO WHOLENESS

The path to wholeness for people with counter-dependent behaviors is far different from the path of those with co-dependent issues. The chart below shows the qualities that each type needs to develop.

people with co-dependency issues need to learn to:	*people with counter-dependency issues need to learn to:*
•become more independent	•become more dependent
•focus on self	•focus on others
•build boundaries	•remove walls
•cope with strong feelings	•identify and express feelings
•identify personal strengths	•identify personal weaknesses
•be intimate with self	•be intimate with others
•be autonomous	•be cooperative
•defend against projections	•take back projections
•avoid unhealthy commitments	•make commitments
•master the world of work	•master the world of relationships
•develop compassion for self	•develop compassion for others
•create sexual boundaries.	•separate sexuality from nurturing.

A STEP-BY-STEP PROGRAM FOR CHANGING YOUR COUNTER-DEPENDENT BEHAVIORS

The main components of a program to eliminate counter-dependent patterns are listed below.

• *Identify your counter-dependent patterns.* Up until now very few people have recognized the importance counter-dependent behaviors play in eliminating addictive behaviors such as co-dependency, or addictions to food, work or activity and substances. Many therapists are puzzled about why the patterns that hold addictions in place are so hard to change. We believe the answer may lie in the not so obvious counter-dependent behaviors that often are ignored in treatment programs.

• *Use the step-by-step holistic approach presented in this book as a map for breaking free from counter-dependent patterns.* This map identifies the key steps in the process and helps you discover where you currently are on your journey to breaking free. These steps involve tranformation work at the physical, mental, emotional and spiritual levels. It is easy to get lost without a map to provide you direction. The steps include

47

remembering what happened to you as a child, identifying the characteristics of counter-dependent behaviors, feeling your feelings, learning re-parenting skills, becoming an autonomous person, learning to take charge of your body, developing a spiritual life and learning to live interdependently.

• *Learn about your developmental needs.* This approach will help you identify the missing elements from your early developmental history that are causing counter-dependent behavior patterns to recycle in your adult relationships. We include various written exercises to help you identify your unmet developmental needs. Once you understand what is missing and where it came from, you are given easy-to-follow instructions on how to get these unmet developmental needs met now in your adult relationships.

• *Learn the essential skills needed to free yourself from counter-dependent behaviors.* An entire chapter in this book is devoted to each of nine core skills. You can first read about why each skill is important and then use the skill-building exercises to develop it more fully. This self-help approach allows you to work on your counter-dependency issues either without therapy or as an adjunct to therapy. We chose these skills because we have found that they help people create more satisfying, intimate relationships. The skills are developing empathy, setting boundaries, reclaiming projections, parenting yourself, resolving conflicts, restoring natural power, communicating about sex, making commitments and developing spiritually.

• *Create committed relationships.* You can create safe environments to meet your unmet needs from the counter-dependent stage of development. This represents an exciting new approach to breaking free. We have found that people, particularly couples, who cooperate in breaking free of counter-dependent patterns discover a doorway to a deeper intimacy. People who are committed to helping each other in this way often discover a sense of soul connection.

• *Develop a broader view of counter-dependency issues.* The social and cultural aspects of counter-dependent behaviors provide a larger context for understanding these developmental deficits in adults. We see that we live in a culture that collectively has evolved to the counter-dependent stage of development. This means that counter-dependent behaviors are not wrong or bad, but simply reflect the stage to which humans have evolved. As you understand that counter-dependent behaviors are both an

48

individual issue and a social/cultural problem, you do not have to be ashamed to admit to having counter-dependent behaviors. Because of the structure of our social and cultural institutions, it would be almost impossible for you to grow up without having some counter-dependent behavior patterns. Therefore, we see the society and culture as part of the problem as well as part of the solution. This book presents a new and interesting perspective that links personal change and social change.

• *Develop a vision of life beyond co-dependent/counter-dependent issues.* We believe this is a necessary and often missing ingredient in breaking free of dysfunctional patterns. You cannot move to recovery from the limitations caused by co-dependent/counter-dependent issues unless you first develop a vision of what your life could be like without them. This book helps you develop such a vision, one that realistically can help you reach wholeness.

• *Do the practical written exercises in the book.* This will help you apply the concepts in this book to your own life. We urge you to take the time to write out the exercises we present, as they offer powerful opportunities for you to deepen your understanding of counter-dependent patterns and learn how they effect your life. These practical exercises, which we have used in our workshops and therapy intensives and with clients, can help you break free of counter-dependent behaviors.

AWARENESS ACTIVITY:
Identifying Your Core Traumas

When you enter a relationship, you usually begin to develop primal trust in this person. This usually involves having a limited "all good" view of who this person really is. You may tend to see your partner as kind, all loving and always available to meet your needs. This view is similar to the blissful state of paradise the child experiences in infancy. Then at some point, something happens that ends paradise, leaving you feeling betrayed, abused or abandoned.

Later in childhood and even on into adulthood, we continue to recreate paradise in our close relationships as a way of breaking free of our core trauma. Each time we do, however, we usually find

49

paradise shattered again by a betrayal of some kind in which someone fails to play his or her role as the perfect parent. Betrayal can become a useful growth experience if we learn to look at what is right about it. (See *Breaking Free of Addictive Family Relationships*, Weinhold, 1991.) It can also help us identify elements of our trauma drama as described in the exercise below.

1. Begin by making a list of the significant traumas or betrayals you have experienced in your life. This can be the times you were betrayed by others as well as the times that you were the betrayer. You can make a chronological list, beginning with the most recent and go to your earliest childhood memory. You can use a few sentences or short phrases to describe each trauma. Then put them in a chronology that begins with the earliest trauma.

2. Review your list, asking these questions.
• What similarities are there between these traumas?
• What was my role in each trauma or betrayal?
• What were the circumstances that set up my betrayals?
• How did I feel in each betrayal or trauma?
• What beliefs, values, assumptions and expectations have I
    formed about myself and about the world as the result of
    these traumas or betrayals?
• How does my earliest trauma replay in each of the other
    traumas?
• What is the drama that has replayed over and over in my life?

3. Now write *"The Story of My Life."* Encapsulate your list of traumas into a mythic or metaphoric tale. Let your story reflect the relationship you see between your early traumas and your life drama.

4. Look at your life drama to see what isn't finished. Examine each event or betrayal to see what you need to do to complete it. Then construct experiences for yourself on your own, in therapy, in a support group or in committed relationships to actually do the completion work.

Chapter Four

THE DISEASING OF RELATIONSHIPS

"In every generation there has to be some fool
who will speak the truth as he sees it."
Boris Pasternak
Great Words of Our Time

In the first three chapters of this book, we have looked at the American family system and identified certain dynamics and deficiencies that help set up conditions that foster counter-dependent and co-dependent behaviors. In this chapter, we begin to look at counter-dependent issues from a broader social and psychological view. We also look at the role our mental health care system plays in keeping people counter-dependent.

THE DISEASING OF AMERICAN LIFE

It is big business today in America to label any compulsive behaviors related to food, drink, sex, relationships or activities such as worrying, gambling, smoking, working or shopping as a "disease." The people who stand to benefit most from the disease model, through the establishment of expensive residential treatment programs, have been successful in getting almost all addictions or compulsive behaviors labelled as diseases, even though there is very little solid research evidence to support this "disease model." Also, there is almost no solid research evidence to support the claims of recovery as the result of participating in these treatment programs. The National Council on Alcoholism (NCA) says that you cannot recover from the "disease" of alcohol addiction anyway and you will always have to identify yourself as an alcoholic or addict. Alcoholics Anonymous (AA) also supports this now widespread disease notion, which originally was developed to

51

counteract the moralistic judgments against alcoholics or problem drinkers who are cured by staying away from alcohol.

While there is some research linking alcohol and genetics, the evidence is mixed and contradictory at this time. What has been found is that some people cannot metabolize the sugar in alcohol and should stay completely away from it. These people have an allergy to alcohol.

Dr. George Vaillant, a physician and a strong supporter of AA, defends calling alcoholism a disease—well, sort of. He argues, "alcoholism is not, strictly speaking a disease — (but) calling alcoholism a disease...is a useful device both to persuade the alcoholic to admit his alcoholism and to provide a ticket for admission into the health-care system." However, he adds, "in the long run, it [the disease concept] is not effective" (Vaillant 1983).

Vaillant also did the largest comparative study on the effects of AA support verses no AA support on long-term abstinence of former alcohol abusers. He found 81 percent of those who quit on their own were still abstinent after ten years, while only 32 percent of those who attended AA meetings remained abstinent after ten years (Vaillant 1983).

The popularity of the disease concept of alcoholism has been spread by the NCA and by AA. In 1956 the American Medical Association (AMA) determined that alcoholism was a disease, even though at that time there was almost no research evidence to support the claim. As noted earlier, the founders of AA used the word "disease" metaphorically, meaning that they believed that alcohol addiction looked somewhat like a disease. Certainly, this concept was useful at that time because of the widespread moral condemnation of alcohol abusers. The AMA, however, saw how useful and profitable it might be to drop the metaphoric use of the term, so they stretched their diagnostic categories to include alcoholism. So definitive and authoritative was this pronouncement that by 1987 (according to a Gallop Poll survey) almost 90% of Americans believed alcoholism was a disease.

Once alcoholism was accepted as a disease, so was the so-called disease of co-alcoholism (now called co-dependency). This was defined as a disease that a person "caught" while growing up in an alcoholic family. This was then followed by the diseasing of compulsive behaviors related to sex, gambling, eating, worrying, smoking, raging, shopping, religious beliefs and being in a destructive relationship. The only compulsive behavior so far to escape the disease label is compulsive working (workaholism).

52

Using the current medical approach, almost any set of behaviors engaged in excessively or compulsively that might have intermittently harmful affects on a person or others that this person relates to is defined as an addiction, which then (and now for the biggest leap) is "automatically defined as a disease."

WHAT IS AN ADDICTION?

Deciding what qualifies as an addiction and what doesn't is difficult enough. The bottom line is usually that some medical expert who is "diagnosing" a particular set of a person's compulsive behaviors decides that this person is "out of control" or unable to exercise reasonable control over these behaviors. This is often based on a subjective judgment that may also be influenced by the socio-economic status of the person with the so-called addiction. In the last half of the twentieth century this medical definition of addiction has replaced the standard definition of an "addiction," which before circa 1900 meant a particular enjoyment found by engaging in a habit. This habit could be related to ingesting certain foods or drink (alcoholic or non-alcoholic) or to taking certain medicines such as herbal tonics or diuretics. As late as 1906, large potent doses of cocaine were part of the mixture in the popular drink Coca-Cola (Grinspoon & Bakalar 1985).

ADDICTIONS AS DISEASES

Defining addictions as diseases is another matter. First, we need to know that there are three kinds or groups of diseases. The first group consists of disorders known by their physical symptoms and are caused by some microbe or virus. These would include polio, malaria, influenza, AIDS, tuberculosis, etc. This list used to include cancer, heart disease and strokes, but recently it has been found that life style changes of diet, exercise and stress management contribute more to lowering death rates than any medical interventions. The standard medical approach to treatment of these diseases is to find the specific microbe that causes the disease and then develop antibiotics that can kill the microbes or prevent their spread in the body. Also in this group are diseases that are thought to be inherited, which include diabetes, cystic fibrosis, Downs Syndrome and hemophilia.

The second group of diseases includes mental or emotional illnesses. People in this group are not diagnosed by taking a blood

53

sample or a brain scan, but are diagnosed through analysis of the person's thoughts, feelings and behaviors, leading to a judgment that these social symptoms are outside the "normal range" of behavior as defined by the accepted social norms. How far they are judged to be outside the social norms determines whether a person is said to have a neurosis, a personality disorder, a psychosis or a character disorder.

The so-called diseases in the third category are called addictions, which are even further away from the microbe/virus-caused physical diseases of the first group. The addictions as diseases theory contends that

- the person inherits a genetic disposition to the addictive behavior
- the addictive behavior exists independently of the rest of a person's behaviors (the genetic disposition takes over his or her body and brain and controls the person's behavior)
- it is progressive and irreversible and if not treated will lead to death.

This logic tends to break down quickly when you apply it to specific situations. When someone addicted to smoking cigarettes gives up smoking, he or she is no longer seen as an addict. However, according to addictionology (the study of addictive behavior), this is not true for people addicted to activity, relationships, sex, food, etc. These people are told that there is no known cure for their disease and they will never get much better. In fact, they are told that they could get progressively worse and die. The best they can hope for is to not get any worse. In the meantime, considerable medical research money is being spent in trying to find a pill or a chemical that will bring relief to the countless millions of so-called addicts (estimates are that 96-98 percent of the population have at least one of these addictive diseases, with many people being diagnosed as having multiple addictions). Those who promote this disease model for addictions usually describe the disease as follows:

- The disease is marked by a loss of control of behavior.
- The sufferer cannot receive education and training to gain control of his or her behavior.
- The disease will get worse regardless of any life style changes.
- The disease is a permanent flaw or trait and sufferers must adjust to this reality for the rest of their lives.
- The disease will eventually kill the person, if long-term treatment is not used.

The only known treatment for the disease is either:
- a support group organized by and for those who share the disease,
- or medical treatment under the care or supervision of a physician or other medically trained specialist that takes place in a hospital or medical clinic.
- People with this disease must not be held responsible for the ordinary moral standards or codes of conduct that others who don't have the disease are expected to adhere to.
- Because people with this disease are prone to deny they have the disease, vigorous attempts must be made to identify such people and inflict treatment on them even against their will if necessary.

This set of criteria allows 20 million Americans to be diagnosed as alcoholics, another 80 million as co-alcoholics, 80 million with eating disorders (if you count obesity), 50 million depressed and anxious people, 20 million addicted gamblers and about 25 million love and sex addicts. Add to this number the countless workaholics, religious addicts, shopping addicts, addicted smokers and spectator sports addicts. Without adding in these additional addictions, this totals to 275 million addicts in this country (Peele 1989), which means there are more than enough addictions for each man, woman and child to have one of his or her own. Only with alcoholism is there any research evidence that supports calling an addiction a disease. Other addictions, in which there is no research evidence of any genetic predisposition toward a disease, should not, in our opinion, be labeled a disease.

I AM MY DISEASE

The disease approach to addictions encourages people to identify with their disease or addiction. They are told to say to people, "I am an addict" or "I am a co-dependent." They are also told that they will always have to identify themselves this way. They are further told that if they make progress, maybe their 12-step group or therapist may allow them to claim to be "a recovering addict" or "in recovery." This is put forth as the best they can hope for in their lives. They are not allowed to identify themselves as having recovered and, therefore, having a disease becomes their primary identity for the rest of their life.

The encouragement to identify with a disease is disempowering and creates another form of co-dependency. How can people break free from addictive behaviors if they are not given any vision of possible change?

It is understandable that identification with the addiction is a necessary step to help some people overcome their denial, but it needs to be reframed. It is much healthier, in our opinion, to have people identify themselves as "someone with an addiction" or "being addicted to an activity, a relationship, to sex, to food, etc." This kind of definition allows for growth and change, so that at some point they can become "someone who has recovered from an addiction" or "someone who is no longer addicted to relationships, sex, food, etc." A developmental definition of addictions allows individuals to reclaim their power and to control their lives. It also provides an essential vision of wholeness.

By identifying yourself as an addict or a co-dependent, you still keep your shame-based identity. Shame means that there is something wrong with you; you are flawed and cannot change the way you are. Remember that the original purpose behind labelling alcohol abuse as a disease was to take the shame and moral judgment out of alcoholism, thus enabling more people to seek treatment. We believe that having people constantly identify themselves as co-dependents or addicts keeps the shame present and drives it further from our conscious awareness.

Diseasing co-dependency encourages people to give their personal power over to medical experts who then are in control of their patient's recovery. People in a powerless position cannot recover, so the disease diagnosis becomes a self-fulfilling prophecy.

THE DISEASING OF RELATIONSHIPS

Since this book is about counter-dependency and co-dependency and how these two problems interact in relationships, we will look more closely at how this disease concept now is being applied to relationship problems.

Co-dependency grew out of the alcoholism field and so it naturally inherited the disease tradition without question, even though there is no research evidence to support any physiological addiction or genetic link. Almost all of the books on co-dependency have accepted this disease model of co-dependency. We believe that this disease orientation poses several additional problems. Most experts on co-dependency say that 96 to 98 percent of the population has co-dependent tendencies. If one were to use the same disease-oriented tactic with co-dependents that is used with alcoholics, namely to have them abstain from the addictive substance, then it would be unsafe for people with unresolved co-dependency and counter-dependency issues to be in relationship with each other. As developmental psychologists, we believe that this disease orientation scares both co-dependents and counter-dependents away from what could be a primary source of transformation: committed, conscious relationships.

Besides offering almost no hope of breaking free, the disease model of co-dependency is producing another interesting reaction. Due to the "diseasing of co-dependency," more and more people are attempting to prove that they don't have this awful disease by escaping into counter-dependent behaviors that make them look good. This includes staying away from making any relationship commitments or not getting very close and intimate with anyone.

Finally, the concept of relationship itself is being diseased by saying that anyone who has a close relationship must be either a love or a sex addict. As a result, many people are avoiding relationships altogether to avoid being diagnosed as a love or a sex addict. A whole new movement of 12-step groups, Sex and Love Addicts Anonymous (SLAA), has become very popular in certain parts of the country. Granted, there are addictive and compulsive behaviors around love and sex, but we believe these behaviors are not the result of a disease.

We believe that all compulsive and addictive behaviors are attempts (sometimes desperate attempts) to avoid certain repressed negative feelings from childhood. This is usually done by finding some mood-altering substance, activity or person to focus on which allows the person to temporarily forget about these negative feelings. Instead of calling it a disease, we see all compulsive or addictive behaviors as:

• adaptive ways to avoid the deep unresolved feelings and issues that people have as a result of not getting some of their bonding and separation needs met in early childhood and
• unskilled attempts to get these bonding and separation needs met as adults.

Sex and love addictions have become such an issue, we believe, because most of the adult population of this culture has severe early developmental deficiencies in bonding. Because people lack the necessary skills for creating nonsexual intimacy and bonding, they use the sexual act to try to get some of those needs met. In reality, some of what they probably are wanting or needing is nonsexual touch and nurturing. This is difficult for most people to get because most men and women in our culture cannot

57

separate sexual touch from nurturing touch in relationships. Some women who have been involved in childbearing and childrearing may have learned to discriminate between sexuality and nurturing during the intimate bonding experiences of holding, touching and talking to a young child. Breast feeding, in particular, helps women develop the awareness of this difference. Most men don't have these opportunities (certainly not breast feeding) and often have not developed this important discrimination.

One of our clients is a classic example of this. He grew up in a family where there was no nurturing touch. He describes his mother as cold and unavailable. When he married, he also married a woman who was cold and unavailable. After the birth of their first child, he felt his wife even less available to him. His need for nurturing touch became more desperate. Because he could not sort out nurturing touch and sexual touch, he ended up sexually molesting his daughter when she was six. He got her to stroke his penis while he stroked her clitoris. After a couple of weeks, he realized the inappropriateness of his behavior and stopped it. He was overcome with tremendous feelings of guilt and shame, which he began covering with addictions to alcohol, sex and work. He finally entered therapy thinking he was a despicable sex addict and child molester. Through therapy he discovered that he had a touch deprivation because of severe bonding deficits in childhood and that he did not know how to get his needs met in nonsexual ways. Through his therapy, he learned appropriate ways to discriminate between sexual touch and nurturing touch and began rebuilding his life.

Men and women who have not learned to discriminate between sexual touch and nurturing touch will seek physical closeness and touch in the only way they know: through sex. Our developmental perspective looks at what is "right" about the phenomenon of "Sex and Love Addiction" instead of labeling it a "disease." It involves "looking for love in all the wrong places" and usually does not satisfy the need for nurturing and bonding, but is the best way currently available for many people.

Sadly, because of the diseasing of relationships, many people in SLAA groups are cautioned against entering a relationship and are told that entering a relationship is like an alcoholic taking another drink. Meetings are often filled with confessions from people who had the urge to get into a relationship, but they called a group member instead or attended an extra SLAA meeting.

Rather than diseasing co-dependency and counter-dependency, we believe the most direct way to address these problems is to help people discover what their unmet developmental needs are and then to help them find direct ways to get these needs met in their relationships. We tell people not to avoid relationships, unless the relationship is physically or emotionally abusive. Rather, we support people in using all their relationships (work, social, romantic, friend, family, spousal) as sources for learning how to get these important developmental needs met in healthy ways. In this perspective, relationships can become an important supportive environment for changing counter-dependent and co-dependent behaviors rather than the cause of the problem.

Besides helping more and more medical specialists get more and more wealthy, the disease model is also threatening to bankrupt the insurance industry. Co-dependency and counter-dependency are now being diagnosed as mental diseases, using either the neurotic category of "Adjustment Disorder" or the more serious category of "Personality Disorder." This allows practitioners to collect third-party payments from insurance companies for treating co-dependency and counter-dependency. Between 1978 and 1984 the number of for-profit residential treatment centers increased by 350 percent and their case load rose by 400 percent (Weisner and Room 1984).

Typical twenty-eight day in-patient programs (twenty-eight days is the usual maximum length for in-patient care that most insurances will pay for) cost the patient's insurance company from $16,000 to $35,000. CompCare, which opened a chain of residential treatment centers, spent $5.8 million on TV ads during the first half of 1988 alone (Alsop 1988). Many of these ads played on people's fears that their undetected disease would eventually kill them or a family member if they didn't seek immediate treatment. This is all taking place in spite of the fact that there are no solid follow-up studies that prove that the treatment approaches most utilized in these centers produce any lasting results.

BREAKING FREE OF COUNTER-DEPENDENT BEHAVIORS

The elements needed to break free of counter-dependent behaviors by getting therapy, attending a 12-Step support group or by changing your relationship patterns are:

- having a strong desire to change
- learning to accept and express repressed feelings appropriately
- being willing to develop new life skills and resources to support desired change
- improving communications skills for work, personal and family relationships
- getting support and encouragement from others
- developing new values and beliefs and
- developing a new vision of life beyond their addiction.

It is possible for anyone to eliminate their counter-dependent behaviors if they incorporate these seven elements into their personal change program, whether it involves therapy, 12-step support groups or committed relationships.

Cost containment procedures are now being instituted by almost all insurance companies, limiting either the number of days of in-patient care, the number of sessions of out-patient care or the dollar amounts for both. What is needed for those who wish to use therapy to help overcome addictive or compulsive behaviors is an effective short-term therapy approach that focuses on the seven success factors listed above. Our Developmental Process Work approach uses short-term therapy along with nontherapy support systems that are based on these success factors. Later in this chapter we will discuss this approach, but first we will examine some of the hazards built into the therapy industry.

THE DISEASING OF THERAPY

There are a number of additional factors that contribute to the popularity of the disease model among therapists. Being aware of these factors may help you make intelligent, informed decisions, if you decide to seek psychotherapeutic help for changing any of your counter-dependent or co-dependent behaviors.

Family History of Therapists. Therapists themselves are not the most stable lot, often suffering from burn-out and other stresses. Interestingly, they have a common profile of developmental unfinished business. As a rule, therapists are first born or the only child and are often pushed through childhood too quickly, without the warmth, nurturing, protection and love that children deserve. They frequently are asked to become a little adult and take care of their parents. They grow up believing that hard work and taking care of others are the only ways to get their need to be appreciated met. They also have low self-esteem and generally are loners, not making friends easily and not knowing how to receive love or how to be intimate. They fit the counter-dependent profile perfectly and often form co-dependent relationships with their clients in an attempt to meet their own unmet developmental needs to be liked and valued (Maeder 1989).

The Training of Therapists. What makes it worse is that most training programs for psychotherapists do not require any self-analysis or personal therapy. Instead, graduate students are often told that psychologists or therapists should be detached, objective scientists who must not let their own values, beliefs and needs interfere with their scientific approach to people. Generally, this teaches prospective therapists to hide any weaknesses or insecurities and instead learn to "look good" to clients and colleagues. This includes wearing special clothing (some even wear white coats), assigning diagnoses to their clients (or "patients" as medically-oriented therapists prefer to call the people they try to help), and using technical jargon that makes others think they are important and smart.

The Risky Business of Therapy. The therapy institution itself has had a "diseasing" effect on both therapist and client. Some of the diseasing effects of therapy are as follows.

• *A long-term orientation to therapy.* The unfinished business of the therapist may cause him or her to distort the real therapeutic needs of the client. The therapist's unresolved co-dependents needs to be needed are often underneath the long-term treatment plans they create for clients. In order to combat this tendency, therapists should have regular, ongoing supervision and be committed to working on their own unresolved family of origin issues as part of their training programs or in their own private therapy.

• *A cognitive orientation to therapy.* Psychoanalytic therapies, such as Freudian analysis and Jungian analysis; psychodynamic therapies, such as Adlerian Therapy and Transactional Analysis; and cognitive therapies, such as Reality Therapy and Rational Emotive Therapy are basically forms of "talk" therapy. Such therapeutic approaches often allow the therapist to remain in a detached and aloof position. Many cognitive therapies do not address the clients' feelings and the deeper kinds of relationship issues that co-dependents and counter-dependents must address if they are to resolve their unfinished bonding and separation issues.

61

One of our clients, who had previously been in therapy with a cognitive therapist, was told by his therapist that he could not express his feelings in his therapy sessions because it might disturb the other therapists and clients in other offices in the building. This is a common ploy by therapists who are afraid that a client who is expressing his or her real feelings might trigger the therapist's own repressed feelings. Most psychotherapy still involves talking "about" feelings without actually experiencing them. (We believe, without actively expressing your real feelings in psychotherapy, you can only learn to better understand the problem and your feelings *about it*.) Talk therapy by itself will not transform the wounds that are at the source of the problem.

• *A financially-based orientation to therapy.* Therapists, like many medically-oriented practitioners, charge what the traffic will bear. As a result, therapy costs have skyrocketed in the past ten years, leaving most clients unable to afford long-term therapy unless they have good insurance coverage. During this same period, insurance companies have responded to cost increases by limiting the dollar amounts they will pay or the number of sessions they will cover in a calendar year. This has effectively excluded most low income clients and has made private therapy "a rich man's" privilege. The poor are required to seek therapy in mental health centers that are understaffed and that often use minimally trained persons as therapists. Some therapists will offer you a sliding scale or reduced rate if you do not have insurance. You may have to ask for this and then negotiate an affordable fee.

• *The use of pathological terminology.* In order to collect third party payments from insurance companies, most therapists have to assign a pathological diagnosis to their clients. Clients are typically labelled as Bipolar (Manic Depressive Neurosis), Dysthymic (Depressive Neurosis), Obsessive Compulsive Personality Disorder, Paranoid Personality Disorder, Schizoid Personality Disorder, Borderline Personality Disorder and so on. The criteria for most of these diagnostic categories are vague and subjective, so that one psychotherapist may assign a certain diagnosis while another therapist may find an entirely different "disease" in the same person. Rarely do these diagnoses directly affect the course of treatment, but they do affect the course of payment by insurance companies. Companies will only pay for about six to nine months of therapy if the diagnosis is an "Adjustment Disorder," while they will usually pay indefinitely for

"Personality Disorders" such as the Narcissistic Personality Disorder or the Borderline Personality Disorder. Guess which diagnoses are used more frequently.

• **The danger of misuse of diagnoses.** These diagnoses easily get into a client's health record, which he or she is usually required to release to employers or other health care providers. In other words, these pathologically-sounding diagnoses can easily fall into the hands of employers or other nonmental health providers who have no understanding of what they mean. People can actually be turned down for promotions at work because of a "questionable" diagnosis in their personnel file. For this reason, business and professional people often prefer to pay for therapy out of their own pocket, even though they have good health insurance coverage. They are afraid that any reference to mental health problems will kill any promotion possibilities. This is especially true in the military service. Any reference on a personnel record to a diagnosis for a mental disorder is often the kiss of death for promotion. It may even result in a less than honorable discharge as well. This leads to an over-emphasis on the denial of any emotional problems and a reliance on counter-dependent behaviors, in order to look good to the authorities in charge.

DEVELOPMENTAL PROCESS WORK: A NEW THERAPEUTIC APPROACH

In using our developmental approach with co-dependent and counter-dependent behaviors in clients, we discovered that many of them can move quickly into more functional lives with focused, short-term treatment. Over the past six years, we have created an approach which we call Developmental Process Work. It is a short-term approach for working with people who seek therapeutic help to overcome the affects of counter-dependent/co-dependent relationship problems. Our approach is based on the following basic assumptions:

• **There is a certain "rightness" about your symptoms.** We ask clients to look at their present symptoms as unskilled attempts to transform themselves. We help them see that what is trying to happen is right and the way the clients are approaching their problems is the best way they know how.

• **You, the client, know more about your process than we will ever know.** As therapists, our job is to follow the client's

63

process, which will eventually reveal to the the client and the therapist what the causes are of the client's problems. This also places the power for change in the client's possession, where we believe it should be.

• **You, the client, need to be in charge of how fast you want to move.** The therapist must adjust to the client's natural pace of problem solving and change. This respects the client's boundaries and allows him or her to maintain personal power and set the pace.

• **All your current conflicts and problems are the result of unmet developmental needs from childhood.** By following the client's process, the therapist and the client will be led to the source of the client's conflicts and problems. This source is usually a trauma or set of traumas occurring sometime in the first three years of life.

• **Any unmet developmental need will continue to recycle in your life until it is met.** The therapist needs to help the client discover these patterns and then suggest ways the client might get these needs met now.

• **It is never too late to get your childhood developmental needs met.** The therapist's job is to teach the client the skills necessary to get these needs met.

• **Therapy should consist of short-term written contracts (3-6 sessions for individual or couples therapy) to work on specific problems.** Initially, group therapy contracts should be limited to 8-10 sessions. These contracts should be evaluated at the end of the specified number of sessions before the therapist decides to go further with the client.

The skills that therapists need to have to be effective with this approach can be easily taught to spouses, friends and family members to use in nontherapeutic settings. The main skills can be summarized as follows:

• Learning to listen to verbal signals and to watch for nonverbal signals that suggest the presence of unmet developmental needs.

• Learning to follow the client's process. This involves knowing what questions to ask and how to read the "feedback" of the client, which tells you if you are doing well at following them or not.

• Teaching the client how to gain access to essential information contained in his or her verbal and nonverbal behaviors. This may require the therapist to have a "tool box" of things to suggest that the client use to gain access to his or her unconscious information, which usually includes unmet developmental needs.

• Teaching clients how to make effective contracts with themselves and others to get these needs met and to complete the developmental tasks left unfinished from their past.

We have found that by using this approach, most clients experience major changes in three to six sessions of individual or couples therapy. In this short period, many of our clients can begin to understand the causes of their unhappiness and conflicts, and they begin to develop new skills for changing their counter-dependent or co-dependent behaviors. Depending on how self-directed and motivated a client is and how much support the client has from a spouse, friends or support groups, he or she may not need any additional therapy beyond the initial series, or may just want to contract for periodic "check-ups."

Long-term therapy may be in order for a small percentage of people who aren't as self-directed or do not have the emotional support they need outside of therapy, or for those with severe early childhood traumas. Severe co-dependent behaviors are often similar to those found in people diagnosed as having a "Borderline Personality Disorder"; and severe counter-dependent behaviors are similar to those found in people diagnosed as having a "Narcissistic Personality Disorder." In these cases, long-term therapy may be necessary to create lasting change. However, many clients with co-dependent and counter-dependent behaviors are still misdiagnosed into these more pathological categories, primarily because of the therapists' desires to receive long-term third-party payments from insurance.

TO DISEASE OR NOT DISEASE

By comparing the behaviors of a so-called addictive disease with how a developmental approach might look at the same behaviors, you will see how our approach differs from the medical approach. Read the following chart which compares some of the classic symptoms of so-called sex addicts and co-addicts (left-hand column), with a developmental explanation of how we might view each of these behaviors (right-hand column):

Characteristics of Love and and Sex Addicts (Brandon 1989)	*UnmetDevelopmental Needs Involved*
• Constantly obsesses about the the sex addict's behavior and motives	• Trying to please others in order to meet needs for recognition, approval and love.
• Compulsive sex is like a drug.	• An attempt to avoid unpleasant childhood feelings such as sadness, grief, anger or fear.
• Believes that sex is the only way to be intimate.	• Needs to be touched and nurtured in nonsexual ways. May have been sexually abused.
• Uses sex as a way to feel validated and complete.	• Did not get enough mirroring or positive affirmations as a child.
• Searches for some magical quality in others to make them feel complete.	• Looking for someone to help them meet their unmet developmental needs for love and acceptance.
• Uses sex as a way to bring excitement and intensity into their life without having to admit to having unmet needs.	• Sex is a way he/she tries to get needs met for nurturing and intimacy
• Drawn to people who are not available to them.	• Fear of being controlled or enengulfed. Sees people as substitutes for unavailable parents who didn't provide effective nurturing.
• In a relationship, they fear abandonment and rejection.	• He/she fears a replay of childhood abandonment and rejection. The need for strong bonding not met.
• When not in a relationship, they feel empty and lonely.	• He/she has many unmet needs for bonding and intimacy, but is afraid to appear needy and dependent.
• They try to lose themselves in romantic obsessions.	• He/she has a strong need to be sex loved and to become a whole and complete person. Sex is a safe way, perhaps the only way, he/she knows to try to get this need met.
• They develop unhealthy dependency relationships and then feel trapped by them.	• Never felt loved as a child. Gives up self in hopes of gaining love. Doesn't know how to be emotion ally separate.

In the traditional methods of treating sex addicts, the illness concept is used to "reassure" them that there is nothing morally wrong with them, that they are just "sick." Carnes (1989) writes, "The illness concept helps affirm the personal worth of the addict...Furthermore, realizing that one has an illness decreases the shame of being out of control" (p. 234). Our Developmental Process Work approach says that the reason you have a so-called sexual addiction is that you have unmet developmental needs from childhood that can be identified and then met in present time. Which would you rather be told, "you have an illness that you may not recover from" or "you have unmet needs that you can meet, thus making it unnecessary to engage in any further addictive behaviors in the future"? Obviously, the latter is more hopeful and more clearly related to the actual treatment of the problem.

Actually, as stated above, the illness concept is used to reassure the client that he or she has done nothing morally wrong, which does relieve the guilt they may feel. However, to tell them they have a disease, a flaw in their make-up, only reinforces the shame that they already feel. Bradshaw (1989) differentiates between guilt and toxic shame, saying that guilt means you *did* something wrong and toxic shame means there *is* something wrong with you which cannot be fixed. The illness concept, as it currently is used, can add to the toxic shame the person may already feel.

We believe, therefore, that the disease or illness concept, while it serves to relieve guilt, ultimately traps people in the shame of their addictions. The developmental approach that we use avoids this altogether and relieves both the guilt and the shame that the client may be carrying.

Knowing that this is an imperfect world, there is a good chance that you will get a therapist who has co-dependent or counter-dependent behaviors or has not worked through his or her own unfinished business from childhood. In order to avoid getting into a "diseasing" relationship with your therapist, we suggest the following guidelines:

HOW TO CHOOSE A THERAPIST

• Interview your therapist before deciding to start therapy. We suggest doing this with at least three people to determine with whom you feel the most comfortable. Many therapists will offer you a free consultation, if you ask.

• Use the inventory at the end of this chapter to check out the therapist for "diseasing" tendencies. If you see some warning signals, don't sign up.   67

- Ask your therapist what he or she has done to deal with his or her own co-dependent or counter-dependent patterns. If you get resistance to your questions, choose another therapist.
- Ask to set up specific written goals, a specific number of sessions and periodic progress checks. If you get resistance to this, choose another therapist.
- Ask your therapist for references from former clients or present clients who you can talk to you about the results they have achieved. Most therapists will claim this is confidential information, but if you insist, they can get permission from their clients to allow you to talk to them.
- If you enter therapy and are not satisfied with the results you are achieving, get a second opinion or discuss this with your therapist. If your therapist does not support your efforts to get the results you want, terminate therapy. This should always be your choice.

IS YOUR THERAPIST DISEASING YOU?

Many therapists are "addicted" to the medical model which allows them to remain in control and keep their clients diagnosed as co-dependent and "diseased." The following inventory may help you identify these diseasing tendencies in your present therapist or may help you spot these tendencies in any prospective therapist.

AWARENESS ACTIVITY:
The Diseasing Therapist Inventory

Directions: Place a number in the blank before each statement to indicate the degree to which this statement is true in your life.
1 = Never   2 = Occasionally   3 = Frequently   4 = Almost always

Does Your Therapist:

_____ 1. Talk too much in your sessions?

_____ 2. Have to look good and have all the right answers?

_____ 3. Ask leading questions, but will not tell you why?

_____ 4. Seem overworked and exhausted?

_____ 5. Sit in his/her "special chair"?

_____ 6. Let sessions run overtime?

_____ 7. Take credit for your progress in therapy?

_____ 8. Refuse to acknowledge or work on his/her own co-dependency/counter-dependency issues?

_____ 9. Let phone calls come through during your sessions?

_____ 10. Use lots of professional jargon and try to snow you with terminology?

_____ 11. Get defensive when you give any negative feedback or ask questions?

_____ 12. Give write-offs or fee reductions to "special clients"?

_____ 13. Tell you what you are doing wrong rather than how you are improving?

_____ 14. Seem formal and distant in sessions?

_____ 15. Wear clothing that sets him/her apart from clients?

_____ 16. Use disease-oriented diagnostic terms to describe your problem to you?

_____ 17. Get threatened if you want to talk to other professionals (get a second opinion)?

_____ 18. Set the goals of therapy for you?

_____ 19. Have unclear therapy contracts that are open-ended and that leave the length and goals of the therapy undetermined?

_____ 20. Get very upset if you have to change a scheduled session?

_____   TOTAL

Scoring: Add up the column of numbers and get a total score. Use the following guidelines to interpret your score.

20 - 40   Little or no damaging effects on the therapeutic relationship. (Very little "diseasing" is present.)

41 - 60   Some damaging effects on the therapeutic relationship. (Some tendencies to "disease" clients.)

61 - 80   Many possible damaging effects on the therapeutic relationship. (Strong evidence of "diseasing" of clients.)

Chapter Five

THE COUNTER-DEPENDENT CULTURE

"There are a number of signs that we in America
may be on the threshold of a period as a nation when we
shall no longer be able to camouflage or repress our despair."
Rollo May
Freedom and Destiny

Each day seems to bring more news of the disintegrating fabric of our American way of life: an economic depression; racial unrest; growing levels of air and water pollution; the breakdown of family structures; a resurgence in the repression of human rights for women, children and minority religious and ethnic groups; continued scandals in high level political offices; deteriorating highways and cities; growing numbers of homeless individuals and families; a rise in the number of violent crimes; and an epidemic number of people involved in breaking free of various addictions. The list is so large that just thinking about the magnitude of the problems can be overwhelming. It is easy to become immobilized in fear, anxiety, helplessness and powerlessness, for it seems as though the whole world is on the edge of collapsing. It is easier to escape into denial through our favorite addiction than to face the truth: something is dreadfully wrong in the world.

The process of remembering what happened to us in our family of origin throws us back into our childhood wounds. Dealing with these wounds and the addictions we've used to deny them tends to make us myopic and truly live "one day at a time." Sometimes the process of breaking free also catapults us back into a child's reality. It is an express intent of this book to provide you with a framework for the breaking free process that empowers you to change your behaviors, to create functional relationship patterns and to improve the quality of your life. One way that we do this for ourselves and for our clients is to provide a larger context not only for understanding addictions, but also for understanding how family patterns create problems in the world. This chapter is about that larger context.

APPLYING THE DEVELOPMENTAL MODEL TO THE WORLD

In Chapter One we identified four successive stages of development (co-dependent, counter-dependent, independent and interdependent) that individuals must pass through to reach psychological maturity, with specific tasks that need to be completed in each stage (bonding, separation, autonomy/mastery and cooperation). This four-stage model of development, which looks at the growth of the individual, is like looking at life through a close-up lens on a camera. If we take off that close-up lens and instead look at life with a wide-angle lens, we also see the individual as a cell in the larger social/cultural system and as a participant in the evolutionary history of all humans.

In this chapter we will apply our four-stage model of development in broader ways. We will show how these stages are really a growth process that can be applied to different levels of our current cultural system and to the evolutionary history of the human species. Applying our developmental model to couple relationships, to the family, to the society and culture, to the United States as a nation and to other nations helps us see ourselves and our problems in a broader perspective. We begin to feel more connected to those around us as we realize that the whole world is working on developmental issues.

We have seen this quite clearly in our recent trips to Russia and Ukraine. When we lived in private homes in the former Soviet republics, we found ourselves deeply immersed in a society that is quite different from ours. Our experience there helped us look more deeply at our model for understanding individual development. As we did that, our perspective about our model deepened, broadening and shifting our focus. We began to to understand the world more clearly and to see the relationship between the development of an individual and the evolution of humans as a whole.

A primary goal of this chapter is to help you reframe your beliefs, perceptions and life experiences regarding counter-dependency and other unfinished developmental issues. Applying our developmental model to the history of the human species helps us see that counter-dependency is also a stage in our evolution as humans. Viewing counter-dependent behaviors from these broader perspectives helps depersonalize our problems somewhat, helps us understand these behaviors in an evolutionary context and helps remove the judgments that many people may still have about dysfunctional adult behaviors in general.

A SYSTEMS PERSPECTIVE OF COUNTER-DEPENDENCY

Seeing the relationship between the "micro" (the individual) and the "macro" (the culture) is useful, for it helps us understand our place in the universe. We can see that common patterns of behavior replay, at each interlocking subsystem level of the larger system: at the individual level, at a couple level, at the family level, at the institutional level, at a national level and at an international level. When you can view development in this way, your world begins to appear less complex and more understandable. When you can view the total development of human consciousness in this way, it helps remove you from the myopia of the moment and provide you with an expanded vision of human possibilities.

A Relationship Perspective

When two people come together in an intimate relationship, there is a period of symbiosis and closeness. This period, which parallels the co-dependent stage of individual development, also has bonding as its task.

Depending on how conscious the couple is about this opportunity to complete gaps in their individual bonding and how willing they are to risk sharing their incomplete bonding issues, they may or may not get their unmet bonding needs met. Regardless of whether the bonding is completed or not, at some point in the relationship one or both of the members will begin to draw away from the intimacy. This person will want to explore the world though new activities or by developing auxiliary relationships. Or one member may become frightened or feel suffocated by the intimacy and want to flee from it by creating some physical and psychological space.

These conflicting pulls between oneness and separateness can reoccur almost daily in some relationships. Most couples do not have the awareness or the skills needed to handle these conflicts. Without an awareness that this desire for some separation is normal developmental behavior, two people in an intimate relationship may try to complete their emotional separation process in destructive ways: by having affairs, by complaining to others about their partner's shortcomings, by escaping into addictions or even by divorcing.

If both parties in a relationship are aware of the feelings of fear or anxiety that accompany the normal need for emotional separation and are committed to dealing with them, then the separation process can become an opportunity for mutual growth. For this to happen, both parties must understand the developmental stages and hold a vision of reaching the stages of independence and interdependence while they work through the issues around separation. This is impossible unless they understand the developmental sources of these issues and have good conflict resolution skills (see Chapter Eleven for conflict resolution skills).

A Family Perspective

Families also replay these same developmental stages. In the early years of the family, when the children arrive and the family becomes bonded, they develop a cohesiveness parallel to the co-dependent stage of individual development. The school years, when the children gradually separate from the parents, parallel the counter-dependent stage of individual development. The college years, when the children live independently but still receive some financial support, parallel the independent stage of individual development. The "empty nest" years, when the children and parents can negotiate various degrees of closeness and separateness, parallel the interdependent stage of individual development. When family members are unaware of how the developmental process applies to the family, they often get stuck in the counter-dependent stage. Here members may try ineffective ways of resolving the separation issues. For example, parents may attempt to hold on to their children too long, causing the children to act out in rebellious ways in order to get separate.

A Religious Perspective

The history of how and why the United States was settled is full of examples of counter-dependent behavior. The roots of some of these behaviors can be traced back to the religious history of Europe. Many Europeans who came to this country were religious dissenters trying to separate from mainstream (parental) religions.

Organized Christianity, which began as the Church of Rome, united Christians under the umbrella of the Roman Catholic Church. This unity, which parallels the co-dependent stage of individual development, lasted until the Protestant Reformation, when many religious dissenter groups formed the Lutheran, Anglican, Greek Orthodox and Russian Orthodox churches.

The process of fragmentation became a generalized movement in religion as the Lutheran church grew into Protestantism. Then as the Protestant Reformation movement developed, other subgroups formed such as the Methodists, Presbyterians and Baptists. This splintering process in religion, which is one of differentiation and separation, parallels the counter-dependent stage of development. Many Europeans were persecuted as dissenters when they chose to separate from the prevailing religious dogma. Their subsequent choice to leave their country and immigrate in large numbers as Quakers, Pilgrims, Puritans and Mennonites extended the separation

In reviewing this history, it is possible to see how these immigrants used the ineffective ways of separating, causing developmental growth to break down. Most of the religious immigrants made "bad" the religion and its leaders from whom they were separating. Making a person or group bad, in order to separate, never works. Because these immigrants did not separate from their early religion or their home country feeling, "I'm okay for wanting to separate and you're okay for staying behind," they brought their unfinished separation issues to this country, where they have been played out repeatedly . For example, both the Puritans and the Pilgrims ended up punishing their members who wanted to evolve religious beliefs of the group, just as their ancestors were punished in Europe. This religious persecution forced them to emigrate to other settlements, just as their ancestors had fled Europe.

A Political Perspective

The political ideals of freedom, liberty and justice for all were carried to the United States by European political dissenters who dared to be different. So strong was their need to differentiate, to break free of restrictive religious or political rules, that they relinquished their homes, vocations and historical roots for a wilderness life of hardship in an unknown continent thousands of miles away. Eventually they established a governmental system that separated politics and religion as a way of preventing legal persecution for their religious beliefs. These European immigrants gradually settled the coastline east of the Appalachian Mountains, living first in separate colonies.

By the time this area became incorporated into a nation of thirteen colonies, many residents of the area again began to bristle at the restrictive laws and decided to separate from the nation and move westward. Some of those who left were drawn by the promise of free fertile land or wealth from gold and silver strikes. Others just didn't like close neighbors and wanted space. The human urge for more wealth, freedom, space and adventure spawned a westward movement in the United States that continued until it reached the Pacific coastline. When there were no more unsettled western areas for people to move to, they headed for the Alaskan Frontier. As Alaska became more densely populated, Americans created spaceships and headed for the moon.

We can see how strong this drive for freedom and separation is in the U. S. A. All four wars that were fought on our own soil were over the issues of freedom and independence. A main issue of the Revolutionary War was the desire by colonists to separate from the British Empire, and the Civil War issue was the right of African American people to be free from slavery.

Freedom and independence (the right to be separate and self-governing) are issues that U. S. citizens will fight for. The U. S. got involved in both World War I and World War II to prevent the aggressive governments of Germany and Japan from taking away the freedom of threatened and occupied countries. The United States did not enter World War II, however, until the bombing of Pearl Harbor made the loss of freedom seem personal and imminent.

In the western part of the U. S., the need to be separate is still particularly strong. In the Rocky Mountains, the "mountain man" and "Marlboro Man" images are alive and well, as people seek remote home sites without the confinements that come with having nearby neighbors or restrictive zoning laws. In California, counter-dependency is evidenced by the custom of "one person, one car." Many Californians consider ride sharing and public transportation as restrictions of their personal freedom. They value highly their ability to come and go as they please. Coordinating schedules with other people and waiting for a bus or train are considered by many to be a loss of their individual rights and personal freedom.

An International Perspective

The recent collapse of the USSR into fifteen republics is an excellent contemporary example of counter-dependent development happening at the international level. Many residents of the republics displayed anger and resentment toward the suffocating domination of "Mother Russia," and expressed a desire to have their own government, defense system, economic system and language. This move toward separation and autonomy ended a long period of nationhood during which a totalitarian government ruled the residents of these republics in a basically co-dependent manner. Communism supported symbiosis, dependency, powerlessness, helplessness and penalized any individual initiative. The citizens of these fifteen republics, comprised of many religious and ethnic groups that speak over one hundred languages, had to adopt a common language (Russian) and to give up their religious and ethnic histories in favor of a single political/social/economic/cultural system known as Communism.

Gorbachev's policies of glastnost (openness) and peristroika (restructuring) supported people's inner desire for differentiation, freedom, individuation and separation. The difficult task ahead for the republics is to survive the challenges of the counter-dependent stage of development: refusing to make anyone bad and creating conflict in order to separate. If they master these challenges, they can move gradually into a new form of government that allows for more independence and ultimately interdependence.

The developing nations of the world often have economic, social and political systems that encourage co-dependent behaviors in their citizens, while most of the developed nations still have systems that encourage counter-dependent behaviors. There are many economic, social and political conditions in the world today that seem to require independent and interdependent solutions. As we become more able to create independent and interdependent solutions at a personal level, we predict that we will be more able to create them at national and international levels.

An Evolutionary Perspective

Looking at human development from its longest perspective—an evolutionary view—helps us to identify basic patterns of behavior that naturally repeat over and over. Gregory Bateson (1972) described this phenomenon as "the pattern that connects." In biology, the phenomenon of repeating patterns is described as "ontogeny recapitulates phylogeny." That is, the development of a human fetus repeats the biological history of the whole human species as it starts from a single cell and moves through all the stages of development in animal evolution (amphibian, reptilian, mammalian).

In archeology there is a similar phenomenon of progressing patterns in the evolution of the human species. Riane Eisler, in *The Chalice and the Blade* (1987), describes a prehistoric culture which she calls the "partnership society." This society had characteristics which correlate with the co-dependent stage of human development: a strong attachment to the (mother) earth, dependency on the (mother) earth and the inability to see themselves as separate from the (mother) earth. The early peoples of this period were primarily hunters and gatherers who wandered from one place to another to find food. About 3500 B. C. the hunters and gathers began to settle down. At this time they began to cluster in villages where they domesticated animals and learned to grow crops. The point at which many cultural historians mark the end of this co-dependent era is the point at which humans first put the plow into the earth.

The formation of villages and eventually nation states can be seen as part of the drive for humans to separate from each other and from the earth. Inside this movement was a desire to dominate the earth and make Her grow food. This movement included a gradual drive to dominate women, neighboring villages, nation states and anything which threatened the survival of the governing group or system. In our current culture technology, war and violence are used to help keep humans separate from from each other and from Mother Earth. Eisler describes this culture as a "dominator society." The contemporary "I'll show you I don't need

78

you" attitude toward (mother) earth and reactionary, rebellious behaviors that place in peril the very existence of the human species are characteristic of two-year-old children who are in the throes of the counter-dependency stage.

The "emerging partnership society" that Eisler describes correlates with the characteristics of the independent and interdependent stages of human development. Both are characterized by cooperation, egalitarian intimate relationships, connectedness, unity and co-creation.

We have found it helpful to chart these three societies that Eisler describes and look at how each society has different ways of viewing the world. By examining these different worldviews we begin to have a longer view of our cultural history. The following chart looks at the evolutionary history of these three societies and shows how they parallel the stages of individual development in humans.

EARLY PARTNERSHIP SOCIETY	DOMINATOR SOCIETY	EMERGING PARTNERSHIP SOCIETY
co-dependent	counter-dependent	interdependent
sensory understanding of the world based on physical senses	mental understanding of the world based on Newtonian physics	spiritual understanding of the world based on quantum physics
tribalism	egoism/individualism	collectivism
humans in harmony with other humans	humans dominate other humans	humans co-create with other humans
God exists in Nature	God exists in heaven	God exists inside of us
humans in harmony with Nature	humans dominate Nature	humans co-create with Nature
tribalism: a local focus on problems	nationalism: a national focus on problems	globalism: worldwide focus on problems
decentralization: nomadic tribes, hunting and gathering,	centralization: cites, agriculture, technology, hierarchical management,	decentralization: an ecology of diverse cultures, appropriate technology, self-organizing, community
superstition	rationalism	mysticism
earth rituals, rites and sacred sites	churches and religious structures	creativity with the gods
undifferentiated unity	separateness & alienation	connectedness, unity in diversity
undiscovered self	denial of the self	fulfillment of the self
sensorimotor and pre-operational thinking	pre-operational and concrete operational thinking	formal operational and unitary operational thinking
material world rules the mind	matter and mind dualism	mind creates matter
ieducation supported survival	education used for socialization and control ling consciousness	education used for transformation and raising consciousness
involuntary simplicity	conspicuous consumption	voluntary simplicity
belief in abundance	belief in unlimited resources	belief in wise use of resources, doing more with less

Being able to understand that there is an evolutionary or developmental force at work in the world removes some of the helplessness and powerlessness that we often feel when we begin to look at counter-dependency issues. This larger view takes us back to ourselves, the only place where change can really begin to happen. To change the culture, the nation or the world, we have to begin by changing ourselves. When enough individuals have successfully completed their counter-dependent stage of development, the counter-dependent culture will change. It is this evolutionary perspective which is embedded in the saying, "Think globally, act locally."

REDEFINING FREEDOM: A CRITICAL TASK

Even the concept of freedom has become entangled in counter-dependent behavior and co-dependent thinking. For an adult with unresolved counter-dependent issues, freedom is often seen as the absence of external control. This kind of thinking is typical of Americans with their strong drive for freedom from persecution, repression, restriction and bondage that comes from some outside source of evil or oppression. This definition of freedom, however, keeps adults stuck with unresolved counter-dependent issues. They tend to see the source of problems as outside themselves and want to rebel against authority figures they believe are responsible for the problems. While this definition helps people develop a sense of individualism, it also keeps them separate and isolated, creates competition, sets up opportunities for domination and competition, emphasizes differences and helps cause wars.

On the other hand, people with unresolved co-dependent issues want freedom from internal responsibility. This "freedom from freedom" perspective keeps them externally focused so that they can blame others when things go wrong. They do not want to be responsible and find passivity, adaptation and enmeshment more comfortable. For example, a person with co-dependent behaviors might say that it is impossible to do anything about the high rates of income taxes here in the United States, because politicians and bureaucrats make all the decisions. This definition of freedom keeps people feeling powerless, inhibits personal autonomy, emphasizes collective sameness, creates individual stagnation and sets up victimization and dependency.

Neither of these two definitions, nor the rebellious or blaming life styles that they create, works very well for individuals or for society. For example, a person with unresolved co-dependency issues will expect to be taken care of with extensive retirement pensions, insurance settlements, unemployment benefits and other kinds of programs that take care of their dependency needs. (People with co-dependent behaviors may look to governmental agencies as their primary caretaker.) A person with unresolved counter-dependent issues may see the government of the United States as the main source of economic oppression because of the high taxes it wages on its citizens, rather than looking at his or her own out-of-control spending habits. Neither definition makes people ultimately responsible for taking care of their own needs or for looking at how their personal behavior is part of a larger problem.

A third and more interdependent definition of freedom requires that people move from these two externally focused worldviews into a definition of freedom that comes first from within—from self-understanding and psychological independence. In this definition people first internalize their power and individual control and then use it effectively externally by acting responsibly to meet their needs and wants. Out of this solid place, people can develop effective social skills and act responsibly to help meet the wants and needs of others.

This means, for example, that people with unresolved co-dependent issues must learn how to take charge of meeting their own needs. There is no perfect parent out there who will look after them. We see this co-dependent attitude permeating much of the thinking of the New Age movement, where people believe that they can manifest abundance without first dealing with the unresolved dependency needs from childhood. This kind of "unlimited thinking," which is characteristic of individuals who have not developed boundaries and learned the lessons of limitation, supports narcissistic behaviors and overconsumption on a planet with finite resources.

People with unresolved counter-dependency issues must recognize that it is not something outside of us ("our evil and oppression government") that is oppressing us economically with high taxes. Rather it is the extravagant and often compulsive spender within each of us (the *internal* source of the problem) that helps create an overspending government. When we decide to live with less and voluntarily simplify our life styles (internalizing the

82

responsibility), then we no longer need to identify ourselves as victims or the government as our persecutor. This is another example of how we can change the culture by first changing ourselves.

People who have developed this third view of freedom are able to perceive the structure of the outer world as a reflection of their inner world. When they are able to create a healthy balance between these two worlds, they will have found true freedom.

THE COUNTER-DEPENDENCY CRISIS

Understanding the relationship between the psychological development of the individual and the psychological evolution of the human race is critical at this time in our history. If we can see the parallels between these two levels of an interactive system, we begin to understand the sources of the problems we face in the world . We also can begin to see that solutions for world problems must address both the individual and the cultural levels of the system.

Let's look again at the individual level, a typical two-year-old child in the counter-dependent stage of development. This two-year-old is focused on separating from the primary caregivers, particularly the mother. Behaviorily, this two-year-old is oppositional to anything adults suggest. The underlying theme of a two-year-old's thinking is, "No! I don't need you. I can do it myself." Power struggles, rebelliousness, egocentrism, outbursts of anger and the need to be right are typical of the two-year-old who struggles to become separate.

If we transpose two-year-old counter-dependent behavior patterns onto the collective level of human society, we see how similar the patterns are to the contemporary behavior of people in the developed countries. Since humans began their gradual separation process from Mother Earth between 5,000 and 10,000 years ago, they have been declaring (unconsciously) to Her, "I can grow food by myself. I can bring you under my control and even dominate you." This forceful declaration of separation from the Earth Mother has been amplified many times. We find contemporary farmers demanding more and more from Her with the use of fertilizers, herbicides and pesticides, in an attempt to increase the yields of their crops. U. S. farmers in particular have become a model for the developing countries in their continued drive for power, domination and individual wealth. This use-it-up, throwaway behavior of Western peoples is stripping the planet of Her natural resources so quickly that the end of many nonrenewable resources is within sight. This has put us at the edge of a global ecological crisis which also has political, economic, social and evolutionary implications.

It is imperative for us to realize that as a species and as individuals most of us are psychologically between two and three years old. We have mature bodies and appear to be adults, but often we relate, react and behave as small children. The implications of this are awesome. We currently have on this planet enough nuclear weapons to destroy the whole world several times over. This does not even take into account biological or conventional weapons! Can you imagine turning this arsenal over to a two-year-old child full of anxieties and frustration about separation? The fact that we are in this predicament at this moment is sobering.

We can no longer view counter-dependency as a medical problem or as a disease. We must look at it as a developmental issue with roots in our early childhood experiences. It must be resolved at the individual level with specific, inexpensive and effective methods of treatment that allow both the individual and the culture to move into independence and interdependency before it is too late.

SUMMARY

Looking at counter-dependency issues from a systems perspective has been useful in helping us to understand the magnitude of the problem. So far in this book we have explored the sources of counter-dependent behavior at the individual, couple, family, institutional, national, international and evolutionary levels. We have also discussed the critical nature of being a society with a high level of counter-dependent behaviors. In Chapter Fourteen we make specific recommendations for addressing counter-dependent behaviors at each of these levels.

CASE EXAMPLE

The United States is an excellent case example of a counter-dependent culture. The highly egocentric behavior of its citizens is focused on material wealth as part of an addictive, consumptive life style in which about six per cent of the world's population consumes twenty-five percent of its resources. These behaviors keep us from having to examine our own values and beliefs and from dealing with the traumatic feelings from our dysfunctional childhoods. Our need to be free from economic, religious, political, social and interpersonal oppression has been carried to an extreme that makes us key contributors to global problems, particularly the environmental crisis at the institutional, cultural and evolutional levels.

The U. S.'s compulsive drive for personal comfort, individual wealth and domination of the environment has helped set the world on a collision course. Television programs exported into developing countries also export expectations that all world citizens should consume excessively. As the developing countries attempt to emulate our bad example, we can expect an even greater depletion of natural resources. Global environmental experts, such as Lester Brown (1988), predict an impoverished planet for our grandchildren, unless there is a dramatic reordering of our values and our priorities to reduce our consumption and pollution.

Insulated inside our single family dwellings, our two cars and our daily job routine, we are able to ignore the shrinking rain forest, the growing hole in the ozone layer, the problems of homeless children and families, and AIDS and growing environmental pollution. In spite of the warnings of many scientists, researchers, and futurists, many people in the U. S. continue to live in their denial.

It is difficult to reach a client consumed in counter-dependent behaviors because his or her defenses against self-examination and self-reflection are so strong. Intervening too quickly sometimes works as a "band-aid" and helps prevent the needed crisis from coming to a head. Effective treatment often requires that the therapist be patient and wait until the client is in sufficient crisis to break down the defenses and denial and begin the journey to wholeness and interdependence. Only then do people (and cultures) with counter-dependent characteristics seem ready to take in new information and begin the process of change.

Unfortunately, U. S. citizens may need a collective crisis to awaken them. We may have to come face-to-face with the loss of our homes, our families and everything we have worked for, before we are ready to stop our denial and begin to deal with the wounds of our childhood, with the problems in our intimate relationships, with the dysfunction in our families and with the crises in the world.

Treating a culture is obviously a more complex matter than treating individuals. It requires a new kind of therapist who has information about the "global family system," who has a micro/macro language and theoretical approaches for dealing with multiple social and cultural levels simultaneously. It requires therapists who are generalists rather than specialists, able to synthesize ideas, information and tools from many fields. It requires therapists who have done their own personal work and cleared their co-dependent and counter-dependent behavior patterns so that they are able to work and live interdependently. These global therapists must be able to move beyond individual therapy and be able to work with large groups of people at one time to facilitate therapeutic processes. They must also be able to teach by modeling, by "walking their walk as they talk their talk."

Once you have begun to develop an evolutionary view of human kind, a developmental view of your own psychological growth and have cleared your life of drama built on old traumas, you are on your way to becoming a global therapist. Self-therapy is also global-therapy.

AWARENESS ACTIVITY:
The Interdependent Living Inventory

It is necessary for all of us to make an inventory of how we are presently living our lives. This inventory may help you become more aware of the choices you have and of the choices you are currently making.

Directions: Place a number fbefore each statement to indicate the degree to which this statement is true for you.

1 = Never   2 = Occasionally   3 = Frequently   4 = Almost always

_____I use natural ventilation instead of air conditioning in my home.

_____I conscientiously turn out lights when not in use.

_____I avoid buying and using unnecessary electrical gadgets such toothbrushes, carving knives and electric can openers

_____I use mass transit or a bicycle whenever possible.

_____I own a car that gets 25 miles per gallon or more

_____I eat less meat and more vegetables and grains.

_____I grow some of my own food.

_____I separate and recycle newspapers, glass, aluminum and plastic.

_____I avoid prepackaged and processed food.

_____I compost my leaves, grass and kitchen wastes.

_____I avoid using herbicides and pesticides on my yard and garden.

_____I grow drought-resistent landscape plants and avoid extensive lawn watering.

_____I actively support organizations such as National Audubon Society and Greenpeace that help preserve the natural ecology.

_____I do not smoke.

_____I vote at local, state and national elections.

_____I attend personal growth seminars and workshops.

_____I am a member of a 12-step group or self-help support group.

_____I participate regularly in family meetings.

_____I volunteer or contribute to a nonprofit social service organization.

_____I participate in citizen diplomacy activities such as home stays in other countries or having guests from other countries.

_____I speak a foreign language.

_____I write to my state and/or national senator or representatives about my concerns.

_____TOTAL

Scoring: Add your number to get a total score. Use the following guidelines to interpret your score.

75 - 100   High degree of participation as an interdependent citizen

50 - 74   Moderate degree of participation as an interdependent citizen

25 - 49   Some participation as an interdependent citizen

 0 - 24   Little participation as an interdependent citizen

Part Two

PATHWAYS TO INTIMACY

Chapter Six

THE ELEMENTS OF BREAKING FREE

"Remember always that you have not only the right to be an individual;
you have an obligation to be one. You cannot make any
useful contribution to life unless you do this."
Eleanor Roosevelt

RECYCLED UNFINISHED BUSINESS

The developmental approach to breaking free of counter-dependent behavior recognizes as a natural law that any development task not completed at the appropriate age is carried forward to the next stages of development as excess baggage. We wrote earlier about how this is as it related to your trauma drama. These unmet needs will recycle over and over again unconsciously in your relationships, until they get met and you heal your core traumas.

Part One of the book describes a developmental approach for understanding the problem of counter-dependent behaviors in adults. By examining the stages of early childhood, we showed how incomplete developmental tasks related to bonding and separation help to create co-dependent and counter-dependent behaviors in adults. We also looked at counter-dependent patterns from a systems perspective, seeing it as a family, institutional, social/cultural and evolutionary problem.

Part Two of the book provides you with developmental solutions to your co-dependent and counter-dependent problems and presents the important skills you will need to learn in order to break free of these restrictive counter-dependent behaviors. We describe the essential elements of the change process needed to both create more intimacy in your relationships and help you look at your life without these dysfunctional behaviors. In this chap-

91

ter, we provide you with an overview of the change process, and in each of the succeeding chapters, we will discuss in detail a specific set of skills needed to break free of counter-dependent behaviors and issues.

The person with counter-dependent behaviors generally has problems with intimacy because of his or her unmet developmental needs related to the bonding and separation process of early childhood. Because these needs were not met when they should have been met, people often try to hide their "neediness" from others and try to use indirect or covert means to get them met. To eliminate these counter-dependent behaviors requires breaking through the protective wall of denial and learning new skills that allow for the development of intimacy and for the development of effective ways to get these needs met now.

Intimacy is so difficult for the person who has unresolved counter-dependent issues because it activates all the old memories and fears of the past of engulfment, invasion, betrayal, abuse and manipulation. In other words, all the feelings, related to his or her unfinished business and unmet needs, will begin to surface for the person with counter-dependent issues when he or she gets close and intimate in a relationship.

The typical co-dependent/counter-dependent relationship dynamic sets up predictable conflicts about intimacy. The person with co-dependent patterns, with intense needs for touch and physical closeness, continually tries to get close to his or her partner with counter-dependent patterns. The counter-dependent partner, always on the alert for signs of engulfment, is prepared to quickly erect protective boundaries. Or the reverse can happen. In structured and in less intimate situations, the person with counter-dependent patterns may be the one to invade the boundaries of the person with co-dependent patterns, by making unilateral decisions or by pulling power plays. Either way, the stage is set for intense competition and conflict usually resulting in very little intimacy. While this is happening, the person with counter-dependent behaviors is usually relieved that he or she doesn't have to be close and intimate. People with unresolved counter-dependent issues have trouble creating intimate relationships where they have equal power. They prefer to be in a one-up positionso they can feel safe in their relationships.

THE SEARCH FOR INTIMACY

Many of us learned about intimacy vicariously, by watching television or going to the movies, because we didn't see much of it in our family where we grew up. We may have assumed that it was only *our* family that wasn't very intimate. Because we didn't spend a lot of time with other families, we supposed that their lives were peaceful and happy like the Cleavers of *Leave It To Beaver* or the Andersons of *Father Knows Best*. When we were old enough to think about sexual relationships, we often learned about sexual intimacy by watching the contrived onscreen romances of television and film stars. Other cultural sources of information about idealized romantic intimacy were television, radio, magazine and newspaper advertisements, Harlequin romance novels, along with popular music, especially country music. Since all of these are filled with distorted and dysfunctional images of what intimacy is all about, there is a good chance you learned lots of misinformation about intimacy just by growing up in this culture.

Such false images of intimate relationships and family life may have made it difficult for you to reconcile yourself with the conflict, competition and fighting that you may have found yourself involved with in your day-to-day experiences with loved ones. Also, if you still get stuck in counter-dependent black/white thinking, you may tend to split your experiences in close relationships into all good or all bad. When your relationship is going well you may tend to see it as all good ("We'll love each other this way forever"). When there is conflict in the relationship, especially the conflict that brings up childhood issues or feelings, then your relationship may look all bad ("Looks like it is time to get a divorce"). Neither view is realistic in close relationships. What most people need is a new definition of intimacy that can be expanded to include both the good times and the not-so-good times.

A NEW DEFINITION OF INTIMACY

If you look more closely at what is trying to happen in the relationship between someone with co-dependent behaviors and someone else with counter-dependent behaviors, as they compete to try to get their conflicting needs met for closeness and separateness, you begin to see that this combination is ideal for activating each other's unmet needs from early childhood. The person with

93

co-dependent needs for intimacy activates the other person's counter-dependent need to protect himself or herself from being invaded or abused. On the other hand, the person with counter-dependent needs for space and separateness can activate the other person's co-dependent abandonment fears and neglect issues. Unless people understand what is really trying to happen in their relationship, they may judge the relationship as all bad and the couple will head for the divorce court. It becomes essential, then, to find a context within a relationship where this troublesome unfinished business can be included in the definition of intimacy.

When we do relationship therapy with parents/children, employees/employers, couples or siblings, we work together as co-therapists. This provides two perspectives on what is happening and also prevents the usual feelings of "two-against-one" triangulation from developing. Our first objective as therapists is to help identify what unmet needs are really trying to get met in this relationship. Once we do this, we can then help people reframe the issues which they brought to therapy in terms of their unmet needs from childhood that they are indirectly trying to get met in the relationship. The next objective is to help them see the wounded inner child in each other and to develop empathy for the pain this child has experienced. When they are able to do that, they are often ready to move to a third step: making an agreement to help each other transform his or her inner child wounds by contracting for corrective reparenting from each other.

Since we have done these steps with each other in our own personal relationship, we often share our own experiences with our clients. We have taught many of our clients how to reframe their conflicts and have taught them how to develop new ways of helping each other break free of their wounds. This process helps them develop a new kind of intimacy so rich and so deep that it can only be described as reminiscent of the paradise of the infant.

Our new definition of intimacy includes the following elements:

- being able to heal the trauma drama through cooperative, corrective reparenting contracts
  (*no competitive struggle*)
- being able to tell each other the truth about who we really are and what our needs really are
  (*no secrets*)
- agreeing to find win-win solutions to all conflicts (*no power plays*)

- being able to share our lives with each other on many levels: mental, emotional, spiritual and physical *(no scarcity)*
- being able to negotiate with your partner to get needs for closeness and separateness met, with opportunities for varying various degrees of both *(no assumptions)*
- being willing to see each other as a complete and separate person with some traits we like and some traits we don't like (no rescues)
- being self-sufficient enough internally to risk the possible loss of the relationship *(no victims)*

When you are able to expand your definition of intimacy to include these elements, every experience in your relationship has potential for intimacy. The relationship becomes a dance that moves you and your partner from one opportunity for intimacy to another. These are the essential ingredients of an interdependent, partnership relationship. We will discuss these essential ingredients more fully in Chapter Thirteen.

CHANGING YOUR COUNTER-DEPENDENT BEHAVIORS

If you are just beginning your work on your counter-dependent and co-dependent behaviors, you may wonder, "Where do I begin?" Please refer to the Step-by-Step Program for Changing Counter-Dependent Behaviors at the end of Chapter Three and the Awareness Activity at the end of Chapter Two. These maps and lists can give you some concrete steps that show you where you can begin, as well as give you an overview of your longer-term work. You can begin to picture how the steps in the program for changing your counter-dependent behaviors can be completed using a variety of resources. Some of the steps are more individual-oriented, some work more effectively in therapy, while others work better in a committed relationship or in a support group. You will need to create your own plan for changing your counter-dependent behaviors.

RESOURCES FOR CHANGING YOUR COUNTER-DEPENDENT BEHAVIORS

Working Alone. It is sometimes easier for someone just beginning the breaking free process to work alone. Reading books, attending workshops and seminars, taking time off from work and relationships to do some reflecting and soul-searching are excellent ways to work alone on your issues. Working alone allows a person with counter-dependent behaviors to feel safe from any invasion or prying. In this safety it may be easier for the shadowy side of the self to emerge, the side that may be insecure, vulnerable, wounded and afraid.

Completing the written exercises in this book is another excellent way of working alone. Keeping a journal on a regular basis, writing and repeating daily affirmations and using exercise, such as walking, hiking, running or bicycling, as opportunities for reflecting are other ways of working alone. Working alone is a useful way to do the mental part of transformation, which enables you to develop an understanding of how the layers of your onion fit together and overlay your original trauma.

Removing the mask of the "false self" is an important part of working alone. Here you can look at how your tough "I don't need anybody" stance, which may have served you so well earlier in your life, may have become a prison that keeps you removed from warmth and intimacy. By understanding what your real needs are, you may be ready to risk changing your behavior.

Working in Support Groups. A person who is experiencing counter-dependent symptoms and who decides to enter a helping program may assume he or she is the only person going through such problems. Outside support can be found through either group therapy or 12-step support groups, both of which offer excellent opportunities to break this belief. When people with counter-dependent behavior patterns participate in a group, the first thing they often learn is how similar people are when they remove their masks. Support groups allow people to share their common struggles and can offer a variety of possible solutions to the problems that counter-dependent issues present.

Support groups may also be risky places for a person with counter-dependent issues, for it requires letting down his or her defenses in front of other people. Those who take this risk, however, usually discover a source of love and support they never before had available to them. Thousands of alcoholics with counter-dependent symptoms have had such experiences when they attended their first Alcoholics Anonymous meeting.

Working in Therapy. Therapy can be difficult at first for the person with counter-dependent patterns, because it requires sharing personal issues with a stranger. People with counter-dependent issues often are therapy phobic. Things usually have to get bad enough for a counter-dependent type person before he or she finally seeks therapy. The person with counter-dependent issues usually enters therapy feeling very scared and vulnerable. Because it is critical for this person to have safety, it is important that he or she finds a therapist he or she can trust. How to find the right therapist was discussed in Chapter Four. You may want to reread that section before looking for a therapist. Cognitive therapy may be necessary at first, before the person with counter-dependent issues has built up enough trust to deal with deeper feeling issues.

Working in Conscious, Committed, Cooperative Relationships. This type of work requires a leap of faith for a person with counter-dependent patterns. It also requires that they begin sharing personal issues with someone else. They may feel scared at first because it requires someone who has counter-dependent issues to become vulnerable and risk being hurt again. For relationships to be successful in supporting change, the partners must agree to the following guidelines:

- close the exits by agreeing to stay in the relationship during a contracted period of time and not run away if there is conflict
- be willing to make some changes in themselves or their behavior, if necessary
- be truthful about who they are and what their needs are
- be willing to resolve conflicts without using power plays, threats or manipulation.

Because co-dependent and counter-dependent patterns are caused by relationship dysfunctions, the best place to heal these dysfunctions often is in relationships. You can create many forms of committed, conscious, cooperative relationships where you can begin to do this, such as those between friends, business partners, parents and children or as a couple.

What the person who has counter-dependent patterns needs to learn from his or her relationships is how to be vulnerable and take risks. Rather than being so guarded about his or her problems or needs, the person with counter-dependent patterns has to learn to ask for help from other people. He or she also needs to develop empathy for others and be less self-centered. Working together in a relationship is a great opportunity for partners to teach each other the things they need to learn and to develop intimacy.

ESSENTIAL SKILLS FOR CREATING INTIMATE RELATIONSHIPS

The development of intimacy requires that people with counter-dependent behaviors have to learn some essential relationship skills. Recovering the capacity to be intimate is a process that is different for each person. Learning to develop intimacy can often take considerable time and effort, because it requires a shift from self-centeredness to other-centeredness. Other steps, such as finding ways to safely release old repressed feelings, can require intensive work, especially considering the strong need for safety and security that people with counter-dependent issues have. The six essential skills that we teach our clients and students who have problems with their counter-dependent behaviors are described briefly below. Each of these skills will be explored in depth in its own separate chapter.

Empathy Training. Empathy is the ability to feel or see the world the way another person does and to be interested in how others think, how they live and what they feel. Empathy happens when we are motivated to learn about other people from a place of compassion and caring. This is a big change for a person with counter-dependent issues who may have learned to gather information about people only as part of his or her need to control, dominate and defend.

Before a person with counter-dependent issues can develop empathy, it is important for him or her to understand why he or she has not yet learned this skill. Certain conditions in our family of origin usually make it impossible or unsafe for us to be empathetic. The key tasks in learning empathy are to let go of the control, give up the domination and break through the self-denial.

Boundary Setting. Boundaries are an important part of the change process for people who have counter-dependent behaviors. As children, they experienced invasions and violations of their physical, mental, emotional and spiritual selves, forcing them to erect walls of defense. The biggest boundary issue for people with counter-dependent issues is having too many personal boundaries. The need for protection and safety while they were growing up in their family of origin required that they create mental, emotional, physical and spiritual boundaries to ward off the assaults of others. As a result, people with counter-dependent issues often have learned to "tune out" what others have to say. Instead, they often try to define the reality of other people by

98

telling them what to think or not to think or what to do or what not to do. People with counter-dependent patterns often develop thick layers of muscles or fat that serve as body armor and discourage intimate touch. They also try to stay in control of situations by telling other people what to feel or not to feel.

The second boundary issue for people with counter-dependent problems is invading the boundaries of others. Their aggressive "I'll get them before they get me" tack is really a disguised defense mechanism that may work reasonably well in the business world, but often fails miserably in the relationship world. This kind of aggressive behavior in intimate relationships helps to set up conflict and helps to perpetuate the battle of the sexes. The task for a person dealing with counter-dependent behaviors is to develop the necessary protection and safety without being overly armored and without having to violate the boundaries of others in the process.

Skills in Reclaiming Projections. Projections occur when people see negative traits in other people, but don't recognize them same ones in themselves. For people with counter-dependent issues, projection is a serious problem because they are often so unaware of their unmet needs. They can see these needs quite clearly in other people and often make harsh judgments about these "needy" people. A typical counter-dependent game is "Courtroom," where they tend to put everyone around them on trial. In this game, all the players who come into the life of the person with counter-dependent issues are taken to court, tried and convicted as bad (no one can meet these people's high standards for perfection). This game is an excellent defense against intimacy because it keeps attention focused on what is wrong with others and keeps the person with counter-dependent behavior from having to look inward. It also helps them stay separate, by acting one-up, staying in control and therefore feeling safe.

Corrective Parenting Skills. Cooperative agreements between people in committed, conscious relationships to help each other meet the unmet needs of his or her inner child can provide a vital foundation for creating intimacy. Relating at this deep level, where old wounds, pain, abuse, abandonment and the scars of growing up in a dysfunctional family are shared, can create connections as intimate as sexual sharing. By creating cooperative contracts that enable people to finally get their unmet needs met, they can transform the relationship from one of pain and conflict into one of breaking free and nurturing.

Conflict Resolution Skills. Intimacy requires that people have skills in resolving all kinds of conflicts. In intimate relationships, people mainly encounter conflicts of needs and wants and values and beliefs. These conflicts can also stir up deep feelings. In order to resolve such a variety of conflicts, it is important that the partners learn skills for working on both external relationship conflicts as well as internal conflicts related to unmet needs from childhood.

Sexual Communication Skills. The bedroom is often the place where true intimacy can fall the shortest for the person with counter-dependent behaviors, for here his or her partner is likely to demand an emotionally honest relationship. Such a demand pushes the person with counter-dependent issues up against his or her wall of defenses. Because the person with counter-dependent patterns did not learn to nurture or be nurtured, it becomes difficult for him or her to move out of the mechanics of lovemaking and into the deeper levels of intimate sharing. As a result, people with counter-dependent issues find ways to avoid sexual intimacy through workaholism, by having multiple sexual partners, or by convincing the partner that he or she is unattractive or sexually deficient in some way.

Once on the path to freedom and wholeness, there seems to be no returning to the old ways. In moments of despair, discouragement and depression, it is sometimes tempting to give up. In these moments, a form of spiritual courage deep inside your soul often pushes you forward, encouraging you into healthier thinking, feeling and behaving.

CASE EXAMPLE

Linda came to Colorado for two weeks of intensive therapy with us, after fifteen years of unsuccessful prior treatment in many other forms of therapy. She had attended a workshop we'd given in her home area several months earlier and in that workshop Linda had a breakthrough experience that encouraged her to come out and do further work with us.

Linda's case turned out to be one of the most bizarre we have worked with. The oldest child of very wealthy parents, she grew up in an environment that from the outside appeared to be quite normal, even ideal. Her parents, however, were some of the most abusive people we have heard of. As a result Linda had developed many counter-dependent behaviors. Her mother fit the co-dependent behavior prototype perfectly: powerless, highly passive, and

100

totally dominated by her tyrant husband. He had the classic counter-dependent symptoms: egotistic, judgmental, perfectionistic and highly demanding. Linda compared her childhood with these parents to growing up in a concentration camp.

In the beginning of her treatment, we devoted several hours of therapy time to helping her reconstruct the pieces of her trauma drama. We examined the dynamics of her parents' relationship; her role in keeping the relationship between the two of them in some form homeostasis; the unconscious psychic agreements she had with each of them; the values, beliefs, assumptions and expectations that she had used to structure her life experiences; the recurring patterns in her list of betrayals; and the original trauma that had scripted her life.

Because of the extreme abuse she experienced throughout her childhood, we knew that her core trauma must have been quite severe. We explored with her the circumstances of her birth. She knew that her mother had been drugged and unconscious and that at one point in the birth process there were difficulties that put Linda's life in peril. The attending physician, who managed to pull her out with forceps, caught her by her right arm as she was delivered. She also believed that the physician held her upside down and spanked her to get her breathing. With this information we were able to begin piecing together with Linda the elements of her trauma drama.

We could see how Linda's birth became a metaphor for her life. Linda's mother continued to play the passive, unconscious role she had played in her birth by "blanking out" whenever Linda was being harmed. Her father, an attorney, picked up the role of the abusive physician. Together the parents recreated over and over Linda's birth trauma. Linda always experienced her childhood as though her life was constantly in danger.

In the privacy of their upper-class home, they subjected Linda to sophisticated psychological and spiritual torture. Linda was kept under constant surveillance like a prisoner. Any time she violated the smallest rule (and there were many), Linda was brought before her parents. Here they described to Linda the nature and severity of her transgression in terms that left her feeling like a criminal. Her father, who played the prosecutor, presented the case against her. He would often call Linda's mother as a witness to testify against her. She was taken before the judge (again her father) where she was always found guilty. Then she would receive her "sentence." When she was small it was often a spanking, but as she grew older it was mostly humiliation, shame, degradation, discounting and name-calling.

In one instance at the age of three, she got scared in the middle of the night and went into her parents' bedroom and awakened her father. He was so angry with her that he marched her down the hall to the bathroom, made her stand in front of the open toilet, pulled down her underpants and then spanked her bare bottom. The force of the angry march down the hall while she was half asleep, the sight and smell of the open toilet and the humiliation of having to stand half naked while her father spanked her so terrorized her that the incident left a permanent scar in Linda's psyche.

The trauma of Linda's birth and other similar early childhood traumas created the theme for her life: "I'm constantly on trial for my life." This theme was woven through various relationships, job situations and even appeared in an experience with a well-known doctor when she conferred with him about psychiatric treatment. Over the years, Linda had accumulated a large file full of old letters, journal writings, newspaper clippings and other materials that she used to document the terror of her childhood. She used this file as a resource to support her "case for the defense," pulling various pieces from it during her therapy work with us to help her prove her innocence to us and to herself over and over again.

The point when she was able to see clearly the core trauma and the overlaying experiences of her life was enlightening for Linda. A flash of comprehension seemed to move through her as she understood for the first time the whole picture of her life. This seemed to shock her into a state of clarity.

As we discussed the aspects of her trauma drama, Janae suggested that she might have become bonded to her drama, attaching to it as she might a doll or blanket, as children often do when there is a deficiency in early parenting. This suggestion startled her and we could see her shift internally as she reflected on this possibility. Janae suggested that this might have been a survival mechanism for her while she was small, because there was nothing else that was safe for her to bond with. In the present time, she now had safe people with whom she could bond and begin to get her needs met. We explored with her the old reality of "I'm constantly on trial for my life" to see how much of it was true in present time. She admitted that she was no longer a child, no longer living anywhere close to her parents and that her life was not in danger.

102

Just speaking this truth released some of the tension in her body as we sat together. Then we led her step-by-step through the Completion Process With Your Parents exercise, designed to help clients understand and complete unfinished business with their parents. (See the Awareness Activity at the end of Chapter Ten.)

By the time the two weeks of therapy were over, we could see a dramatic change in Linda's appearance and behavior. She appeared lighter, softer and gentler. She radiated an incredible loving energy. She also spoke gently and acted more centered. The angry, agitated woman whom she had brought to therapy two weeks earlier had been transformed.

After Linda's return home, she kept us posted with progress reports that were a continual affirmation of her life change. In one letter three months later Linda wrote, "My healing has held up. My body is very peaceful. I have reduced my sleeping needs from eight to five hours and wake up feeling rested. All this healing is a gift, a blessing and a miracle." In other exuberant letters she described the joy she was finding in burning and throwing out the many boxes and stacks of "defense materials" that she had collected for so long. The process of letting go of her trauma drama had been a joyful and healing one for Linda. We receive periodic letters from her and she is continuing to make excellent progress in the two years since we last saw her.

AWARENESS ACTIVITY:
How to Identify Your Unmet Developmental Needs and What to Do About It

The following chart can be helpful in identifying your unmet developmental needs. Read through the list of developmental needs and place a check mark next to those that you believe you may have missed. Next check the adult indicators of unmet needs to see if you identify with any of them. Then check the corrective parenting activities to see what you can do to get these needs met now.

BONDING NEEDS *Co-dependency Stage* (0-6 months)	ADULT INDICATORS OF UNMET DEVELOPMENTAL NEEDS	CORRECTIVE PARENTING ACTIVITIES TO MEET BONDING NEEDS
1. To be born into a comfortable environment with soft lights, soft music, warm temperature and with adults dressed in ordinary attire	• Frequent attacks of anxiety and fear • Frequent upper respiratory problems (bronchitis, asthma, shallow breathing, pneumonia)	1 • Learn breathwork techniques such as re-birthing • Reenact your birth and set it up in an optimal way
2. To have maximum skin-to-skin contact with both parents for the first 24-36 hours after your birth	• Trouble relaxing, chronic body tension • Feeling deprived of nourishment, compulsive eating, drinking, sex	2 • Get a regular massage or infant massage • Ask to be held and rocked
3. To have immediate and extended family available at your birth to bond with	• Feeling unconnected or isolated from others, being a loner • Trouble trusting that others will be there for you	3 • Reenact your birth by asking people to play the part of family members • Do physical trust experiences—trust fall, trust walk
4. Being received in a loving way and assured of immediate care so that the adrenal stress reaction is not activated	• Trouble relaxing, chronic body tension • Addicted to activity or stimulation	4 • Do things to nurture yourself, like taking a warm bath • Learn meditation and relaxation techniques
5. Being allowed to nurse right after birth	• Compulsive overeating or drinking • Compulsive buying or hoarding	5 • Get fed from a baby bottle while being held • Being held, rocked and sung to • Taking charge without guilt assertiveness training

6. Allowing the child to be in charge of birth process as much as possible	• Passivity, letting others lead • Being afraid to try new things	6• Learning to ask directly for what you want • Make a list of things you wanted to hear from parents and have someone hold you and say these things to you
7. To have your True Self mirrored back by parents and other adults	• Low self-esteem, undervaluing self • Lack of awareness of your needs	7• Look at yourself in a full-length mirror and affirm positive things about your body, your abilities and who you are • Support people in asking directly for what they want; no rescues
8. To develop effective ways to let others know your needs	• Inability to ask for what you want • Not knowing what you need	8• Ask for comfort and support when identifying and expressing deep feelings
9. To bond with mother, father and other family members	• Feel insecure and fearful • Difficulty in trusting others, avoidance of touch	9• Ask to be held, rocked and sung to • Ask to be given a baby bottle while being held and given unconditional positive mirroring
10. To have your needs respected and taken seriously by important caregivers	• Feeling uncomfortable or isolated from others • Denial of your needs	10• Look for things you have in common with people when you meet • Ask to be held and comforted when feeling sad or scared
11. To be touched and stroked in loving nonsexual ways	• Avoidance of touch • Feeling deprived of nourishment; compulsive eating or drinking	11• Ask for hugs and physical, nonsexual nurturing (being sung to, etc.) • Develop self-nurturing skills

SEPARATION NEEDS *Counter-dependency Stage* Early exploration and full exploration phases (6-16 Months)	ADULT INDICATORS OF UNMET DEVELOPMENTAL NEEDS	CORRECTIVE PARENTING ACTIVITIES TO MEET SEPARATION NEEDS
1. To be correctly mirrored by significant caregivers	• Feeling unloved by others • Needing admiration and attention from others	1 • Ask for positive, unconditional mirroring from others • Buy a teddy bear or doll to hug, sing to and hold as a symbol of your inner child
2. To have available caregivers who enjoyed being with you	• Feeling unloved or unwanted • Feeling abandoned or engulfed by others	2 • Join a support group • Do original pain work in therapy
3. To have support and encouragement to explore your world safely	• Easily bored, needs others to stimulate interest • Have a hard time relaxing, chronic anxiety	3 • Ask for support from others to help you explore your world • Take risks by trying new things, set goals and make plans to achieve them, develop a vision for a better life
4. To discover how your world works by trusting your senses. t	• Rejecting help from others even when you need it • Striving for perfection, hard to admit a mistake • Being unable to trust your senses	4 • Use your senses more often to learn more about familiar things • Ask someone to take you on a trust walk

SEPARATION NEEDS Early separation and complete separation subphases (17-36 Months)	ADULT INDICATORS OF UNMET DEVELOPMENTAL NEEDS	CORRECTIVE PARENTING ACTIVITIES TO MEET SEPARATION NEEDS
5. To have your feelings supported and accepted by significant others	• Denies problems and/or discounts the importance of problems • Excessive need to look good	5 • Learn empathy skills • Learn to distinguish between your nurturing needs and sexual needs
6. To get positive support for exploration by receiving twice as many "yeses" as "nos"	• Rebellious and fearful of control by others • Self-centeredness, low tolerance for frustration	6 • Integrate your power, relationship and information skills • Ask for support when you need it to explore new things
7. To get support to be emotionally separate from your mother and father	• Trouble being close to others emotionally and physically • Seeing yourself and others as all good or all bad	7 • Learn to receive without resistance and set effective boundaries • Learn to reclaim projections and use perception checks effectively
8. To get support for expressing all your feelings	• Intolerance of the mistakes of others • Inability to feel deep feelings	8 • Consciously commit yourself in a relationship where you can give and get emotional interdependence • Learn win/win conflict resolution skills
9. To be allowed to express negative feelings without the threat of loss of love	• Excessive need to be right or to have the final say • Striving for perfection	9 • Uncover and learn to love your shadow parts • Create safe ways and places to express old anger and rage effectively
10. To learn to ask directly for what you want and need	• Rejecting help from others, even when you need it • Denial of your needs and wants • Expecting others to read your mind	10 • Learn to take charge of getting what you want without guilt • Agree to ask for what you want 100% of the time

107

Chapter Seven

EMPATHY:
A PATH TO INTIMACY

"The impact of someone's failure to listen...
the absence of response has painful, numbing consequences."
Clark Moustakis
Who Will Listen

WHAT IS EMPATHY?

The development of genuine empathy is a key skill for people with unmet counter-dependent needs to learn if they wish to establish and maintain intimate relationships. One of the most clearly defining characteristics of a person with unmet counter-dependent needs is his or her strong self-centeredness. The person with counter-dependent behaviors is using almost all of his or her resources to keep from feeling any unwanted feelings and to keep others from finding out his or her hidden weaknesses and insecurities. People with counter-dependent issues also need other people to give them praise and admiration, thus reassuring them that the other person doesn't see their frailties and that their secrets are still intact. At a party, these are the people who talk on and on about their own life when you ask them something about themselves. If they ask you anything about yourself, it is usually out of deference to social norms or in order to manipulate you. If you stop asking them about themselves, they will find a way to end the conversation and move on. In such situations the person with counter-dependent issues may reveal a real lack of empathy for others.

Empathy comes from the German word *einfuhlung,* which means "feeling into." It is the ability to understand another person pretty much as you understand yourself. Someone with

109

empathy is able to "crawl into the skin of another person" and see and feel the world the way that person does. This usually means being able to listen to another person so well that you can repeat back to them what they said in such an accurate way that the other person feels seen, understood, respected and supported by that person. It does not necessarily mean you agree with what the other person said, but it does indicate that you understand what he or she has said.

There are three components to empathy. The empathic person is able to:

1. understand the other person's feelings, yet is able to remain separate from that person
2. communicate an understanding of the situation or events that may have triggered these feelings and
3. communicate in such a way that the other person feels accepted and understood.

Carl Rogers (1961) said that empathy was the most effective skill we know for "...improving a person's relationships and communications with others" (p. 332). You need to use both verbal and nonverbal listening skills in communicating with empathy. They include attending, following and reflecting (Bolton 1979). Later in the chapter, we will include skill building exercises for each of these skill areas.

WHAT ARE FEELINGS FOR?

People often confuse feelings when they communicate and misuse them. They say, "I feel that you are trying to control me" (they mean "think" instead of "feel") or they may say, "You made me mad." (They mean "I chose to get mad" because no one makes another person feel anything.) Also, people often think that they need to justify their feelings, give reasons for their feelings or wait until they think they are justified in expressing a feeling; for example, "I told him not to call me after 10:30 p.m., so I really let him have it when he called me at 10:35 p.m."

What most people don't know is that each of our basic feelings has an important purpose. There are six basic feelings, each with a separate distinct function. They are as follows:

BASIC FEELINGS AND THEIR FUNCTIONS
(Weinhold & Weinhold 1989)

Feeling	Function
1. *Anger*	Your natural response to not getting your wants/needs met. You may also feel scared to ask directly to get your needs met and get angry instead, hoping to get what you want without asking directly.
2. *Fear*	Your natural response to perceived physical or emotional danger. You may not believe you can think and feel at the same time, and therefore may not think to check out whether or not there actually is a real danger. You may also use fear to cover your anger.
3. *Sadness*	Your natural response to the loss of a person, object or relationship (real or fantasy). It is an important part of "giving up" something you were attached to. There may also be some anger connected with the loss.
4. *Shame*	Your natural response to crossing some personal or social limit about what is appropriate. Healthy shame helps us monitor our behavior in public situations and also helps form our ethical code.
5. *Excitement*	Your natural anticipation of something good happening for you. Fear and excitement are often closely related. Some children never got permission to show excitement.
6. *Happiness or Joy*	Your natural satisfaction at getting what you want or need, or for doing something effectively. Some people don't know it's okay to be happy. They may be addicted to struggle.

WHY PEOPLE WITH COUNTER-DEPENDENT ISSUES DIDN'T LEARN EMPATHY

If, during the counter-dependent stage of development, you wanted to be comforted and nurtured after feeling scared by some exploratory encounter, and instead were made fun of or rebuffed in some way, you may have developed protective defenses against further hurts. You will attempt to prove to your parents that you are strong and do not need anyone. Repeated experiences like this will convince you that you should not tell others when you are feeling scared, insecure, sad or confused. The message you internalize is "Take care of yourself and don't trust anyone else." This pattern of behavior requires that a number of defenses be built to make sure that no one finds out your real feelings and uses this against you.

People with counter-dependent issues who didn't get these important needs met often become hypervigilant, watching everyone and every situation to determine if they are going to be laughed at or hurt. This takes an inordinate amount of energy and does not allow much additional energy for "getting to know" people, beyond seeing them as a potential threat.

Frequently, the mothers and fathers of adults with unmet counter-dependent needs were unable to support the independent strivings of their children. Mothers may have needed to complete their own bonding connections with their sons and daughters that they missed in their own childhood. If you were taught that your needs were not as important as your mother's needs, you may have relinquished your personal needs. Often a mother or father tries to create the perfect child to show off to the world. You may have been taught not to show your feelings because feelings are signs that you are less than perfect. You may have been rewarded for doing things well, but that could lead to pressure to keep doing things to please your perfectionistic parents. You may have been told that you can do anything as long as you "look good" and do what your parents say.

As a result, you may have developed counter-dependent traits that allow you to be quite capable (although you may worry about failure), but you may not feel very lovable. You may realize that you were used as objects to satisfy your parents desires and dreams, which was the price tag for your getting parental approval and recognition. You may have a lot of rage and sadness about not being loved for who you really are and, at the same time, you may have built defenses to avoid feeling these feelings. The

112

person with counter-dependent issues, in reaction to the loss of the True Self, often will inflate the false self to look like the real thing. Inside, this person feels fragmented and cannot risk the emotional closeness of an intimate relationship which could bring up his or her unwanted feelings and weaknesses. There is literally no time and energy available to focus on another person and if the person with counter-dependent behaviors did, he or she may fear that there would be serious consequences such as abandonment or rejection. Many people with counter-dependent patterns are addicted to perfection or at least to "looking" perfect. This may have been the only way they had to get any needs for recognition or approval from perfectionistic parents.

SELF-DEFEATING CORE BELIEFS OF PEOPLE WITH COUNTER-DEPENDENT PATTERNS

Some of the self-defeating core beliefs of people with counter-dependent issues are the following:

- If I pay much attention to the other person, I will lose myself (which I have trouble holding on to anyway).
- If I listen to what others say, I'll get talked out of my own beliefs and views.
- If I get close to someone, they will see how unlovable I am and reject me.
- If I listen to other people's feelings, it may stir up my own.
- If people get to know me they will see how weak I am and lose respect for me.
- If I open up to someone, I'll be abandoned and may die.
- If I cry, I will never be able to stop.
- If I get angry, I might kill someone.
- If I expressed my pain, it will be unending and I might go crazy or die.
- If I could not handle the pain of rejection, I do not know what would happen to me.
- If I am not in control, I will not get what I want.
- If I am not in control, people will take advantage of me; they will control me.

THE FEMININE FORM OF SURRENDER

Surrender means "letting go" and it actually has two forms: The masculine form involves letting go of guilt and being able to take charge of one's life without feeling guilty. The feminine form involves letting go of judgments and being able to receive information, love and caring from another person without resistance. Generally, women are more likely to have learned the feminine

113

form but not the masculine one, while men may know the masculine way, but have a very poorly developed feminine side. It is important for both men and women to develop each of these two forms of surrender in order to have an intimate relationship. People with counter-dependent issues have a difficult time receiving without resistance and so they are not able to be very empathic. Most counter-dependent type people resist anything that the other person is saying or doing that they perceive as threatening to them; this is part of their built-in protection system. So, the person with counter-dependent behaviors must be taught to let go enough to listen to and take in what others say and to do without resistance. Frequently, they will evaluate what is said to them before deciding to even think about it. If you get quick responses or negative responses, you know that what you said has been evaluated, but probably not considered very carefully. The masculine form of surrender will be discussed in Chapter Twelve.

Letting go is one of the primary tasks of people with counter-dependent issues and learning how to surrender is vital to the development of intimate relationships. The following case example illustrates how vital it can be.

CASE EXAMPLE

The following is a first-hand report of change by one of our clients. We asked him to tell his own story of how he has uncovered and subsequently changed many of his counter-dependent behavior patterns.

"When I first learned about developmental needs people should get met in early childhood, I was quite dismayed. In the course of my birth and early childhood experiences I received few or none of those things which are now recognized as essential for healthy, successful development.

"I was born via C-section. There was little apparent bonding with anyone in my family. My mother has told me of her feelings. She perceived me as an ugly baby and didn't particularly like to hold me or care for me. Obviously I wasn't nursed and, in fact, I was schedule fed according to the infant rearing practices in vogue in 1940. According to my mother, my father questioned his paternity and showed little interest in me.

"My half sister, 10 years older than myself, showed some interest. Her background of physical and sexual abuse precluded my being able to have a healthy and truly nourishing relationship

114

with her. My memories of infancy, recalled in regression, center around hours alone in isolation, crying out for love, attention, and with her. My memories of infancy, recalled in regression, center nourishment and not receiving them. In what I think was a desperate attempt to get my needs met, I created repeated crises of pneumonia. Frequently I had to be rushed to the hospital and put in an oxygen tent. This was regarded as a bother and inconvenience by my parents and my mother has told me that she considered just letting me die on more than one occasion.

"I did bond to a considerable degree with our family dog. She became so protective of me that my mother decided to get rid of her when I was about four. At that time I reconciled myself to a life of loneliness and isolation.

"My father left for Word War II when I was three. I then became an object of competition, between my mother and sister, for the male energy in the household. The abuse I experienced from them left me with a deep mistrust of women. These experiences of abuse also became the foundation for patterns of sexualizing love, physical touch, nurturing, and for bonding with female perpetrators. After my father's departure for the war, my mother took a lover. After the war my parents attempted unsuccessfully to reconcile their differences and their marriage finally ended in divorce.

"The dynamics in my family created betrayal and failure as my model of intimate relationship. My sister and mother fought bitterly. My sister, who was a bright and gifted person, left home at 16. I lost track of her soon thereafter. At this point, neither my mother nor I know of her whereabouts, life, or circumstances.

"At the age of seven I was sent off to a boys' prep school. My mother and I corresponded irregularly and my father visited every couple of weeks or so. My sense of life as an isolated and lonely experience deepened. One of the older boys 'befriended' me. Subsequently he took me out into the woods near the school and raped me. He also threatened me with death if I ever told anyone. I was already experienced as a keeper of family secrets. I kept that secret, even from myself, for 43 years.

"My next recollection after the rape was being in the school infirmary with my body covered with boils. I could keep a secret, but I couldn't contain my rage. I felt betrayed by my father, who I thought should have been there to protect me. I felt betrayed by my 'friend' and began a pattern of mistrust of male friendship, and found myself bonding with male perpetrators. At the age of eight

115

I felt alone, insecure, unworthy, and concluded that there must be something inherently wrong with me. I had become a shame-based person.

"I managed to hide my shame well enough to graduate from college and go on later to become a successful businessman. I still had difficulty in my relationships with men, however, where my employers, colleagues and customers appeared as male perpetrators. My 'success' came from my willingness and proclivity to put myself in a 'one down' position. Since I had no formal business training, I often placed myself in the role of student/learner and cultivated business relationships quite successfully from that place. I also became skilled at faking strength and power and was able to negotiate business contracts for the benefit of my employers. Inside I felt insecure and powerless concerning my own position in the company. Much of my time in business I felt intimidated by many of the men that I met in a business context. Eventually I had to leave the corporate world when I was asked to make business decisions that were in conflict with my own values and sense of integrity.

"I twice married and divorced women who were very aware of my deep levels of pain. I believe that we were drawn together because of our similar histories of abuse. Although there was a great deal of healing in both relationships, we lacked the skills and guidance to take it any further than we did.

"The patterns of betrayal, neglect, mistrust, fear of intimacy, abuse, sabotage, failure, and denial, however, played out again and again in my life. Eventually I left the corporate world and took refuge in nature. My connection to nature has been a consistent thread throughout my life. I also began cultivating a spiritual life through the practice of Yoga and meditation. These activities helped ease somewhat the sense of isolation and detachment I experienced in my human relationships. My inherent longing and drive to complete my unmet developmental needs, coupled with my mistrust and fear of intimacy, produced a constant cycling between the extremes of co-dependent and counter-dependent behavior patterns. I became a master of the dance of intimacy. I could use intimacy to support my dysfunction and, at the same time, as a key to healing. The grief, frustration, and lack of fulfillment that I experienced in the co-dependent part of relationship dance are well known to me, as is the illusion of healing that comes when I flip into the counter-dependent phase.

116

"For reasons of which I am not exactly clear, perhaps through a kind of grace, I have held the vision of myself as a healed and happy person, as well as a member of a healed and functional family, extended family, community, and society in which I would be a participating co-creator and interdependent partner. The pursuit of this vision has guided me on an extraordinary adventure of life in which I have known the depths of sorrow and despair and the pain of failure, frustration and disappointment. It has also provided me with a depth of compassion and understanding that now supports me in helping others heal their childhood wounds.

"I have been a spiritual seeker and finder much of my life and in recent years a man of prayer. My work with spirit guides and teachers of Native American Indian descent has taught me more about my connectedness to all beings and things of this world and to the world of spirit. My Native American practices have also showed me the value and power of ceremony and prayer in my life.

"Through my training in Native American traditions, I became aware of my bondedness to Mother Earth. I have spent many hours out on the land being nurtured and comforted by Her. She became the one mother I could depend on for solace and healing. She has been my primary source of parenting for many years.

"Only recently did I risk bonding again to humans. I knew that my only pattern for bonding in relationships was to bond with perpetrators and create abusive relationships. I had never found people, however, who were safe enough or who really understood the nature of my childhood wounds with whom I could work to change this pattern.

"The isolation from other humans and my loneliness finally grew too great for me to bear. I knew from the conflict and pain in my life that the unresolved issues from my childhood were sabotaging my adulthood. After I met Barry and Janae, read their book on co-dependency and saw their therapeutic approach, I decided to enter therapy with them. My first session was bonding work with Janae. For about forty-five minutes she held me while I cried, releasing the years of suffering from abuse, abandonment, neglect and rejection. It was the first time in my life that I felt safe enough to let down my protective walls at a deeper level than I had previously been able to do and really allow someone to see my pain. It was also the first time that I allowed myself to be comforted by another human. Always before I had retreated inside myself or gone out on the land to my Earth Mother.

"In subsequent sessions with both Barry and Janae I did corrective parenting work with them. I asked to be held, mirrored, sung to and appreciated for who I am. Having two safe, loving, available people to provide my missing developmental needs healed a deep place inside of me. For the first time in my life, I experienced in my body the feeling of being loved by someone who was not a perpetrator. I now knew the feeling of two kinds of relationships: safe and loving and unsafe and abusive. Because I can tell now the difference between healthy and unhealthy relating, I have choice. If the relationship feels safe and healthy, I know I can stay. If it feels like the unsafe and unhealthy pattern from my past, I know I need to leave quickly.

"Breaking through patterns based on a history such as mine has opened up a whole new world for me at the age of fifty. At this point in my life I have come to believe that I chose my family of origin and do not now see myself in anyway as a 'victim of circumstances.' I am grateful for the opportunity to be alive to clear what I believe are my karmic patterns. I know that my parents did the best that they could, given their own histories and conditioning.

SKILL BUILDING ACTIVITIES:
Learning to Be Empathic

Verbal and nonverbal behaviors are an important part of learning the skill of empathy. They include the following **nonverbal attending skills**:
- Lean forward slightly toward the other person when listening to him or her.
- Face the other person squarely and maintain good eye contact.
- Maintain an open position with arms and legs uncrossed.
- Maintain an appropriate distance between you and the other person.
- Mirror the body movements of the other person as much as possible.
- Avoid distracting motions and gestures.
- Keep environmental distractions at a minimum.
- Remove any physical barriers such as desks or tables.

Verbal attending skills include the following:
- Most people use either visual, auditory, kinesthetic (movement) or proprioceptive (feeling) verbs in their sentences. If you listen to which kind they use most and respond using the same kind of sensory verb, people will feel more understood. For example, if I say,

"I *saw* the whole problem *clearly*" (visual) you might say, "You got a good *look* at the big *picture* didn't you?" On the other hand, if you were to reply, "I *hear* that you have a better *feel* for the problem now," I probably would not think you understood me.

- Stay focused on what the other person is saying. Don't use the situation to get into your own agenda (e.g., "That reminds me...").

The second set of verbal skills are called **following skills**. The important following skills to remember are as follows:

- *Door openers* help get someone started, such as "I'm interested in what you think about that" or "Do you want to talk about how you are feeling? I will listen."
- *Minimal encourages* keep things going. Say things like, "Tell me more" or "Really?" or "And?" or just an "mm-hmm" that says keep talking.
- *Open-ended questions* help the person keep talking. It is more effective to say, "What's going on?" than to say, "Are you sad?" This gives the speaker more room to expand on the message.
- *Attentive silences* allow the speaker to reflect on what he or she has said. This may be uncomfortable at first, but if it is used often it becomes a natural part of communicating.

The third set of verbal empathy building skills are called **reflective listening skills**. They are as follows:

- Use *paraphrasing,* a concise response that captures the essence of the content of what was said, *but* uses your own words. To use the exact words of the other person is called "parroting" and should be avoided.
- *Reflective Listening* involves paraphrasing that captures the feeling tone or feelings that were spoken. For example, a friend might say, "I'm not sure what to do. Every time I think I am going to get the job, someone else is picked." Your reflective listening response might be, "You sound really frustrated and discouraged."
- *Reflecting Meanings* are a way to combine both feelings and content. Using the above example, a response that combines both content and feeling might be, "You really seem discouraged and sad about this job hunting process and you probably just want to give up sometimes." The main message should be "You seem to feel____ because_____." Always make it tentative so the person can agree if it fits and they can correct you if it doesn't. This helps bring more clarity.
- *Summary Reflections* are helpful when you have covered lots of ideas, feelings and topics or at the end of a conversation. It is a brief restatement of the main ideas or feelings during a longer conversation. It makes sure that you are still "with" the person and may help the speaker clarify the main themes of the conversation. You might say things like, "Let me see if I am still following this. You said____

119

and _____, is that right?" Or you might say, "It seems to me as I listen to all this, that you main concern seems to be _____."

Reflective Listening Skill Practice Exercise

Test how well you can identify the feelings in the following statements. Read each statement and then write, in one or two words, the feelings involved in each statement. Disregard the context. When you are finished, compare your answers with the authors' and decide which ones best reflect the unwritten feelings.

The Person Says   *The Feeling Is*

1. "I'd like to go on a vacation this summer, but I don't know if I can afford it."
2. "She thinks she is so smart. Just because she got a promotion. Big deal!"
3. "Why do things always turn out this way for me? I never seem to get what I want."
4. "I'm so stupid. I don't know what I would have done if you hadn't helped me."
5. "This is the best relationship I have ever had and I sure don't want to lose it."
6. "Gee, I'm not having any fun today. I can't think of anything I want to do."
7. "Look, I just bought myself a new dress. What do you think?"
8. "No one would want to be my friend. I don't have much to offer."

Reflective Meaning Exercise

Reread each of the statements in the *Reflective Listening* exercise and write out a reflective response that captures the essence of the feeling and the meaning.

Answers to Reflective Listening Skill Practice Exercise:
1). fear, 2). anger, 3). sadness, 4). shame/happiness, 5). happiness/fear 6). fear, maybe anger, 7). excitement, 8). fear.)

Chapter Eight

BOUNDARY SETTING

"Remember, no one can make you feel
inferior without your consent."

Eleanor Roosevelt

BOUNDARIES: A COUNTER-DEPENDENT
PERSPECTIVE

Boundaries provide a structure to help us avoid invading
another person's space and also to protect us from those who
might invade our space. They serve as fences do in neighborhoods
so that we can identify what is "ours" and what is "theirs." As
Frost said: "Good fences make good neighbors." Boundaries allow
us to be separate physically, mentally, emotionally and spiritually. They provide us a way of feeling safe in our relationships.

By creating physical boundaries, we feel more in charge of our
body. These boundaries allow us to protect ourselves against
invasions, such as abuse, sexual aggression and people coming too
close physically. We develop postures, muscles or even fat to
armor our body against some potential violation of our space.
Emotional boundaries also allow us to have feelings and to
express them and to know the difference between our feelings and
the feelings of others. Mental boundaries permit us to have our
own thoughts and perceptions that we know are different from the
thoughts and perceptions that other people have. Spiritual
boundaries help us know the part of ourselves that seeks tran-
scendence or a connection with some Power higher than ourselves.

People with unmet counter-dependent needs, because of their
history of invasion and abuse, never learned to create appropriate
boundaries. They were in such need of protection while growing
up that they had to create walls instead. The boundary issues for
people with counter-dependent behaviors are 1) having too many

121

boundaries and 2) invading the boundaries of others. This is opposite of people with co-dependent behaviors, who usually have few or no boundaries and are often invaded by others.

BOUNDARY WORK IN THERAPY

We find that working with clients who have counter-dependent issues in individual therapy usually takes longer than working with those with co-dependent behaviors, because the person with counter-dependent behaviors is often more removed from his or her feelings. When a client who has counter-dependent issues comes for therapy, we begin by supporting his or her need to maintain rigid boundaries. This approach, looking at what is right about this person's behavior, is important for two reasons. One, it supports their need to look good. This reduces the anxiety that many people with counter-dependent behaviors have when they enter psychotherapy. Two, it helps to develop the kind of client/therapist rapport that the person with unmet counter-dependent needs will need to begin taking off the mask of the inflated false self and to reveal the wounded inner child. Reframing the problem is especially important for people with counter-dependent issues because, like most clients, they come to therapy expecting the therapist to take a "critical parent" role and tell them what they are doing wrong and how bad they are.

We have found that clients who have counter-dependent issues initially need support rather than confrontation and criticism. Being a supportive therapist can help create the kind of safe environment that many people with counter-dependent issues needed during their childhood and never got. In a safe and supportive environment they can explore the circumstances which originally created their need to create rigid boundaries. A safe environment also helps the person with unmet counter-dependent needs get validation for the abuse and violation experiences of his or her childhood. This "naming" of the abuse is an important step in helping them identify their experience correctly. This is particularly important to the person who often is cut off from the reality of his or her wounded inner child.

In therapy, it is also important to help people with unmet counter-dependent needs see that their early decision to erect walls was done out of necessity and without much choice. Most people with counter-dependent issues had their power of choice taken away when their boundaries were violated so early and so

122

often. When this fact is spoken, many clients with counter-dependent issues will visibly lose some of the tension in their body. This kind of support is critical to helping the client remove his or her layers of armoring. We go very slowly, encouraging these clients to take as long as they need to let down their protection. We acknowledge their history of violation and do all we can to avoid becoming another perpetrator of abuse in their life.

This kind of supportive work often creates a new experience for the client with counter-dependent issues, one in which he or she feels safe to think, reflect, explore and choose freely what and how to change. As children, people with unmet counter-dependent needs were always in a reactive state, ready at any moment to respond to a potential threat of physical or emotional harm or invasion. Going slowly, building trust, creating safety and establishing rapport as an ally rather than as an authority are critical in the development of a successful therapeutic relationship with clients with counter-dependent issues.

As a client, you can help yourself break free by bringing some of these ideas into your therapy. It is highly appropriate for you to co-create your therapy treatment by choosing a therapist who supports your goals. Your relationship with your therapist can become one of several relationships where you work in committed, conscious and cooperative ways to get your counter-dependent needs met.

CREATING APPROPRIATE BOUNDARIES

People who have unmet counter-dependent needs are usually hypervigilant, watching for the next incident of invasion or abuse. In their hypervigilant state they often identify the first signs of a possible attack or invasion and make a perceptive countermove first that is designed to short-circuit their opponent's move. This aggressive nature of people with unmet counter-dependent needs, with their "I'll get you before you get me" behavior, makes them a frequent violator of other people's boundaries. It also means people will perceive them as aggressive. If aggression is a problem for you, there are several things you can do to help overcome this tendency.

• Release the stored and repressed feelings of your early childhood violations and/or abandonments. This will reduce your fear of having them be exposed accidentally. The releasing of these feelings may have to be done in therapy or in a safe relationship.

123

- Learn to discriminate between real and imagined threats to yourself. Perception checks are a good tool for sorting this out (see Chapter Nine).
- Learn new ways to protect yourself from invasion that do not involve invading the boundaries of others.
- Learn to ask your loved ones for feedback and help, if you need it. They may indeed experience your invasions before you are aware of them.
- Clean up any violations you become aware of as soon as possible. Demonstrate your willingness to deal with the problem.

KINDS OF BOUNDARIES

Effective boundaries are necessary in four areas: physical, emotional, mental and spiritual. Let's look at each kind as they pertain to counter-dependent behaviors.

Physical boundaries. Physical boundaries allow us to have domain over our body and over our possessions. They let people know how physically close they can come to us. Physical boundaries allow us to say how and when we want to be touched and who we want to touch us.

Counter-dependent people often grew up with their physical boundaries being continually violated through some form of abuse. They might have been spanked, hit, beaten, slapped or disciplined in other ways to intimidate and control them. Their parents may have even invaded them in the guise of love and affection by teasing, touching, tickling, kissing and "rough housing" with them without permission.

Children learn two typical kinds of responses as the result of such invasive experiences. The first is to avoid all physical touch. They do not allow people to get very close to them and they avoid getting too close to other people. They usually do not enjoy snuggling, cuddling and other kinds of nurturing activities unless these are associated with sexual foreplay.

The second typical response is to invade the boundaries of others. This invasion allows people with counter-dependent issues to maintain their offensive position which serves them in two ways. Invading boundaries, especially in the same abusive manner that they were violated as a child, allows these people to unconsciously pass on some of their own pain. This passing on of child abuse and pain to others is called the "vicious cycle of cruelty" (Weinhold, 1988). People who have unfinished counter-
124

dependent issues learn that it is not safe to express their true feelings to those who have wounded or abused them. Instead they learn to express their anger toward someone they perceived as weaker. The second way that invading others serves people with unmet counter-dependent needs is that it helps them avoid dealing with their old feelings or avoid facing their "neediness."

Breaking free of the wounds you carry because of physical abuse and learning to create healthy boundaries begins by paying attention to your body and the bodies of those around you. Notice how your body responds when you anticipate a violation coming. Does it recoil, tighten or stiffen? Do you hold your breath? As soon as you notice this kind of cue, you can pause for a moment and examine what real choices you have.

Old choices might include an escalated attack to overpower your opponent quickly, or throwing up a wall of defense based on fear and anger or running away. New choices might include using assertive "I" statements that protect you and also allow you to stay in relationship with the other person ("When you borrow my car without asking, I feel angry and violated. What I want from you is for you to ask permission before you use or borrow any of my belongings. Are you willing to do that?" or "When you touch my body...").

Emotional boundaries. Emotional boundaries involve the way that we relate with others at a feeling level. Having healthy emotional boundaries allows us to differentiate between what we feel and what others feel.

People with counter-dependent needs often deny their current feelings as a way of protecting themselves from feeling their old feelings. Counter-dependent people also deny the feelings of other people because that too can stir up the old feelings.

There are more ways that people with counter-dependent patterns violate the boundaries of others:

• *Discounting* is one common way. Discounts involve devaluing someone's thoughts, feelings or behavior. It can also involve minimizing the importance of something you have done that affects others.

• *Manipulating* is another common way of violating others' emotional boundaries. Manipulation is a way of using indirect methods of communication to try to get what you want, such as the dynamics involved in the Drama Triangle.

• **_Diverting_** the focus of attention is also a common form of emotional manipulation that people with unmet counter-dependent needs use to divert attention away from their own feelings that are emerging.

Examples of discounting and refocusing statements are, "Oh, you're not angry. You're just a little upset." "You get upset too easily anyway when things don't go your way." "You should do something about your short fuse." These kinds of emotional discounts and manipulations are painful for the friends and family of the person with counter-dependent issues to deal with. They are not allowed to have their own true feelings and instead are expected to adopt the point of view of the person with counter-dependent issues. These defenses keep others off balance, making it difficult for them to stay with their feelings and maintain their own focus.

Breaking free of the wounds of an emotional violation requires that the old, unresolved issues and repressed feelings from your childhood be released. This is best done by working with a therapist or with your partner in a committed relationship. Only by releasing these old feelings in a safe, supportive environment will you be able to refrain from emotionally violating others and stop the vicious cycle of cruelty. Changing these counter-dependent behaviors also requires that you have accurate information about the true function of your feelings so you can use your feelings appropriately.

Mental boundaries. Mental boundaries involve the way that we view the world. They allow us to know what we value, believe, think, want and need, so that we can separate out our perceptions and experiences from those of others.

A common boundary violation that people with unmet counter-dependent needs try is to define the reality of other people. They will often assume that they know what others think, particularly their children, their spouse and their subordinates, without ever asking them. Another common violation of mental boundaries is interrupting someone while they are talking, thus preventing them from completing their thought. Punishing, ridiculing, and overruling the opinions of others are also common violations of mental boundaries. Defining another person's ideas as crazy or stupid is also a common way that people with counter-dependent issues invade other people's mental boundaries. Carl Roger's (1981) said, "If we accept as a basic fact of all human life that we

126

live in separate realities; if we can see those differing realities as the most promising resource for learning in all the history of the world; if we can live together in order to learn from one another without fear; if we can do all this, then a new age could be dawning."

Denial is another form of mental violation. People with counter-dependent issues often deny their own problems or another person's perceptions as a way of maintaining control and domination.

Breaking free of the wounds that were caused by having your mental boundaries violated when you were a child requires that you develop stronger object constancy: the ability to hold yourself as an object of worth even when others attack your thoughts or ideas or when you make a mistake. To develop object constancy and break free of your old wounds often requires that you find a safe space inside yourself where you can explore your own ideas, beliefs, perceptions and experiences. Here you can begin to construct your own way of looking at who you really are and how the world operates outside your family of origin. Keeping a journal is an excellent way to begin exploring your own internal world. A journal also helps you work through some of your needs to be perfect, to look good and have others recognize your accomplishments. You are only in relationship with yourself when you are writing in your journal.

Another important way a person with counter-dependent needs can develop effective boundaries is to learn to make and keep effective agreements. People with counter-dependent behaviors often have trouble with both parts of agreements. They often make agreements they can't keep because they want to look good and they don't keep agreements because they don't want to be controlled. When they break an agreement, they often try to blame it on others or on circumstances beyond their control.

Spiritual boundaries. Spiritual boundaries allow us to experience higher, more transcendent aspects of ourselves. They allow us to feel the unconditional love of a higher power or greater force in the universe. Spiritual boundaries also help us to develop object constancy, the ability to love ourselves even when we feel imperfect. When children are violated spiritually they fall out of love with themselves and disconnect from their spiritual self. This kind of experience is often experienced as terror.

Terror is a combination of shame and fear that promotes perfectionism and highly controlled behavior. Statements such as "God will punish you!" and "You're going to burn in hell for that!" are common forms of spiritual terrorizing that people with counter-dependent issues experienced in childhood. As part of the perpetuation of the vicious cycle of cruelty, they often use this same spiritual weapon on others, especially their children. The child learns to view God and his or her parents as violent, unpredictable and punitive. In this way the person with counter-dependent behaviors can use God as an ally in his or her attempt to control others.

Another form of spiritual violation is "playing God." People with counter-dependent issues will often play God by putting themselves on a pedestal, refusing to reveal their humanness. This stance can violate the spiritual boundaries of those who attempt to approach them with love and kindness to find comfort.

Transforming spiritual violations usually takes much longer than any of the other violations because the soul of the person is often damaged. To reach into the soul of a damaged person requires a lot of skill, patience and unconditional love. Transformation requires that the wound be gently opened and cleansed with tender compassion. This may involve hours of having someone be present to listen and to hold us as we venture out to reveal our wounds as well as support our vision of change. When the wound is finally healed, there is room for an influx or flow of love from the Divine. In 12-step programs this is often described as a "spiritual awakening."

SUMMARY

As you begin to develop an awareness of how you, as someone with counter-dependent needs, have had your boundaries violated and how you have violated the boundaries of others, it is important to remember that you were wounded because of the ignorance of other people and that you have also wounded others in your ignorance. As a child, you may have needed the protective walls you constructed to protect yourself from feeling your feelings connected to abuse or abandonment or boundary violations. Also, if you hadn't constructed firm boundaries to protect yourself from the physical, emotional, mental and spiritual violations in your family of origin, you might not have survived your childhood as well as you did.

128

The task at this point in your life is to determine whether or not the walls of your boundaries still serve you well. Do you still need so much protection? What is it costing you to be so protected? Are you still in so much danger? Are you as weak and vulnerable as you were as a child? Can you learn new ways to protect yourself that still support more intimacy with yourself and with others? Only when you feel safe and ready should you take steps to create new ways of communicating and relating that allow you to take down your walls.

CASE EXAMPLE

Jeff had many of the characteristic counter-dependent behaviors. He was very bright and hard working, but had real difficulty with intimate situations and stayed as far away from feelings as he could. He used his boundaries to wall off his feelings and avoid close intimate situations where he perceived he could get hurt.

In therapy, we had explored the reasons behind his fears of intimacy, looking for events in his childhood in which his boundaries had been violated. He recently had remembered an incident of childhood sexual abuse. Sexual abuse is one of the most damaging kinds of boundary violations, for it crosses through all the levels: physical, mental, emotional and spiritual. It leaves the victim permanently scarred, often with feelings of having been terrorized.

Jeff's brother, who was eight years older, sodomized him when he was six. This experience was extremely traumatic for Jeff. When he told his parents about the abuse, however, he was blamed for the incident. Neither parent supported him in his feelings of shock and hurt. His mother actually spanked him and shamed him horribly as punishment. His father withdrew from disciplining him, but said nothing in his defense.

In the session he had with us, he spoke of two issues related to this incident that he wanted to work on: his anger toward his brother and the lack of support from his parents. He said, "I really need to get angry at my brother, but I can't. It is still so difficult for me to get angry." *(This told us that getting angry would be an important part of Jeff's work.)*

Janae said, "Do you have a picture of yourself getting angry at your brother?" Jeff thought for a moment and then shook his head, "No, I don't." *(This indicated to us that Jeff was not yet ready to confront his perpetrator. Had he been ready, he would have had some image of it. So we shifted.)*

129

Barry said, "Maybe you need to deal with your lack of support from your parents before you can deal with your brother." As Barry said this, Jeff leaned back and supported himself with one of his hands. *(This was a positive signal, indicating that we should work on the support issue.)*

Barry asked him how he would like to work on the support issue with his parents. He indicated that he wanted us to play his mother and father and reenact the scene where he told them about the abuse. We agreed to do that. Then Barry asked Jeff what he wanted to get out of this particular roleplay. He said that he wanted to replay the scene with a new ending. What he wanted was to get support from both of his parents for his feelings and for them to protect him against his brother.

Barry asked Jeff what he wanted him to do as his father. He said, "I want you to tell my brother off and then protect me from my mom's anger and shame." At that point Barry turned to an imaginary brother and told him, "You leave Jeff alone! You have no right to do this to him! Get away from him this instant and don't you ever do this to him again!" *(By now Jeff had moved behind Barry and huddled up small as if hiding from his brother. He looked and sounded like a scared seven-year-old.)*

Then Barry turned to Jeff and asked him how he was doing. He said, "I'm scared, Dad. Will you hold me?" As Barry held him, he told Jeff how sorry he was that he had not protected him when Jeff needed his father. Barry also assured him that he would not let his brother hurt him again.

When Barry asked Jeff what he needed from him to help him deal with his mother, he said, "Will you go with me to talk to her about how she hurts me when she criticizes and shames me?" Barry said he would do that.

The two of them moved toward Janae, who was playing his mother. Jeff began to talk to her about her hurtful remarks and how they affected him. As he talked, he began moving slowly behind Barry until he was completely hidden from his mother. Barry turned to look at Jeff and said, "You seem to be hiding behind me. Are you scared?"

Looking relieved that I had come to his aid, Jeff said, "Will you talk to her for me?" *(I knew that he also needed modeling on how to be appropriately angry with his mother, so that he could deal with his brother later.)*

Barry told Jeff's mother (Janae), "If you ever spank him like that again, I will turn you in for child abuse. What you did to Jeff

130

was abusive and it has to stop." At this point Jeff reported that he was afraid that his mother might go away and that he would lose her. So then Barry added, "This boy needs a mother and a father. If you don't know how to raise him, ask me."

Jeff then started to talk to his mother from his sheltered position behind Barry. He told her how he felt when the incident happened and asked her to support his feelings and not criticize him. She was able to respond to his request and he began to relax and move out from behind Barry. *(At this point I knew that Jeff was integrating an internal protector and didn't need me to play that part for him any longer.)*

We asked Jeff if he had gotten what he wanted from the session, and he said he had. He now knew what appropriate anger looked like and that he had finally gotten the protection he had always wanted from his parents. *(These were important missing developmental pieces for Jeff that would allow him to defend himself in future situations where he formerly would have felt victimized.)*

AWARENESS ACTIVITY:
Boundary Building Exercise

In this exercise you will learn how to create appropriate boundaries rather than walls. You will also be able to experience what it feels like to be both the invader and the one being invaded and determine which role you feel most comfortable in. Toward the end of the exercise you will learn how to raise and lower your boundary, allowing you protection when you need it and intimacy when you want it. It is important as you do this exercise that you maintain a high awareness of what is happening at all times in your body.

Directions: This exercise is best done on a floor with a pile carpet or a surface where you can draw a temporary circle on the floor with your finger. You need to do the exercise with a partner and each of you needs to take turns following the set of instructions given below. Choose a partner and sit on the floor across from each other. Decide who is going to begin acting as the person who is invaded and who will play the one who invades. This person will complete the exercise first. Your partner will play the invader. At the end of this exercise you will exchange roles so that you both get an experience of playing invader/invadee. You will both find directions for each role in the exercise.

Part One: No Boundaries

This part of the exercise is designed to have you really feel what it is like not to have protective boundaries. Partners sit across from each other about three feet apart. Your partner should start making some sort of aggressive or threatening nonverbal move toward you. Do this slowly and with awareness. Notice how it feels to have someone approach you this way without warning. What feelings emerge? What reaction do you notice in your body? What thoughts come into your mind?

Part Two: Boundaries, No Protection

1. *Partner One:* Now draw an imaginary circle around yourself while sitting on the floor. Use your finger to trace the parameter of the circle in the carpet, if possible, or use string, magazines, pillows or whatever you have handy. Feel what it is like to have the circle (boundary) around you.

Partner Two: Feel what it is like to be outside this circle and not have a boundary like your partner has.

2. *Partner One:* When you have your boundary (real or imaginary) created, tell your partner outside the boundary to begin playing the invader.

Partner Two: Using one hand, gently invade your partner's boundary. Each partner should pay attention to how it feels to play the particular role (invader or invadee). Ask yourself if you like the role you are playing.

Part Three: Creating Boundaries with Protection

This part of the exercise is for developing an awareness of what an appropriate boundary looks and feels like.

Partner One: Using the boundary created around you as a base, now create an imaginary egg-shaped sphere that completely surrounds you. As you set the sphere in place, notice how it feels to have this imaginary protection around you. Next, charge your egg with your own energy by breathing it full of breath through quick bursts of breathing, by radiating out energy from your whole body or by imagining it full of some color, sound or other kind of comforting support.

Partner Two: Notice what it feels like when your partner begins to isolate him or herself from you with this protective egg. Do you notice any emotions coming up for you? Do you have any other kind of response?

Part Four: Protecting Your Physical Boundaries

In the next part of this exercise you will learn how to protect yourself against physical boundary violations.

Partner One: When you have your egg full of protective energy, ask your partner on the outside of your boundary to physically invade you by slowly moving one hand toward your egg. As the hand comes toward you, you can protect yourself in two ways. First, use the energy in your egg to make it impenetrable by your partner. Second, if the hand gets inside your egg, make a countering move with your hand to block your partner's hand. Use only enough force to stop the encroachment and to assert your strength. If you undermatch the oncoming energy, you set yourself up to be victimized. If you overmatch the oncoming energy, you set yourself up as an aggressor.

Partner Two: Invade your partner in a way that feels appropriate for him or her. If you are working with a timid partner, use less forcefulness. If you are working with a stronger partner, then you can use more force.

Part Five: Protecting Your Mental Boundaries

Partner One: Think of something that people say to you which causes you to lose confidence in your thinking so that they can invade your mental boundaries. Perhaps it is some kind of message that says that you are stupid, dumb or crazy. Now share this message with your partner outside your boundary. Then return to the safety inside your egg, making sure it is full of energy or whatever kind of protection you have filled it with. Your partner is going to repeat the message you just shared with him or her while you stay in the safety of your egg. When you have your egg ready, indicate to your partner when you are ready to begin.

Partner Two: Speak back the disturbing message that your partner shared with you. You can repeat it with different inflections and then begin to add variations of your own that you intuitively sense will fit with the original message.

133

Boundary Setting

Partner One: Continue to keep the shell of your egg impenetrable. Use the protective devices you have created (color, sound, energy) to keep out your partner's attempts to invade your mental boundaries. You can close your eyes, look away from your partner or sing a song to yourself if you need to. When you are able to do this successfully, you can tell you partner to stop. If your partner's words begin to penetrate your shell, ask him or her to stop while you recharge your egg. Continue with the exercise until you know you can protect yourself against mental violations without difficulty.

Part Six: Protecting Your Emotional Boundaries

Partner One: Remember the kinds of things people do or say to you which cause you to give up, modify or hide your real feelings. It could be some kind of seductive "please rescue me, I'm helpless" message or one that says, "You're so important. We really need you to do this job," which appeals to your need to be important. Now share this message with your partner outside your boundary. Then return to the safety of your egg, filling it again with protection. When your egg is ready, give your partner the signal to begin the invasion.

Partner Two: Speak back the message your partner shared with you. Use body language and voice inflections that amplify the feeling part of the message. For example, if your partner's message has a victim tone in it, look and sound like a real victim.

Partner One: Continue to keep your egg impenetrable as your partner gives you your message. Give yourself comforting messages if you need to, saying such things as, "My feelings are mine and they are okay." When you can successfully resist your partner's message, tell him or her to stop. If you have difficulty at any point, stop the invasion and recharge your egg. Continue until you can protect yourself against violations of your emotional boundaries

Part Seven: Protecting Your Spiritual Boundaries

Partner One: Think of the kinds of things that people have done to violate your spiritual boundaries. It could be some kind of terrorizing statement that invokes the wrath of God. It could also be something that attacks you in the very core of your being through shame, humiliation or judgment that makes you want to
134

die. Now share this message with your partner and return to the safety of your egg. When you have it filled with protection, tell your partner you are ready to begin.

Partner Two: Repeat back the message your partner shared with you in a way that reflects a Divine Pronouncement. Look and sound like an authoritative God or parent.

Partner One: Hold your own strength, resisting your partner's attack and abuse. If you need to pray or ask God or some other higher power for support, you can do that. When you can successfully resist your partner's message, tell him or her to stop. Stop the process at any time, if you have difficulty resisting, and recharge your egg. Continue until you can protect yourself against violations of your spiritual boundaries.

At this point it is time for partners to reverse places. Partner One should remove his or her actual or imaginary boundary mark on the floor before moving on to repeat the exercise with his or her partner.

When both partners have learned how to protect themselves from physical, mental, emotional and spiritual violations and can actually feel the protection that the egg sphere provides, it is time to move on to the next part of the exercise.

Part Eight: Moving in the World with Protection and Boundaries

In this part of the exercise you will learn how to take your egg with you as you are out in the world. Both partners should make sure that they have their egg around them. If you were the first *Partner One,* you should take time to firmly reestablish your protective egg. When both partners have their eggs in place, they should stand up, imagining their egg as a hoop with handles. Picking up your egg/hoop, begin to move around the room. Notice how you react as you encounter your partner and as he or she comes close to your egg. Do you have an impulse to make your egg stronger and invade them? Or do you find yourself giving up your boundary? As you move, try to keep your boundary intact. Stay out of your partner's egg and keep yourself totally separate.

Part Nine: Raising and Lowering Your Boundaries

This is a very important step for people with counter-dependent issues who have little experience in allowing other people inside their boundaries. It is important to go slowly and experiment with this step.

As you walk around the room with your partner, notice when you feel safe and when you feel unsafe. When you can identify the safe people, try opening and closing your egg as you come close to him or her. You can imagine a sliding door, a window blind with a pull string or little lens-type holes that open and close as images for how you might let others inside your egg. Become aware of what it feels like to actually be in charge of who enters your space and how much they can enter it. It is the ability to raise and lower the shell of your protective egg that really allows you to be in the world safely and still be intimate. For many people with unmet counter-dependent needs this kind of exercise will provide the first experience of both safety and intimacy.

Part Ten: Touching and Maintaining Boundaries

This can be the most difficult part of the exercise, for it requires that you actually let someone completely penetrate your egg while you still maintain your boundaries. This exercise also requires that you learn to give off nonverbal signals that are congruent with your desire or lack of desire for being touched. It also requires that you learn to read the nonverbal signals of other people about their desire or lack of desire for being touched. This kind of learning is valuable for the person with counter-dependent issues who never had an opportunity to develop these skills.

As you walk around the room, nonverbally let your partner know whether or not you want them to touch you. Give off clear signals with your face and body about your position on being touched. Also notice when your partner invites you to touch him or her. Learn to read their nonverbal signals about how much and where to touch. Approach them slowly and cautiously, so that you can stop quickly if you reach the limit.

Part Eleven: Discussion and Interpretation

Now discuss with your partner what you learned by doing this exercise. Talk about ways you can use this information in your life. Make a specific plan with your partner on how you are going to use what you learned to create healthy boundaries for yourself.

Chapter Nine

ME AND MY SHADOW: RECLAIMING PROJECTIONS

"When a man points a finger at someone else, he should
remember that four of his fingers are pointing at himself."
Louis Nizer

WHAT ARE PROJECTIONS?

In the clever little ditty about "me and my shadow," the singer/
dancer is in relationship to his shadow as he relates how they stroll
together down the avenue. However, a person with counter-
dependent issues is *not* in relationship with his or her shadow and
may not even know he or she has a shadow part. The "shadow" in
psychology usually refers to those unwanted aspects of yourself
that you are unaware of, or try to ignore or tend to see only in other
people. Seeing your own shadow in other people and judging them
for being the way they are is known as "projecting." Projecting is
a way that a person with unmet counter-dependent needs avoids
or hides aspects of himself or herself that he or she had learned as
a child were unacceptable.

People with counter-dependent needs tend to be more aware of
the unfinished business of others and often are totally unaware of
their own unmet needs. People with counter-dependent issues use
projections to keep themselves from having to look at and face
their own unfinished business. If they are in relationship with a
person with co-dependent behaviors, that person may be seen as
the "sick" or needy one in the relationship. This often "enables" the
person with counter-dependent patterns to avoid looking at his or
her own shadow.

HOW AND WHY WE DEVELOP A "SHADOW"

Our shadow consists of all those aspects of ourselves that we try to keep hidden from others and from ourselves. These are usually the aspects of ourselves that our parents or teachers or society said were wrong, deviant, bad, unruly or uncivilized. Our parents may have told us things like, "Don't be so active, sit still," or "Don't play with your food," "Sit up straight," "Don't play with yourself, that's bad and dirty," or "Good girls don't get angry," and "Big boys don't cry." We then learn to hide all of these rejected or unacceptable feelings, thoughts and behaviors. We put them away in a "bag," so to speak. Hiding these natural aspects of our True Self, at a young age, allows us to please others and just plain survive. As we grow up, we drag this bag of unwanted or unappreciated traits behind us everywhere we go. For most people, by the time they are nineteen or twenty they have put almost everything of value about themselves into this bag: their creativity, their passion, their sexuality, their ability to have deep feelings, their energy, their spontaneity, their hungers, their enthusiasms, their dreams, and whatever else that they deemed frivolous, unattractive or unacceptable by others.

What's left? The only things left are those behaviors, thoughts and feelings that peers, parents, teachers and other adults found acceptable or nonthreatening, which is usually not much of who we really are. The person with counter-dependent issues usually becomes overidentified with his or her "false self" and is still trying to look acceptable enough or nonthreatening enough, in hopes of getting his or her unmet developmental needs met. People with counter-dependent issues hope that if they do enough of the right things, they will get the respect, love and recognition they have always wanted. Of course, this doesn't work. Instead, they find themselves on a treadmill, doing as much as possible to look good to others, but feeling empty inside.

One of the core beliefs of people with unmet counter-dependent needs is that they are "not enough." They are not lovable enough, handsome enough, good enough sons or fathers or daughters or mothers and so on. They hope that no one will notice that they aren't good enough and fear that people somehow will find out. This belief often drives their behavior. Everything they say and do may come out of this belief.

The main way a person keeps the real self or True Self from accidentally popping out of his or her bag is to keep the focus on

138

"unacceptable" things that *others* do and say. This is where projection becomes a useful defense. Interestingly, when we project a quality of ourselves on others, it is like giving it away and it becomes hard to reclaim it, if and when we want it back. For example, a man projects his ability to deal with feelings onto his wife, and lets her feel all the feelings. Then when one of his children has a problem with feelings, he has to let her handle it. It is difficult to reclaim these split-off parts, but that is exactly what a person with counter-dependent issues must learn to do.

THE SHADOW AS THE INNER CHILD

The "shadow," which most people with counter-dependent issues regard with fear and distain, turns out to be none other than *their own inner child.* The awful closet full of monsters or the bag that they have been dragging along all these years contains the important elements of their True Self that they were taught to disown. Many times when people with counter-dependent needs realize how they have lost touch with their inner child, they actually weep about the losses they have experienced. It is necessary to mourn the loss of your True Self or your inner child and then begin the often scary and painful process of reclaiming those parts of you that you cast aside in order to be acceptable to others.

Breaking free of counter-dependency requires facing your weaknesses, insecurities, fears and "shadow" parts and then learning to love each one of those parts as you would love a hurt and rejected child. In therapy, we ask clients to buy themselves a doll, teddy bear or stuffed animal to represent their inner child or their split-off parts. By hugging this bear, doll or stuffed animal or by saying loving things to it, they are learning to love those parts of themselves that they were told were unlovable, bad or unacceptable. One of our clients is a businessman who travels a lot. He bought a travel bag just for his teddy bear on his business trips. Others strap their bear or doll into the passenger seat of their car and carry on a conversation with their inner child to and from their work.

THE ROLE OF SHAME IN CREATING PROJECTIONS

The most effective way that many parents used to get you to hide an aspect of yourself they didn't want to see was to use shame.

139

The message with toxic shame is "There is something wrong or unacceptable about you." You might have heard, "Shame on you, for talking back to your mother, you are an insolent brat!" Or, "Shame on you for playing with your genitals, you have a filthy mind."

Guilt and shame are different. Guilt implies that you did something bad or wrong and you need to stop it. While guilt involves conditional negative messages such as: "You have done something bad," shame involves "unconditional" negative messages such as: "You are a bad person." Although there were elements of having done something bad in the shame example above, the underlying messages are "You are bad" and "There's something wrong with you."

Bradshaw (1988) writes "... I had one of those life-jolting discoveries that significantly changed everything. I named the core demon in my life. I named 'shame'" (p. VII). He adds, "Toxic shame is unbearable and always necessitates a cover-up, a false self. Since one feels his True Self is defective and flawed, one needs a false self which is not defective and flawed. (*Once one becomes a false self, one ceases to exist psychologically)*" (p. VIII).

Bradshaw lists the following characteristics of toxic shame:
1. It becomes a core identity which provides you with a sense of being flawed and defective and also powerless to change.
2. It causes you to hide your inner feelings and thoughts from others and it means you must guard against letting other people see these inner thoughts and feelings.
3. It causes people to constantly guard against exposing these qualities to yourself.
4. It is experienced as an inner torment or a sickness of the soul.
5. It produces shame about shame, so you are ashamed to have toxic shame and won't admit shame. In order to hide your shame you may try to shame others. It is like a kneejerk reaction; you are shamed in some way and you quickly get the monkey off your back by shaming someone else.

Bradshaw also discusses three ways that people learn shame. The first way involves identifying with shame-based role models, usually our parents. The second way is through the trauma of abandonment, where you may have been abused, neglected or forced to abandon yourself in order to take care of your parents. This usually means that you learn to distrust your needs, feelings and natural instincts. You may feel ashamed for even having
140

needs, feelings or instincts. The third way that toxic shame develops, according to Bradshaw, is that we experience profound betrayal and a violation of primal trust when we are shamed as a child and there is no time to grieve this loss and no support available to help us grieve. This original pain needs to be identified, expressed and supported before toxic shame can be released.

You can see that toxic shame helps explain why people with counter-dependent patterns split-off aspects of themselves. Until they identify the core shaming experiences that created their original pain (traumas in the trauma drama) and are given help in expressing this pain, they will not move through the shame.

HOW TO SPOT PROJECTIONS

- If your reaction to an incident is far greater than the incident called for (The "making a mountain out of a mole hill" phenomenon).
- If your feelings remind you of some previously painful situation. (You are "rubber-banded" back to an earlier trauma. For example, when your partner yells at you, you quickly begin to feel and behave as a three-year-old and see your partner as your omnipotent mother or father.)
- If you find yourself in a conflict where you are totally focused on what the other person said or did. This over-focusing is usually to avoid a feeling you are having or a way of avoiding looking at your part in causing the conflict.
- If you find yourself using loaded words like "always" or "never" to describe the situation.

PERCEPTION CHECKS: SEPARATING REALITIES

An important communication skill that people with counter-dependent patterns need to learn is the "perception check." When you find yourself projecting blame on others or when you think your partner is doing or saying something to put you down, it is important to check your "perception" of what he or she is doing or saying. For example, in the therapy session described below, Jane said to Art, "I don't think you really want this relationship to work. You just want to blame it all on me like my mother did and then leave (like my father did)." I asked her if she would label that as her "perception" of Art and ask him if any of what she said was true

141

"for him." She hesitated, but finally said, "Art, is any of what I said true?" Art replied, "No Jane, I really want this relationship to work, and I am not going to blame it all on you and then leave."

It is also important that the "grain of truth" in Jane's perception is also acknowledged, so I asked Art to tell me what, if anything, *was* true about Jane's fears. Art thought for a minute, then he said, "Jane, I was at the end of my rope and threatened to leave you last week. I can see now that could cause you to be afraid." I asked Jane if there was anything she wanted from Art and if there was, then to ask him directly for it. She replied, "Art, when you threaten to leave me I get really scared; will you agree to not make threats like that anymore unless you are really going to leave?" Art answered, "Yes, I'm willing to make that agreement."

Almost all projections can be handled in this manner, if both people are willing to help each other. It is also helpful to remember that the person who is not caught up in a projection may recognize a possible projection before the other person does. To help the person who is doing the projecting, the other person might say, "It looks and feels as though you might have a projection operating here. Are you willing to take a look at what you are saying or doing to see if there is a projection involved?" Or you can simply ask the person with a possible projection if he or she is willing to do a "perception check" with you.

HOW TO TAKE BACK PROJECTIONS

It seems as if most people spend the first twenty or thirty years putting things into their shame bag. Then comes the task of the next twenty or thirty years: realizing what they have done and trying to take back these split-off parts of themselves. With proper support for our True Self from the beginning of our lives, we would not have to put away or hide parts of ourselves and, therefore, would not have to use projections as a way of denying our True Self.

Robert Bly (1989) writes about a five stage process for learning to understand and take back projections. Most of the first four stages involve trying to make projections work for us. He says that in stage one we try as hard as we can to keep the projections intact. In stage two we realize that our projections don't always work. For example, our spouse is loving toward us and wants to get close. What can we do in these situations when it is hard to see them as bad or uncaring? He says this dilemma is frightening for a person with counter-dependent issues because this brings up old fears and insecurities. This person may try to provoke or manipulate his or her partner back into the shadow role he or she wanted them in. The ultimate solution that many people choose at this stage is to have children and project things they don't want to look at on their children. Children can't fight back. They are always doing things they shouldn't be doing, so they make great targets for projections.

In the third stage, according to Bly, things break down so badly that you have to use moral rightness to justify your actions. Parents may claim they were doing it "for your own good" when they punish you severely. The message is, "Don't question my authority, I am right." If the family is religious they may even pull in God: "God will punish you if you don't behave or listen to me."

In stage four, people with counter-dependent patterns may let down their guard and begin to see what they are doing. You may begin to see that they have diminished yourself through the projection process. This may lead you to take inventory of your life and decide to change your life. You also may get into therapy or join a support group and at this stage begin piecing things together.

In the fifth stage, according to Bly, the task is to "eat" your shadow. This means you must face everything you have pushed away from yourself or pushed onto others. You have to chew up, swallow and digest all that you have been afraid of. By reintegrating these split-off parts, you can begin to feel deeper feelings, feel passionate about life, become more spontaneous, and become more healthful and spiritual. According to Bly, people who have eaten their shadow tend to "be" more than "do" and show more grief than anger. They often find they have much more energy, need less sleep and are more wise and discerning in their decisions.

The following case example shows how projections operate for people with counter-dependent issues in relationships. It also shows some of the tools you may need to begin to reclaim your shadow.

CASE EXAMPLE

Art and Jane, who were having serious relationship conflicts, came to me (Barry) to start couples therapy. We negotiated a three session contract to see if we could work together effectively and to determine whether or not they were getting what they wanted. During the first session or two, I had tried to help them see what was causing their conflict. We tried to identify the unfinished business that each of them had brought into the relationship.

I thought they were really gaining lots of insight, so at the beginning of the third session, I was pleased to hear Jane announce, "I have been thinking about our last session and I now realize what the biggest problem in our relationship is." I asked, "What is it Jane?" To this she replied, "It's him," as she pointed her finger at her husband and then launched into a nonstop shaming litany of all the things that he had done or not done to her that ruined "the relationship." This was obviously an attack in which she tried to project blame for everything that was wrong with the relationship on the other person.

Apparently, I had moved too fast for Jane and she got really scared that she would be blamed for all their relationship problems, similar to the way she was blamed for all her parents' relationship problems. I was able to recognize Jane's terror and immediately knew that she had been triggered back to a childhood memory. It wasn't "Jane the angry bitch" talking, but "Jane the scared child" who was yelling at her husband. I let her know I saw her scared child, "You look really scared Jane, just close your eyes and sink into that feeling." She did this and she began to sob. Between sobs she told her story about when she was six and one night her father, who was drunk, crawled into bed with her and sexually molested her. The next day she told her mother, who immediately ordered her father out of the house and they divorced.

Later on Jane's mother periodically would blame Jane for breaking up her parents' marriage. Jane's mother never remarried and lived out the rest of her life as an angry, miserable victim. Jane believed that her parents' divorce actually was her fault and took all the blame for her mother's unhappiness. Whenever she got into a conflict with her husband, Art, she became afraid that the same thing was going to happen again.

This illustrates how projections get set up and how frequently behind these projections, such as the ones that Jane had, there is a shamed little child. Projections are often difficult to sort out in a relationship because there usually is an element of truth about the accusation. In Jane's case, she actually believed that Art did *all* those things she accused him of doing because he really had done a *few* of them.

144

SKILL BUILDING EXERCISE: Suggestions
for Reclaiming Your Projections
(How to eat your shadow)

- Get involved in body work to loosen up those tight and constricted places in your body that you used to armor yourself. Massage, deep tissue work such as Rolfing, Lomi work, Trager work or Myotherapy may be a good adjunct to your psychological work.
- Develop your creative and artistic talents—try dance and movement classes, clay, drawing or playing a drum to awaken lost resources.
- Make a list of the projections you have used and who you have projected things onto.
- Go to these people on whom you have projected and tell them you are taking back your projections. Ask them to give the projections you put on them back to you, which also could mean asking them to help you learn things that they know and you don't.
- Do things to awaken your senses. Do things that increase your sense of smell, taste, touch, sight and hearing.
- Do free writing. Put pen to paper and write whatever comes into your mind for, say, ten minutes. Do not lift the pen from the paper; record everything. This can open up creative doors in your mind.
- Buy a teddy bear, doll or stuffed animal and use it to represent aspects of yourself that you thought were not acceptable. Learn to love and care for this object as you learn to love and care for those aspects of yourself.
- When you meet someone new, attempt to find out things about them that you have in common with them. This may help you feel more connected and open to people.
- Use perception checks with others when you are aware you are having unusually strong reactions to what they are doing or saying. Say, "I'm having a reaction to something you said and I want to check it out. Did you mean...?"
- Buy or make masks to represent your internal demons, witches or ugly giants. Wear the mask and try acting out that part. Try writing out a dialogue with this part, asking it what it represents and what it has to teach you. This can be fun and you can learn more about these hidden parts.

SKILL BUILDING EXERCISE: Facilitating Blame

Blame is one of the most destructive forces in relationships and one of the most common ways that projections are used in relationships. The following exercise can be done alone or with a partner, particularly when there is some mutual blaming involved. If you are doing this alone, it can be strictly a writing process; or you can use a pillow or empty chair to represent the other person, if you want to dialogue with that person. If working with a partner, you can each write and then each read the other's "blame sheets," or you can speak these blaming statements directly to each other. If you are working with a partner, you may want to alternate completing each step.

Step 1 - *Blame It All on Them*. In a conflict where you think the other person is to blame, you may need to take a good look at any secret blaming you are holding onto. Write out all the things that you are blaming the other person for. Make them 100% to blame for what happened. Get it all on paper or speak it all to your partner. Your partner's job is to make sure you have not taken *any blame* for what happened. If you are doing this alone, read and evaluate your written blame sheet and correct it if you actually accepted *any* of the blame. Notice how this feels for you. It usually feels good to blame everything that happened on someone else.

Step 2 - *Blame It All on Yourself*. This time you need to look at yourself and blame everything that happened on yourself. Again, write or speak this out completely. If you have a partner, his or her job is to make sure in this step that *you* accept *all* the blame. Again, notice the feelings you have in accepting all the blame. Compare these feelings to those in Step 1.

Step 3 - *Whose Responsibility Was It?* Responsibility is different from blame in that it means "ability to respond." This time look at what happened from the perspective of "How much ability to respond did I have in this situation?" "How much more experience and information did I have about this situation?" "How did I use my ability in this situation?" Write or speak your answer to this question, and communicate it to your partner, if appropriate.

Step 4 - *What Have I Learned?* Ask yourself, "What could I have done differently if I had used my ability to respond more effectively?" Write or speak your answer to this question and communicate it to your partner, if appropriate.

146

Chapter Ten

CORRECTIVE PARENTING: HEALING YOUR INNER CHILD

"You grow up the day you have your first real laugh at yourself."

Ethel Barrymore

CONNECTING WITH YOUR INNER CHILD

Many people with counter-dependent issues grow up cut off from their inner child. They put aside many of the qualities of their inner child long ago, either to protect themselves from parental shame and abuse, or they never realized these qualities because of parental neglect. As adults, unfortunately, they often treat their inner child the way they were parented as children. You may give your inner child shaming and abusive messages like the ones you heard growing up. Using the examples below, create your own list of messages you use to shame and abuse your inner child.

- "Stay out of my way."
- "I don't need you in my life."
- "Don't embarrass me."
- "Don't make any demands or have any needs."
- "I don't have time for you."
- "I don't like you."
- "I don't like your feelings."
- "I hate you."
- "You must be crazy."
- "You can't do anything right."
- "You are so stupid!"
- "You'll never amount to anything."
- "Why would anyone love you?"

147

HEALING YOUR INNER CHILD

After you have established a solid contact with your inner child, you will need to remember as much as you can about the circumstances in your childhood that caused you to put your True Self aside. The awareness exercises in the first part of this book may help you begin to piece things together. If you need further help, the book *Breaking Free of Addictive Family Relationships* contains many exercises that can help you remember what happened to you as a child and can help you better understand what you set aside as a child and why.

Taking charge of the healing process is also very important. You cannot wait for someone else to do it for you. The hopeful message of this book is that despite the wounding your inner child suffered through abuse or neglect, you can learn to heal these wounds as an adult. You can learn ways to get your unmet developmental needs met and repair the damage to your inner child. For the most part, it is not a question of unlearning something. It's really an opportunity to learn something new for the first time that you did not get a chance to learn as a child.

John Bradshaw (1990), in his book *Homecoming: Reclaiming and Championing Your Inner Child*, writes about ten nurturing rules to use when you "parent" your inner child. These are sort of a "Bill of Rights" for healing your inner child. They are the birthrights you gave up as a child and now can reclaim as a part of healing your inner child. They are listed below:

1. You have the right to feel all of your feelings. There is no such things as a "bad" feeling. You can learn effective ways to use your feelings to get your needs met.
2. You have the right to want whatever you want. You can actively seek what you want by asking for it directly.
3. You have the right to what you see and hear. You have the final say about what you see and hear.
4. You have the right to have fun and play whenever you want to. You can decide when, where and with whom you want to play.
5. You have the right to tell the truth as you see it. You can listen to how others see things and still decide what is true for you.
6. You have the right to set your own limits or boundaries. This helps you feel safe and secure.
7. You have the right to your own thoughts, feelings, behaviors and your body. You do not have to take responsibility for anything that is not yours.

8. You have the right to make mistakes. There really is no such thing as a "bad" mistake. Mistakes are good because they help us learn.
9. You have the right to privacy and a responsibility to respect the privacy of others. Do not consciously violate the privacy of others.
10. You have the right to have problems and conflicts. You don't have to be perfect to be loved.

WORKING WITH FEELINGS

The most essential part of healing your inner child is to remember and express any repressed feelings from childhood. These unexpressed feelings are like an anchor filled with old patterns of thinking and behaving that doesn't allow you to move forward. Children are often punished for expressing angry or sad feelings, or they witnessed others being punished for expressing these feelings. In addition, many of our core feelings of fear of abandonment and grief, rage and shame were too overwhelming for a young child to express, even if he or she had supportive parents. So, even with effective support, people still grow up without feeling or expressing many of their deepest feelings that they experienced during childhood.

One of the universal feelings of childhood is abandonment. Mostly children experience some emotional or psychological abandonment when parents and others do not support or mirror their True Self. The illusion that the young child carries is that the parents are perfect mirrors for him or her and that they will mirror back the child's True Self. When parents don't do this, the child experiences an abandonment of this True Self. After numerous such episodes, the child eventually may abandon his or her own True Self, believing that his or her parents know more about who the child really is than does the child.

The other common form of abandonment is physical abandonment. Young children under two cannot tolerate a prolonged absence from a parent they are bonded to. For example, if parents go on a vacation and leave the young child with a sitter or relative for a week, the child may experience this as abandonment. If a mother goes to the hospital to have another child, this can be a double abandonment (physical and emotional), because when she returns all of her attention may be on the new baby. It is important for parents, even if they are leaving a small child for a

149

short period of time, to look the child in the eyes and tell him or her that they are leaving and when they will return. Even if the child doesn't understand time concepts, he or she will understand the feelings of the message. One of our clients with a severe eating disorder told us that when she was two years old, her grandmother distracted her by feeding her cookies in the kitchen while her parents sneaked out the front door and left for a two-week vacation. This client now suffers from intense abandonment fears in her relationships and cannot eat when these fears appear.

Masterson (1988) also says that underneath the depression that often accompanies an experience of abandonment are over-whelming feelings of panic, terror, rage, shame, grief, despair and emptiness. Depression of our feelings then serves to keep these overwhelming feelings out of our awareness. The problem is that while these feelings were too overwhelming for a young child, they no longer are for an adult. Most adults, however, behave as if they were still one or two years old and are afraid to feel these core feelings. No adult has ever died from feeling his or her core feelings, no matter how overwhelming the feelings might seem. Lots of adults have repressed their feelings and died from ill-nesses caused by repressing them.

People who come into therapy and are depressed are usually not in touch with these deep core feelings. It usually takes some time to build enough trust before clients will risk sharing their deepest fears and depression. More and more medical research is confirming what many mental health people have believed for a long time. This research shows that most degenerative diseases, such as cancer, heart disease, arthritis and strokes, may be caused by repressed core feelings. These feelings get stored in the body and place chronic stress on all the internal systems of the body, until something breaks down and a person gets sick.

Alice Miller (1981) writes about the importance of grieving the loss of your True Self and the loss of your innocence in childhood. It is true that you never can go back to childhood again. It is gone forever, but you can go back and feel those important feelings and then move on to complete what was left incomplete in childhood. There probably isn't an adult alive today that doesn't have some unfinished business left from his or her childhood. Most people try to work around it and compensate for this deficit in some way; the way, for example, a person with a disability might try to develop some other aspects of himself or herself to compensate for the

150

handicap. Perhaps your unmet developmental needs have motivated you to develop certain aspects of yourself that you wouldn't have developed otherwise. Nevertheless, this unfinished business still remains and still holds us back in some way. You no longer have to settle for having a handicap. You can repair the damage and free yourself to live a happier, fuller life.

The following graph shows the layers of feelings that people create. The outer layers serve as layers of defense against experiencing the core feelings. Notice that both positive and negative feelings are part of the core, so gaining access to these core feelings can also lead to more joy, love, ecstasy and bliss.

THE LAYERS OF FEELINGS

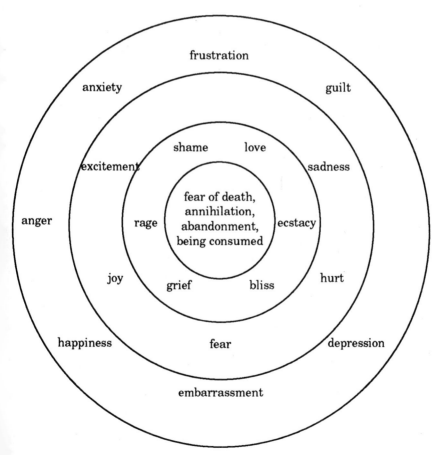

The process of uncovering and expressing your core feelings most likely will need to be done in therapy. Group therapy is generally better for this because the group seems to provide the safety net and support that people need to break through their fear of these feelings. Often witnessing other group members doing deep emotional work triggers emotional responses that you can't hold back any longer. Self-help or 12-step support groups are not usually structured to handle deep emotional work, but they can provide useful cognitive support before and after emotional work is done.

A final word of caution about abandonment. Rage, which is one of the core feelings, is also a common response to abandonment. When rage comes out, people can hurt themselves or someone else. Rage needs to be expressed in a safe environment using the group members to help the person safely express the rage by holding the person's arms, legs and the head. You will need to work with a therapist who has been trained to facilitate rage work. Rage work, if done correctly, can be done quickly and with very beneficial results. Be sure that the person does not have any medical problems that would be exacerbated by the rage work, such as heart disease or high blood pressure. Another effective though less violent form of rage work is to have the person squeeze and twist a towel. (This is particularly good if someone feels like choking someone else who abused him or her.) Another effective way we use to get people to express intense anger is by beating on a bed mattress or a vinyl bean bag chair with a tennis racket. The vinyl makes a loud cracking sound when hit with a tennis racket that many people find particularly satisfying.

CORRECTIVE PARENTING SKILLS

Learning corrective parenting skills means taking charge of healing your inner child and actively championing that child. This requires letting go of the illusion that your parents or other parent substitutes will still provide you what you need, if you are only perfect enough, clever enough, or obedient enough and finally deserve it. The only way you are going to heal your inner child is to ask for what you want from others and yourself. Let's look at four sets of corrective parenting skills that will help you do that.

Identifying Your Unmet Developmental Needs.   Each developmental stage has specific needs that must be met if the child is going to complete the task for that stage. It is important to know what these needs are for if you grew up without these important needs satisfied, you may not even know what you missed. At the end of this chapter you will find the needs that you should have gotten met listed under each developmental stage. By identifying these needs you will know what you need to do to begin corrective parenting work on yourself.

Developmental Permissions. These are the positive supportive messages that you should have received as a child. If you didn't get these kinds of messages and/or got many unsupportive negative messages, you may still need to hear these words from others as well as learn how to give them to yourself. These include, "I'm glad you were born," "You belong here," " I love you just the way you are," "You are lovable and capable," "You can ask for what you want and need," "You can trust your inner knowing," "You can think for yourself," and "I will not abandon you." Also, check back to the list you made of things you wish you had gotten from your parents ("Sins of Omission") to see if there were any developmental permissions contained in the list that you can now ask for.

After you have identified the developmental permissions that you are still needing to hear, you will need to ask someone of your choosing to say these messages to you. If you wanted to hear them from your mother, you may want to select a female to say them to you. If you wanted to hear some from your father, select a male to say them to you. Be aware of any resistance you might still have to hearing these messages. You have learned to live since childhood without these important messages and may have convinced yourself that you really don't need to hear them. Ask for them to be said repeatedly until you lower your resistance or just acknowledge your resistance and wait for another time. When you are ready, you will "let in" this support.

Corrective Parenting Contracts. Once you have identified your unmet developmental needs, you can make contracts with your friends, spouses and loved ones to get their help or assistance in meeting these needs. Pick only people who you feel safe with and who are committed to supporting your growth.

Many opportunities occur in intimate relationships for this kind of cooperation and support.   When a couple agrees to cooperate and support each other in getting their unmet developmental needs met, many rich opportunities for a depth kind of love and nonsexual intimacy can develop. True love grows out of the union of two people where the other's best interests are at least equal to our own. A truly loving person is able to receive his or her real self, brokenness and all, and to support and encourage the other person's attempts to become a whole person.

A corrective parenting contract between a couple may get transacted in the following way:

Mary: "John, when you raise your voice in the middle of an argument with me, I feel scared like I did when I was a little girl. I was never able to respond to my father when I was little. I know now what I would have liked to have said to my father when he did that to me. Would you be willing to play my father for about ten minutes and help me finish this with my father?"

John: "I don't want to be your father. I want to be your husband."

Mary: "I know you are not my father, but when you do certain things you remind me of my father. I want to take care of this unfinished business, so that I no longer need to see his face instead of yours when we get in an argument."

John: "Oh, well, if that's the case, sure—I can play the role of your father for a few minutes."

Mary: (Now talking to her father) "When I was small and I did things you didn't like, you would yell at me, and I got scared of you. You were so much bigger than I was that I felt powerless to tell you how I felt. I want to tell you now. Will you listen to me and not at me?"

John: (As Mary's father) "Yes, I will listen to you and I won't yell at you."

Mary: (Now sobbing quietly) "I really wanted you to talk to me and play with me, but it seemed like you were always too busy and that the only attention I got was when you yelled at me. I wondered what I had done to make you hate me so. You were so hateful to me. I still need you to tell me that you love me. And I need you to hold me and tell me things that you like about me. Will you do that?"

John: "Yes, I do love you, Mary, and I would like to hold you and comfort you." (Now holding and rocking Mary) "You are a wonderful little girl. You are smart and so full of life and joy. You are very lovable and I'm glad you are my daughter. I'm very sorry I didn't tell you these things when you were a child. I had my priorities backwards then and I was always too busy for my children. I regret that deeply. Is there anything else that you want me to tell you as your dad?"

Mary: "No, that is all I can think of now. Thank you, John, for playing my dad and telling me those things. It really helped. I could feel myself relaxing in your arms as you said those things. I think it will really help me to stop seeing you as my father and to see you more as John."

Corrective parenting contracts are usually short-term agreements like the one above, which are designed to help each person take care of unmet developmental needs in a clear, conscious way. They work best with people you feel most bonded to, but they can be used in a variety of settings with different people in your life. Everyone who comes into your life could be someone you could contract with to finish some unfinished business. Be sure to do this work with people who are safe and who will not take advantage of your vulnerability. It is absolutely necessary to get the person to agree not to use the situation to act out any sexual feelings. It is not appropriate for this person to be sexual with you if you have regressed to feeling like a small child.

Self-nurturing skills. One of the hardest things for many people with counter-dependent patterns to do is to nurture themselves. They need to learn how to take care of themselves and their inner child. It is often important for adults with counter-dependency issues to buy a doll, teddy bear or stuffed animal to remind them of their need to nurture themselves. It is very hard for many adults to carry a stuffed animal or a doll around. They are embarrassed and self-conscious, but those who do this and persist through their fears and embarrassment often report that this did make it easier for them to begin to nurture their inner child.

It is sometimes necessary to contract to do one thing every day to nurture your inner child. Many adults use substitutes for the nurturing such as alcohol, drugs, sex, material things and food as ways to try to comfort themselves. These do not work very well and they usually have addictive side-effects.

Following is a list of possible activities that you can use to nurture your inner child. You can decide which ones are best for your inner child.
- Get a regular massage.
- Soak in a hot tub or soak in a bath tub with bubble bath or bath oils.

- Take time during your day to be alone and reflect on your inner child.
- Take regular walks in nature.
- Take a regular nap each day.
- Meditate quietly in a special place or room of your own.
- Listen to beautiful music.
- Have a friend hold you or give you a back rub.
- Write in a journal about your inner child healing experiences.
- Write regular letters to your inner child telling him or her the things you like about him or her.
- Sit or stand in front of a mirror and learn to love all of your body parts. Say loving things to your inner child.
- Write developmental permissions and dictate them into a tape recorder. Play them on the way to and from work or before you go to bed at night.
- Talk to your inner child every day. Use your teddy bear, doll or stuffed animal to represent your inner child and talk to him or her.
- Sing to your inner child. Make up songs that affirm your inner child.
- Take your child to the circus or the park to play.

CASE EXAMPLE

We first met Julie in one of our workshops. At that time she was seeking more meaning in her life. She had a new home, a new car, two young children, a graduate degree and was living "the good life." After ten years of the same job and the same husband, she was realizing that something was missing. The hollowness of her day-to-day experience had forced her to look at her life. When she came to therapy initially, it was to do private work with me (Janae).

She had targeted her marriage as the place where she was most unhappy. Dissatisfaction in her relationship with Doug had been building and she was at a point where she was considering having an affair. Her initial issue in therapy was exploring whether or not she should leave Doug.

Our first task was to look at what really was happening in Julie's life, especially between her and Doug. We began to review her childhood and young adulthood in an effort to connect the present to her past. As we did this, some interesting things emerged. First, Julie was a twin. She had two brothers, one of which was her fraternal twin. She also almost died at birth because neither her parents nor the delivering physician expected twins. In fact, the doctor had begun to suture her mother after her brother was born before anyone realized there was a second baby. She had begun to breathe the amniotic fluid and was in danger of suffocating by the time she was delivered. Because of her small size and respiratory problems, she was kept in an incubator at the hospital for almost a month before she was taken home. Her brother, who was larger, went home after a few days. Julie and I examined this early history together and looked at what she would have needed for her birth to have been ideal. The gap between the actual and the ideal became a framework for her therapy work.

She made several calls to her parents and talked to them about the circumstances of her birth and the period following her birth to see if there were any other details that would be helpful. She also talked with her twin brother to see what she could learn. Conversations with both parts of her family helped her remember things about her birth.

Julie decided she wanted to do a session of co-therapy with Barry where she could use Developmental Process Work to relive her birth. She thought this would help her remember some of her feelings associated with birth and would help her learn more about what wasn't finished. She asked Doug to come with her to act out the role of her twin brother in this session, while we agreed to be her parents and also to facilitate the session.

The evening that we did the session, Julie arrived with a scenario that she wanted to use as the script for reliving her birth. She asked Doug to curl up with her on the floor and directed us to get our large blanket and cover them up as though they were inside the womb. Julie and Doug began a dialogue as baby brother and sister as they waited inside their mother to be born.

Julie remembered that through most of her life she had felt that her brother, Tim, had abandoned her. He had come out of the womb first, had gone home first and had joined the male world. She had never felt close to him as a result. She identified Tim as a bad person and the cause of a lot of her problems. Julie believed if he hadn't abandoned her she would not have had so many problems in life.

Back in the "womb," however, the dialogue began to create a different story of their relationship. Julie remembered that she was afraid to be born first and that it was too scary for her to leave Tim. Because of her fright at separating from Tim, she persuaded him to be born first. It was at that point that her plan backfired and she ended up being trapped in the womb. This birth trauma required that she be hospitalized in an incubator for a month, separating her from both her mother and Tim.

We suspected that Julie had never been able to express her feelings of fear and abandonment related to her traumatic birth. We asked her if she would like to relive her original birth and see what feelings might come. She agreed to do that. She and Doug recreated a prebirth dialogue. ("I'm scared to go out without you, Tim. Will you go first? I'll come right behind you.") Tim (Doug) slipped quickly out of the "womb" and left Julie there alone. We quickly covered her with the blanket and simulated the doctor suturing up her mother.

In a moment, Julie was in a panic of fear and terror as she remembered her near suffocation. We quickly uncovered her and held her, while repeating to her the things she told us she had wanted from her parents and didn't get. *(This provided her with some essential developmental permissions and also reparenting.)* After she had been sufficiently comforted and was calmed down, she looked at us and said, "Now I want to do it right." Then she looked at Doug and asked, "Will you do this again with me?" He took a deep breath and smiled at her and said, "Sure." *(At this point, Julie took charge of creating a Corrective Parenting experience for herself.)*

Back into the womb they went. They went through another prebirth dialogue, this time with Julie insisting that she go first. After a few moments, Julie slipped out through an opening in blanket. Janae caught her and held her quietly. Then Julie called to Tim to come out. Barry caught him as he emerged. The four of us sat quietly together for a time, as the two of us played their parents and spoke welcoming messages to them.

Near the end of the session, we discussed with Julie what she saw as the connection between her relationship with Tim and her relationship with Doug. She thought for a moment and then gasped loudly, sitting upright. "I have been trying to get Doug to abandon me the same way that Tim did. My attraction to other men and the temptation to have an affair were things I knew Doug would never tolerate. If he found out, he would leave me for sure. I see now how I was trying to get Doug to be Tim."

We helped her look at how her birth trauma had created a life drama. Julie could recall how she had felt abandoned all her life by men: first her twin brother, followed by her older brother, her father and several boyfriends. Now she was trying to get Doug to play the abandoning male in her drama.

We also looked for other things that might be unfinished about her birth. She remembered the awful loneliness of being in the incubator in the hospital for that month. Julie contracted to come in for another session to work on her feelings of loneliness using a Corrective Parenting contract with Janae.

In that next session, we recreated the incubator with Julie inside it. For a long period she lay quietly. *I (Janae) thought that there were unexpressed feelings from this incident, so I decided to recreate the original scene by leaving the room for a while.* I left and closed the door loudly enough that Julie would know I was gone. I could still see and hear her through the glass in the door and could monitor the situation closely. In a minute or two Julie began sobbing. The sobbing grew louder and louder until I knew from her crying that she was reaching core feelings.

At that moment I reentered the room, pulled back the blanket on her "incubator" and encircled her with my arms. She reached around my neck and clung tightly to me. I held her this way for fifteen or twenty minutes, until she calmed down. She began to share with me how the terror of her time in the incubator had returned, how she felt so powerless to get anyone to come and how she had feared that no one would come and she would die. *(At that point I could see how the incubator incident was already a replay of her original trauma and her life drama had begun.)*

The unfinished piece of healing in this part of her birth process was to replay the scene and provide the missing Corrective Parenting. I asked Julie if she would like to go back to the incubator period again and get what she missed the first time. She said she thought she was ready to do that. She curled up on the floor, and I rebuilt the incubator with sofa cushions and a blanket. After a few moments of quiet, I asked her what she would like to have had when she was that tiny baby, if she could have asked for it. She said the scariest part was being alone and missing her mother. What she wanted, this time, was for me to be her mother and come and get in the incubator with her.

I made the incubator a little larger, got down on the floor and wiggled my way under the blanket with her. By this time she was beginning to feel the emotional exhaustion of the session's experience. She nestled into a little ball, curled up beside me, let out a long sigh and fell asleep. For several minutes we lay together in our peaceful hideaway. Eventually she moved her body out of its constricted position and her eyes fluttered open. Smiling happily when she saw me still there, she stretched and sat up. I also sat up. *(I could see Julie was shifting out of her regressed state and returning to her normal state of awareness, signaling this part of the work was complete.)*

For a few minutes we sat talking about the session, discussing what else might yet be incomplete. She said that she tended to make her life feel lonely and barren like her incubator, so we discussed the kinds of self-nurturing activities she could do to help relieve these feelings. She came up with several that she contracted to do on a regular basis. She shared how helpful it was for her to be able to see how she could change her childhood belief that "life is an incubator" by creating supportive new experiences for herself.

Julie was able to find other missing pieces in her life drama and made separate therapy contracts to work on them. Over the course of several months, she was able to move out of her old patterns. She could see how the "something is missing" belief she had at the beginning of therapy was more accurately "something is unfinished."

Once Doug and Julie saw how Julie's primary attraction to Doug was for him to play the role of Tim in her life drama, they reexamined their relationship. They began to see how incompatible they really were in many other aspects. Julie, for instance, was emotionally a newborn child. She could see the developmental gaps she had in her childhood and that she had never really been autonomous. She had always been under the care and supervision of someone who played a parent role with her. She had never really been an adolescent and learned how to relate appropriately with boys. She had never dated anyone but Doug and felt she needed more experience in the world of male/female relationships.

She was honest with Doug and said that he really was married to an emotional child and that she needed to grow up some more before they could have a truly adult relationship. She wanted to separate and try living alone for a while. Eventually they decided to divorce. They brought their children to therapy for one session. Jeff, their three-year-old, had trouble verbalizing his feelings. He did work at releasing his frustrations nonverbally, however, as he methodically broke a whole box of sixty-four crayons into little pieces. When we all saw how cathartic the experience was for him, we began cheering him on. He eventually got up on his feet and jumped up and down on the crayon pieces. We all were overjoyed that Jeff could really express his feelings. Doug and Julie agreed to a cooperative parenting contract that would meet Julie's need for some alone time and also support their children's need for continuity in parenting.

The loving and gentle way that Doug and Julie were able to separate and to use their experience as a growthful one, honored who they really were and what they really needed. It was incredible for us to be a part of such a loving experience. We acknowledged their loving attitude toward each other and the way they were able to create a new pattern for couples to separate and not make each other bad.

AWARENESS EXERCISE:
Completion Process With Your Parents

This exercise is designed to be done with a trusted partner or therapist who will guide you through the process and also support and witness your experience. This exercise can take up to two hours with each parent, depending on how much previous work you have done with your parents. It lets you play both your part and your parents part in a role play situation. Sometimes it is possible to do this with your real parents, if they are willing. In that case, we recommend doing the exercise in therapy where you will have skilled support if the process becomes difficult or breaks down because of the intense feelings that emerge.

1. Decide which parent you will first complete with. Invite your image of this parent (or parent figures) to sit down in front of you to go through a process in which he or she will speak his or her truth and will listen to and validate your truth.
2. Tell this parent about any unresolved feelings (pain, grief, shame, resentment) that you have toward him or her.
    a) Tell this parent what he or she did or didn't do that hurt you. (Use your two lists from the Sins of Omission and Comission at the end of Chapter Two to do this.)

b) Tell this parent how you felt when he or she did or didn't do these things (physically discharge any feelings if necessary).

c) Tell this parent how each of these things affected your life.

d) Tell this parent what unhealthy telepathic agreements you are aware that you made with him or her. ("I'll do this for you if you do this for me.") Tell him or her why this was unhealthy for you.

3. Tell this parent the new healthy agreement you want from that parent and ask him/her to agree. ("What I want from you now is... Are you willing to agree to that?")

4. Change seats, assume the role of your parent and answer this question.

5. Therapist or partner checks for completion of this part of the process. Did the unhealthy agreement get stated clearly? Were the feelings expressed? Was the new healthy agreement stated clearly?

6. Now as your parent, respond to the other things your son or daughter has said to you.

a) As the parent, receive what the child has said. Tell your child your real feelings.

b) Reflect back the facts and feelings. Let your child know the truth about what he or she has said to you.

7. Again switch seats and reflect back to your parent what he or she has said. Add any thoughts and feelings this brings to your awareness. Is this the truth? If not, ask him/her again to tell you the truth.

8. Switch seats and become your mother or father again, and by using intuition, sense what it was like to be that parent. Begin with your parent as a child, moving through the years to his or her adulthood, sharing what life was like for him or her. As the parent, look at the influences that caused you to be the way you were as a child growing up. Communicate anything further you wish to communicate to your child about your life.

9. Change seats and become yourself again. Take in what your parent communicated. See if there is anything further you wish to communicate to your parent.

10. Release your parent from your expectations and blame releasing your parent to find his or her highest good in his or

her own way. Accept your parent as he or she really is (if you can now). Say, "I release you from my expectations and blame. You are free to find your highest good in your own way, if you choose. I accept you as you really are." (Note! If you are not ready to release your parent, tell them that instead and tell them why and are not ready.)

11. Forgive your parent (give back anything you took on that you don't want). Say, "I now give back to you your shame, your fears..."

12. Forgive yourself. Give back to your True Self (reclaim) all the things that you have denied yourself and that you now realize you truly deserve. Say, "I now give back to myself my self-respect...,etc."

13. Affirm your choice to take charge of your own life and to use your free will to create the life he or she wants. Say, "I now agree to live my life differently from now on. In order to do that I will (will not)...."

14. Therapist or friend gives feedback to you regarding the completion of the whole process.

15. Repeat Steps 1-14 of this process with your other parent.

(Note! Give yourself time to integrate what you have learned from this process before repeating it with your other parent.)

Chapter Eleven

CONFLICT AND INTIMACY

"The meeting of two personalities is like the contact
of two chemical substances: if there is any reaction,
both are transformed."

Carl Jung

Most people have never seen a conflict resolved in a win/win
way. This is unfortunate, because it is impossible to move out of
dysfunctional patterns of behavior without encountering conflict.
As you saw in Chapter Three, the relationship interactions in the
trauma drama and the Drama Triangle are both fraught with
possibilities for conflict. Conflict is sometimes also an signal that
you may be involved in some sort of psychological "game" (see
Games People Play by Eric Berne [1961]). In this chapter we will
present some effective tools for working with conflicts in new and
optimistic ways that help bring you closer to those you love.

LIMITING BELIEFS ABOUT CONFLICT

When we teach classes or run therapy groups in which a
conflict erupts, many of the participants are ready to crawl under
the nearest table or run out the nearest door. This lack of
experience in seeing and believing that conflicts can be resolved
without people getting hurt emotionally, physically, mentally or
spiritually creates a whole set of negative beliefs and feelings
about conflict. Below are some of the most common beliefs people
have about conflict:
- Conflict is bad.
- Conflict is scary.
- Conflict is disruptive.
- Conflict is destructive.
- Conflict means someone loses.

- Conflict means someone will get hurt.
- Conflict is difficult to control.
- Conflict escalates and expands.

People with co-dependent and counter-dependent patterns tend to approach conflict differently. For people with co-dependent patterns, conflict often is approached more passively. That is, they enter a conflict expecting to end up in the victim role. The best they can hope for is to make people feel sorry for them so they get their needs met. People with counter-dependent patterns tend to enter a conflict more aggressively and usually end up in the persecutor role. By staying in this role, they hope to hide their needs for closeness and intimacy and meet their primary need for safety by keeping people away.

HOW PEOPLE WITH CO-DEPENDENT PATTERNS HANDLE CONFLICT

Conflict is one of the most difficult things for people with co-dependent patterns to experience. When conflict emerges, people with co-dependent patterns are almost always "rubberbanded" back to their childhood, where there was conflict in the family and they felt small, powerless and afraid.

Such negative experiences about conflict motivate these people to avoid anything to do with conflict situations and creates dilemmas in their relationships. What these experiences set up are situations where people have to choose between entering a conflict or getting their needs met. If they avoid the conflict and stay passive, then they may be able to avoid their childhood feelings. On the other hand, if they stay passive, they probably will not be able to ask for what they want or get their needs met. This kind of either/or choice creates a dilemma, requiring them to use manipulative or indirect methods, such as playing victim, to get their needs met. In this way, they hope they can circumvent the direct conflict which they so fear.

What doesn't work about this approach is that:
- it supports game-playing, where people use manipulation, the Drama Triangle and other power plays between people
- it creates more undercurrents in relationships which increases the likelihood that even more conflict will occur
- it keeps people separate
- it interferes with intimacy.

HOW PEOPLE WITH COUNTER-DEPENDENT
PATTERNS HANDLE CONFLICT

All the things listed above that make conflict a negative experience for people with co-dependent patterns create a positive experience for the person with counter-dependent patterns, who is interested in using conflict to avoid intimacy in the first place. Conflict is a valuable defense system of a person with counter-dependent patterns, because it can be used to distance people quickly. Playing manipulative control games that keep relationships in an uproar allows the person with counter-dependent patterns to maintain reasonable distance and security against having to deal with his or her feelings.

In a typical co-dependent/counter-dependent relationship, for example, conflict serves as a valuable regulating mechanism. When there is too much intimacy, the person with counter-dependent patterns may begin to feel old feelings of suffocation from the past. By moving immediately into the persecutor role, he or she can quickly create heated conflict, which causes separation between the partners, quickly diffuses the feelings of suffocation and reinstates a feeling of safety. If there is too much space in the relationship and the person with co-dependent patterns begins to feel old feelings of abandonment, he or she can go quickly into victim and create a conflict which is designed to pull his or her partner into contact. This will help diffuse the feelings and reassure the person with the co-dependent patterns that he or she is not about to be abandoned.

While conflict serves as a valuable tool in modulating the amount of closeness and separation in dysfunctional relationships, it also prevents intimacy and keeps participants from dealing with their old feelings and their unmet needs for bonding and separation that are left over from childhood. For a growing number of people who want intimacy, living with unresolved conflict no longer serves a useful purpose.

NEW CHOICES, NEW OPPORTUNITIES

Eventually people (particularly those with counter-dependent patterns) understand that their closed, defensive and protected responses in a conflict situation ultimately caused them to feel isolated, lonely and alienated. This is the point where they may decide to make new choices. The other choice, besides being afraid and protecting themselves, according to Jordan and Margaret Paul (*From Conflict to Caring* [1989]), is what they call the "path of learning." This path focuses on two kinds of learning: learning about the other person and learning about yourself. Both of these kinds of learning require development of empathy which was discussed in Chapter Seven. Only compassion and caring for your own wounded inner child and the wounded inner child in others can help you to use conflict situations to learn more about yourself and other people.

Having an awareness of your own woundings and the woundings of others is like taking down the major barrier on the road to intimacy. Once this barrier is down, however, you can see by looking down the road ahead that you are in uncharted territory. You will need a road map to help you find the way. This road map involves several parts.

First, it is necessary to reframe the idea of conflict. Rather than seeing the path full of unknown beasts that can hurt you, you can look at the path as one full of unknown challenges and opportunities to learn and grow. Second, it is necessary to provide a sturdy vehicle to get you through the ruts and wrong turns, a vehicle that can survive the marshy wetlands and the unpaved roads of the high places. Such a vehicle for dealing with your conflicts would have gears that allow you to reverse or change direction if needed, and a lifetime guarantee. In other words, a vehicle you can depend on. Third, it is necessary to develop a vision of win/win conflict resolution that keeps you headed toward closeness. This means that the vehicle would need a compass or homing device to help you navigate the road toward intimacy. With this kind of preparation, you can locate the perils of conflict as you head toward deeper and deeper intimacy.

THE PARTNERSHIP MODEL: A ROAD MAP

In 1986 we began looking for a road map for dealing with conflicts after spending six months living in Switzerland. We had gone there to study with a Jungian analyst named Arnold Mindell. During our studies there we began to develop the first piece of our map, showing us how inner conflicts are mirrored in outer conflicts.

While we were there studying, the nuclear reactor at Cherynobl station exploded and we were irradiated while walking the streets of Zurich. We were unaware of the danger, as were most all of the
168

people in the countries neighboring the Soviet Union. The delay in notifying countries in the path of the nuclear fallout was mostly a result of the isolationist policies of the Soviet Union at that time. That was an important lesson for us, for we could see the inherent danger of neighbors not speaking to each other at the global level. We could see how conflict between neighbors, if not resolved, could eventually erupt as conflict between neighboring countries.

In addition, while we were living there, American planes bombed Libya and tried to kill General Omar Kdahafi. As temporary expatriates, we learned quickly that many Europeans did not appreciate American aggression against one of their volatile neighbors. This helped us see the effects of a self-serving action by the United States and their lack of concern for the welfare of our European neighbors. Both of these experiences made us very aware of the importance of having tools and maps for working with conflict. We decided that we wanted to do something to become part of the solution, and that would require us to take personal action.

After our return to Colorado we established a nonprofit, tax-exempt organization, The Colorado Institute for Conflict Resolution and Creative Leadership (CICRCL). Between 1986 and the present we organized two international conferences on conflict resolution, offered numerous workshops, seminars and trainings and field tested our own model for working with conflict with many different groups. During this period, we looked at what was working in the field of conflict resolution, what wasn't working and what was missing. From this research we developed our own approach for working with conflict, which we call The Partnership Model. Some of the assumptions of this approach to conflict resolution are listed below:

- Conflict is an opportunity for growth and intimacy. Many people avoid conflict because they fail to see the opportunities present in conflict situations. Resolving conflicts effectively brings people closer together and helps them work more cooperatively.
- A comprehensive approach for resolving conflicts is needed to help people deal with many different kinds of conflict.
- Each person involved in a conflict has an important role to play in the resolution of the conflict. Individual initiative is encouraged.

169

- When people are given explicit, practical and easily learned tools, they can learn to resolve conflicts quickly and effectively.
- The sources of all major conflicts in the relationships between adults can be found in the unmet developmental needs or unresolved conflicts from their childhood.

The Partnership Model is structured as a linear map that you can follow when you encounter conflict. As you follow the map you will find you can take different "roads" or options, depending on the kind of conflict you are having. Each option has specific worksheets that you can use to guide you through the conflict, as you will see in the map shown below.

AWARENESS ACTIVITY:
The Partnership Model for Resolving Conflicts

Partnership Worksheet #1
Preparing Yourself for Conflict Resolution

Directions: Using a current conflict, fill in the blanks below to help you get a better understanding of how to manage a conflict.

Part 1: The Inner Experience of Conflict

a. I know that I am in conflict because_____.
   (I experience: tight stomach, mind goes blank, sweaty palms, dizziness, rapid breathing)
b. Where I feel this conflict in my body is_____.
                              (place in body where I feel the conflict)
Part 2: Centering

Now take a deep breath and breathe into the area of your body where you feel tension. As you breathe into the place where you feel tension, visualize the tension lessening. When the tension has released, refocus your attention to your belly by placing your hand about two inches below your navel. Breathe into your belly area while you also imagine your energy going downward toward your feet, firmly anchoring them in the earth. Let yourself feel the flow of energy between the earth's core and your whole body. Notice how your body feels when you breathe and visualize using your energy in this way so that you can train yourself to quickly center yourself when you experience a conflict.

Part 3: Identifying the Feelings Involved in the Conflict

a. When I think of this conflict, I feel _____.
(name of feeling)

b. When I identify this feeling, it tells me _____.
(identify the function of this feeling)

Part 4: Identifying Your Typical Behaviors in Conflict Situations

The way that I typically deal with these feelings and body symptoms is _____.
(describe your usual response in a conflict situation)

Part 5: Diagnosing the Conflict

The way that this conflict effects me is _____
_____.
(tangible effects of conflict on me = needs/wants conflict)
(no tangible effects of conflict on me = values/belief conflict)

Part 6: Deciding How to Approach the Conflict

Option 1: **Defend** yourself by encountering the conflict directly.
• Use Worksheet #1 to get yourself ready to approach the conflict.
• Use Worksheet #2 for conflicts of wants and needs, or
• Use Worksheet #3 for conflicts of values and beliefs.
• Use if the conflict is not resolved using Worksheets #2 or #3.

Option 2: **Deflect** the conflict by stepping aside and deciding not to encounter the conflict. The person you are in conflict with may be too powerful, maybe over-reacting or aggressive or may be someone you feel unsafe to work with on conflicts.
• Use Worksheet #4 to determine what in you attracts these kind of people to you.

Option 3: **Deepen** your awareness. You can work alone on the conflict when the other person is unwilling or unable to work on it with you.
• Use Worksheet #4 to deepen your awareness of your part of the conflict.
171

Option 4: **Discover** the sources of your conflict by looking at your past and your unfinished business in past relationships. Work with a partner who will help you get to the sources of the conflict. Again, use Worksheet #4 as a guide.

Part 7: Establishing Ground Rules for Dealing with the Conflict Situation

a. Agree on a time frame for the conflict resolution session.
b. Each person states his or her perceptions of the conflict. Get agreement on what the conflict is before trying to resolve it.
c. Each person shares a desired outcome. Ask: "How would you like to have this conflict resolved?"
d. Take turns presenting the problem according to the instructions on Worksheets #2, #3 or #4.
e. Avoid complaining and ask for what you want directly from the other people involved. If someone is complaining to you, ask them what they want from you.
f. If there are obvious projections present, deal with those first. Have each person directly address the person who they had the original conflict with (usually parents) whom your partner can role play with your help. Then deal with any present-time elements of the conflict that are left over, if anything.
g. Agree to try out any agreements you make for a specified time to see if they will work.
h. Learn to accept relapses. The old behaviors that cause the conflict may not change immediately. If that happens, ask the person who has a relapse what he or she wants or needs to do to be successful in changing his or her behavior.
i. Also agree to get back together at the earliest possible time, if the agreement needs to be modified.

Partnership Worksheet #2
Intimacy Building Activity: An Eight Step Method For Resolving Conflicts Of Wants And Needs

Directions: The person who feels the conflict more should initiate the process. In some cases, only one person in the conflict knows this method so he or she needs to go first.

1. **Describe objectively your perception of the problem or behavior.**
   ("I noticed that you didn't clean up your dishes after you ate last night.")
2. **Share the way you feel toward the person or problem.**
   ("I felt angry with you when I saw them laying out.")
3. **Describe the tangible effects or results of the problem or issue on you and/or your relationship.**
   ("When I have to clean up your dishes in the sink, which is extra work for me, I don't want to be close to you.")
4. **State clearly what it is you want from the other person.**
   ("What I want is to be able to feel close to you. In order for me to feel good about being close to you, I need for you to keep your agreement to clean up your dishes after you eat.")
5. **Ask the person clearly for what you want.**
   ("Would you be willing to do that?")
6. **Use reflective listening.** Pause for a perception check to determine the other person's feedback or perceptions about the conflict. Do not allow yourself to get bogged down at this step in defending, blaming, escalating or complaining.
   ("When I get angry at you about these things, you look like you are upset with me. Is that true?")
7. **Negotiate if there are differences between what you want and what the other person is willing to give or do.**
   "I sometimes don't have time to clean up everything before I leave for work. Would it be all right if I just stack them in the sink until I get home and then do them?")
8. **If you are unable to negotiate the differences (usually because it is a conflict involving beliefs or values) agree to disagree or use Partnership Worksheet #3.**
   ("I see that we just don't agree on this issue and I can accept our disagreement. Will you also agree to disagree?" or "Will you agree to explore our differences using Partnership Worksheet #3?")

Partnership Worksheet #3
Intimacy Building Exercise: A Seven Step Method
for Resolving Conflicts of Values and Beliefs

Directions:

1. **Take turns listening to each other's views of the conflict using reflective listening. Be sure to identify the feelings as well as the content.** ("It seems to you that I am trying to control you and you also seem a little angry and scared to me. Do I understand accurately what you are saying and feeling?")

2. **Take turns finding the sources of your value or belief conflict.** ("What experiences have you had in your life where you have felt people were trying to control you?") Again, listen and reflect back the feelings and content for each other before going on to the next step.

3. **Take turns finding the sources of your feelings.** ("What other times in your life have you felt this way?") Focus on the feelings here and reflect back what you hear from the other.

4. **Determine any shifts in awareness.** ("Based on your exploration of the sources of your beliefs and your feelings, do you have any new perceptions of your values or beliefs?") Take turns restating any new perceptions to make sure you understand them.

5. **Now determine areas of agreement and disagreement.** ("I think we now agree that what we identified as control was really a desire for more relationship. Because of our past history of having people try to control us, we are prone to be indirect with each other. This could be a problem for us.")

6. **Make plans to handle any areas of disagreement.** ("I think if either of us is feeling controlled by the other in any way, that person should bring it directly to the other one and we can talk about it again.")

7. **If this conflict brings up strong feelings and reactions,** you will need to consult Partnership Worksheet #4 to help locate the source of these strong feelings and reactions.

Partnership Worksheet #4
Intimacy Building Exercise:
Identify the Sources of Your Conflict

It is important when looking for the sources of a conflict to remember that you are never upset for the reasons you think you are. If the conflict brings up strong feelings, that is always a signal to look deeper for the source of the conflict. Listed below are some of the common sources of conflicts with questions that you can ask yourself to help you identify the source of the conflict. Once you identify the source of a current conflict, you can begin to look at what is unfinished in some past relationship. When you identify what is unfinished you can complete the old issue by contracting with someone to work through the old issue. You may be able to do this with the person with whom you are actually in conflict or you can contract to do this with a friend, partner or a therapist.

A. *Family Patterns Source* — Ask yourself these questions:
- "Does this person remind me of anyone from my family of origin?"
- "Have I experienced this or similar conflicts in the past?"
- "What is the unfinished business from my family that I am attempting to complete with this person?"
- "What kinds of people or behaviors tend to produce recurring conflicts for me that are related to things that happened to me in my family of origin?"
- "What feelings can't I express in this conflict? How does this inability relate to what happened to me in my family of origin?"

B. *Co-dependent Source* — Ask yourself these questions:
- "Does this conflict bring up my fears of abandonment or a fear of not getting my needs met?"
- "Am I having trouble trusting this person? Who does he or she remind me of?"
- "Am I acting like a victim in this conflict?"
- "Am I clinging to or trying to control this person by playing manipulative games?"
- "Do I have trouble asking for what I want from this person?"

C. ***Counter-dependent Source*** — Ask yourself these questions:
- "Does this conflict bring up my fears of invasion or abuse?"
- "Am I pushing this person away to avoid dealing with my fear of intimacy?"
- "Am I acting like a persecutor in this conflict?"
- "Am I making the other person bad so that I can feel justified in going away?"
- "Am I talking about my conflict with a third party and creating secrets?"
- "Am I taking sides in this conflict rather than supporting the other person's feelings?"

D. ***Other Sources*** — Ask yourself these questions:
- "What is it about this person that reminds me of some part of myself that I don't like?"
- "How does this relationship conflict reflect an internal conflict of my own?"
- "How is this conflict related to a universal or global issue?"

We advise you to use this model when any conflict comes up. When we teach this model in our workshops and classes, we have people follow the worksheets step-by-step to work through a conflict. With the model as a road map, you will find navigating your way through conflicts can be a joyful ride that allows you to see life in new ways and to feel closer and more intimate with your companions in conflict.

CASE EXAMPLE

Ed and Lynette came as a couple to one of our conflict resolution classes. It was a second marriage for both and they were committed to making this relationship work. Each had two children from the previous marriage. Ed's two children were older and had lived more with their mother in another state. Lynette's children were high school age and both lived with them. When we asked for volunteers in the class to work in front of the group on a personal conflict, they came forward.

Before beginning to work on their conflict, we asked them to describe the usual way they try to resolve conflicts. The process would break down when Ed would get very rational and logical at a time when Lynette was trying to share her feelings with him. The more she struggled to share her feelings, the more rational Ed would get. When the tension got to a certain level of uncomfortableness for her in this struggle, Lynette would begin to pull away emotionally. She would become silent and uncommunicative or even walk out of the room. Ed would become agitated at her leaving and pursue her. He would keep asking her questions or follow her if she would leave the room. They were both unhappy that so many of their attempts to resolve their conflicts ended in frustration and even more anger. Part of what they wanted was to learn how to really have a good fight and get through it. We agreed that we could help them develop new ways of resolving conflicts as we also addressed a particular issue they had.

Their conflict involved whether or not Ed's twenty-year-old daughter Amy, and her two-year-old child, could come from out of state and move in with them temporarily. After a stormy adolescence and an unplanned pregnancy, Amy had gone on welfare and was now struggling to finish junior college. Ed was having a difficult time watching his daughter and granddaughter living without much emotional or financial support. He felt badly that neither of his children had been able to live in the warm and caring home that he and Lynette had created together. He still yearned to make up for some of the losses they had experienced as a result of the divorce between him and Amy's mother.

Lynette clearly stated her resistance to Amy's proposed move: "I feel overwhelmed at the thought of Amy moving home. She shuts me out and I feel like an outsider. I'm scared something might happen to Ed and me."

Barry asked, "What are you scared might happen between you and Ed?"

"Well," Lynette replied, "Amy could come and monopolize Ed's attention and he wouldn't have time for me. He might even choose between her and me and we could end up getting a divorce."

Janae asked Ed if he was aware of how Lynette felt. He said, "Yeah, I've heard all this before. I just get angry that I've done so much for her kids and now she refuses to help one of mine. It doesn't seem fair."

At this point Lynette put her head down on her knees, curled one foot over the top of the other and got very quiet. Ed watched her closely. (*The lowered head and the curled foot indicated that Lynette was probably moving into an inner child feeling state. This was a signal that Ed was in that moment a player in her drama and that she was working on unfinished business from the past.*)

177

Janae commented, "Lynette, I notice that your feet are all curled up. Who is it that is curling up her toes?"

Lynette, looking shy and innocent, said, "My little girl. She is thinking about how Ed might leave her. He sounds so angry that I won't do what he wants me to. I'm really scared."

"Who in your past left you?" asked Janae. "What happened when you were a little girl that makes you afraid that Ed will leave you?"

"My dad died," said Lynette sadly. "I get afraid Ed will go away too."

(At this point we began to look for the unexpressed feelings from some trauma in her drama.)

"Ed," said Barry, "I'm going to ask you to move over to the far side of the room for a minute. Would you do that as an experiment?" "Sure," said Ed.

Barry turned to Lynette and said, "I want you to look up for a moment and see that Ed has gone. He has left you and he might not be back. How do you feel when you think about that?"

Lynette broke out sobbing. "It's my dad. He left me and I wasn't done. I miss him so *much*."

Ed began to speak to Lynette from his place on the other side of the room, so we motioned for him to come join us again.

Janae turned to Ed and asked, "Did you know that Lynette still missed her father so much?"

By now Ed was becoming emotionally moved by Lynette's pain and grief and was moving close to her. "No, not in the way that I know it now. Lynette, I know that you were still little when he died and that you didn't get to say good-by to him."

"I didn't get enough hugs or spend enough time with him," she said. "Even before he died, I wanted to play and do things together but he was never there because of his drinking." Then she looked up at Ed with teary eyes, saying, "You gave me the chance to get that feeling of being close and safe. I'm afraid if Amy comes that you will give her all your love and there won't be any left for me. You'll go away just like my dad did and I won't see you again."

Barry added, "So you've been seeing Ed as your father each time that you get in this conflict. Is that true, Lynette?"

"I guess so. I didn't know it though. I just thought I was afraid we would get a divorce."

Barry questioned Lynette, "If you could talk to your dad right now, Lynette, what would you say?"

"I'd tell him what I missed growing up."

Barry came back with the key question: "Lynette, would you like Ed to play your father and do that right now?"

"Yes, if he would. Will you, Ed?"

"I sure will," Ed said, smiling.

Ed came close to Lynette, wrapping himself around her to hold her like a little child. Lynette, looking and sounding about seven-years-old, began telling Ed all the things she wanted to say to her dad when she was a little girl. Ed rocked her back and forth as she talked, speaking softly to her in turn as he answered her back. After a few moments Lynette stopped speaking and laid quietly in Ed's arms.

After a short break, Ed, Lynette and the class group returned to review what had happened. Lynette was able to identify how much bonding and closeness she had missed with her father. She could see how much of that need she was unconsciously bringing into her relationship with Ed. Lynette also now was aware of the way she projected her father onto Ed when he began sounding logical and rational. For her, Ed's unresponsiveness to her feelings was like an abandonment. She could see that she pulled away in the midst of their conflicts to protect herself from feeling the old pain of her father's abandonment.

Lynette asked Ed if he would contract with her to help fill her unmet needs with her father for holding or nurturing, for time to play and for time to talk. He said that he would really like to do that.

We asked Lynette and Ed if they had gotten what they wanted from their work with us. They looked at each other and glowed for a moment and looked at us. They didn't have to say another word. It was obvious to everyone that they had broken through an important barrier to intimacy. They told us later that they experienced a dramatic increase in intimacy in their relationship following this session. They have continued to resolve their conflicts by helping each other identify the unmet developmental needs that surface during their conflicts and are committed to helping each other get these needs met.

Chapter Twelve

PILLOW TALK:
SEXUAL COMMUNICATION

"On the stage...masks are assumed with some regard to
procedure; in everyday life, the participants act their parts
without consideration either for the suitability of scene or for the words
spoken by the rest of the cast: the result is a general tendency for things
to be brought to the level of force even when the theme is serious enough."

Anthony Powell

COUNTER-DEPENDENTS DO IT FAST

The bedroom is where the person with counter-dependent
needs may have his or her worst problems. Many people with
counter-dependent behavior patterns have difficulty with the
level of intimacy and closeness that ongoing sexual relationships
require. As a result many of these people have learned to be
emotionally absent during lovemaking as a way to avoid intimacy.
They may be able to handle the mechanics of lovemaking, but they
are usually unable to handle the mechanics of intimacy that go
with it. They are often interested in getting sex over with as
quickly as possible, so they don't have to deal with their anxieties
and fears.

COUNTER-DEPENDENT VS. INTERDEPENDENT SEX

The contrast between these two forms of sexual contact can be
really quite striking. The following chart shows the major characteristics of each form of sexual encounter.

Counter-dependent Sex is...	Interdependent Sex is...
• performance-oriented, based on how well you perform for your partner	• communication-oriented, based on you taking charge of your own pleasure and asking for what you want
• ritualistic and mechanical	• spontaneous and creative
• as an escape from problems	• a celebration of the resolution of problems
• manipulative and controlling; requiring lots of effort	• relaxed and effortless
• physically satisfying	• physically, emotionally and frequently spiritually satisfying
• comparative and competitive	• intimate and cooperative
• followed by feelings of emptiness and loss	• followed by warm, connected feelings
• used to avoid past problems	• used to work through past problems

Part of the problem of sexual intimacy for people with unmet counter-dependent needs is caused by the way our society distorts sexual behaviors and the meaning of sex. Another part of the problem usually can be traced to some kind of unintentional or intentional sexual abuse in the childhood of a person with counter-dependent behaviors. We will first address the social causes of the problem.

THE SEXUALLY ADDICTED SOCIETY

There is a tremendous amount of sexual hype in our society that we can't escape from. Sex is flaunted in television commercials, billboards, magazines, newspapers, books, videos and movies. We are subjected to a daily bombardment of socially accepted forms of sex that distort our notions about how sex should be. We spend billions of dollars trying to look sexy, smell sexy, taste sexy, feel sexy and act sexy. From dieting to surgical procedures to exercise, we use everything we can to look beautiful, thin and sexy. Women are portrayed as sex objects to sell everything from soap to suntan oils, from automobiles to garage door openers! Recently, we have seen the use of sexy male bodies to sell items such as shaving lotion, cologne and clothing "that will drive her mad."

What people are actually buying is not a product, but a fantasy. The fantasy promises us that looking good or looking

182

sexy is the best way to make it in the world. This is the reduced version of the American Dream in which people try to live the perfect fantasy instead of facing the imperfect realities of life. Many people with counter-dependent behaviors have bought this one completely because looking good is what it is all about for them. They hope that *if* they can look sexy enough or confident enough or perfect enough no one will ever suspect them of being the weak, insecure, uncertain people they actually are. Because we live in a society that is obsessed with youth, sex and looking good, it is easy for the person with counter-dependent issues to hide: at least, that is until they find themselves in an intimate, emotionally close relationship.

Many males with counter-dependent behaviors buy pornography or call the phone numbers on the television ads and listen to women talk to them in sexual ways. In this way, they can have a "sexual" relationship with a fantasy person without having to "get involved" in an actual relationship. They may masturbate and fantasize a sexual encounter which appears to be safer than the real thing and therefore more satisfying. Excessive masturbation can be a way a person with counter-dependent issues satisfies a strong sexual desire, without ever having to be intimate with someone. This is usually learned in families where there is no nurturing available. The child may turn to masturbation as an alternative or confused way of getting the nonsexual "good feelings" he or she needed and wanted. Because of this childhood experience, the person with counter-dependent issues may still try to get his or her nurturing needs met through sex. People with unresolved counter-dependent issues often have their need for nonsexual nurturing and their need for sexual satisfaction or intimacy confused or intertwined.

SEXUAL ABUSE AS A CAUSE OF
COUNTER-DEPENDANT BEHAVIORS

Despite the sexual distortion produced by our society, far more sexual distortion is produced if the person with counter-dependent issues was sexually abused during childhood. The two main kinds of sexual abuse are intentional and unintentional. People who experienced unintentional sexual abuse either got poor modeling about sex, were not given accurate sexual information or were given distorted information about sex being "dirty" or "bad." Intentional sexual abuse refers to deliberate acts of sexual

183

violence and abuse. Most people with counter-dependent behaviors, however, have no memory of any sexual abuse from their childhood and have no idea that behind their inability to be intimate as an adult may be a traumatic incident or series of incidents of unintentional or intentional sexual abuse from their childhood.

There are several reasons for this memory loss, which is similar to the memory loss of Vietnam veterans who were in combat and later could not remember what happened. People who experienced either combat or childhood sexual abuse suffer similar symptoms, like disturbed sleep, nightmares, phobias, addictions and other obsessive-compulsive behaviors—but they may have no memory of these events.

This loss of memory is now diagnosed as Post-Traumatic Stress Syndrome. Often through therapy the memory of the traumatic event returns, and the person can learn to express all his or her feelings that were part of the original trauma. For many adults, the memory of childhood sexual abuse does not return for twenty or thirty years. In a recent landmark case, two daughters won a large damage suit against their father who sexually abused them almost forty years earlier. The memory of this abuse remained hidden from these women until they sought therapy for sexual dysfunctions (*Gazette Telegraph*, May 16, 1990).

In childhood sexual abuse, particularly if it was with a parent or trusted adult, there is an even greater tendency to repress the memory. Children, during the first six to eight years of life, have a natural need to see their parents as perfect. This provides them with the security they need to grow up. Without this illusion, they fear they will not survive. When sexual abuse occurs before the age of eight or ten, it is actually easier for the child to blame him or herself than to blame it on imperfect parents. Children believe that they must have done something bad to have had bad things happen to them. Sexual abuse perpetrators, to protect themselves, often threaten children with messages like "you will be sent away to an orphanage if you tell," or "you are a naughty boy or girl and you will be punished if you tell anyone about this." This causes people to develop counter-dependent symptoms and to grow into adulthood believing that they are bad, worthless, unlovable and shameful. This distortion leads people with counter-dependent symptoms to hide any childhood sexual abuse even from themselves. This also helps them maintain the childhood belief that their parents were perfect and, therefore, keeps their "security blanket" intact. They believe they need this security blanket because they are such flawed and unworthy people. They also believe they are incapable of changing who they are.

We have some anecdotal data from our therapy practice that suggests that gays and lesbians frequently are victims of intentional or unintentional sexual abuse, and this abuse may have affected their sexual preference. A daughter who was unintentionally or intentionally sexually abused by her father when she was a child may be afraid of men and turn toward females for intimacy. Sons who were invaded sexually by their mothers may have trouble being close to women and choose intimacy with men as a solution. However, there also are healthy reasons why people might choose to be gay or lesbian. The important point is that it needs to be a choice, not a reaction to the early abuse. More research has to be conducted to determine all the factors that influence sexual preference before definite conclusions can be drawn.

In addition, it is clear from our clinical experience that sexual abuse and eating disorders are totally connected. If you are a compulsive eater or dieter, then it is very likely you also have experienced childhood sexual abuse. Carla Wills-Brandon's book, *Eat Like a Lady: Guide For Overcoming Bulimia* (1989), is an excellent resource on this topic, as is Marion Woodman's book, *Addiction to Perfection* (1982).

UNINTENTIONAL AND INTENTIONAL SEXUAL ABUSE

Part of the process of unraveling this complex form of denial and repression is to get some good information about what constitutes sexual abuse. Frequently, acts of unintentional sexual child abuse are not even recognized as such by those who were abused, even though they still suffer from the effects of being sexually abused in this way.

There are two categories of sexual abuse to examine. First is unintentional sexual abuse from parents who are ignorant of what constitutes sexual abuse. This unintentional form is quite common. Second is intentional sexual abuse where the parent or adult knew they were abusing their children, but could not stop or would not stop. Let's look more closely at each category.

UNINTENTIONAL SEXUAL ABUSE

The following list of unintentional forms of sexual abuse represents a consensus list developed by therapists and other experts in the field of child abuse. As you read this list, place a check mark next to those items that happened in your family. We have taken items for this list and the one on intentional abuse from similar lists in Carla Wills-Brandon's excellent book, *Is It Love or Is It Sex?* (1989). The reader is referred to her book for further information related to these lists.

_____Parents did not give you any age appropriate information or talk to you about human sexuality while you were growing up.

_____Parents did not give you specific information or talk to you about menstruation or normal sexual development in adolescence.

_____Parents gave you false information about masturbation, where babies come from, what the role of sex is in a relationship, etc.

_____Parents refused to answer your questions about sexual development.

_____Parents invaded your privacy while you were in the bathroom or your bedroom (not knocking on a closed door before entering or asking permission before entering).

_____Parents used religion to shame and condemn any of your sexual curiosity.

_____Parents gave you very little appropriate nonsexual touching or hugging.

_____Parents had you bathe or sleep with them after you reached school age.

_____Parents exposed you to pornographic magazines or materials when you were a child, without any information.

_____Parents exposed you to sexual jokes and sexual remarks.

_____Parents forced you to sleep or bathe together with your opposite sex siblings when you reached school age.

_____Parents walked around the house nude or with only underwear and/or skimpy negligees.

_____Parents talked to you about the details of their own sex life and/or talked to you about any sexual problems they were having.

_____Parents shamed you if they caught you masturbating or exploring your genitals.

_____Parents called you degrading sexual names like whore, slut, hot number, or sleaze.

_____Parents made fun of your sexual development or teased you for having breasts or growing hair around your genitals.

_____Parents encouraged you to assume a surrogate spouse role by confiding in you about their adult problems.

Some children are "parentized" to be an adult partner and given special titles such as "Daddy's Little Princess" or "Mama's Little Man." This is called covert incest where no actual intercourse or inappropriate touching of you occurred, but where there was active sexual energy present. Later there usually is an attempt by the parent to control your sexual life. When girls get older and ready to start dating, fathers will overcontrol and not allow any dating. Boys may find their mothers examining their underwear or grilling them for details of what happened on a date.

INTENTIONAL CHILD SEXUAL ABUSE

There are also many intentional acts of child sexual abuse that when you were a child you may not have realized were sexually abusive. We have compiled a list of the obvious and the not-so-obvious intentional acts to help you correctly "name" any intentional sexual abuse that might have occurred in your childhood. As you read this list, place a check mark next to those items that you remember from your childhood. You may also want to check those items where you have no conscious memory, but have a "feeling" or intuition about it.

_____Parents or other adults gave you wet or open-mouthed or lingering kisses on your mouth.

_____Parents or other adults touched, washed or stimulated your genitals while giving you a bath or dressing or undressing you.

_____Parents or older siblings watched you dress or undress or watched you take a bath after you reached school age.

_____Parents or other adults forced or encouraged you to be sexual with siblings or other children.

_____You had your genitals or breasts touched or tickled by a parent, older sibling or other adult while engaged in "horseplay" or "rough housing."

_____You were forced to watch while another child was molested or raped.

_____You were masturbated by a parent, older sibling or other adult.

_____You were forced to masturbate them.

_____You were forced to watch while they masturbated themselves.

_____You were forced to strip down or stand naked in the corner under the guise of punishment.

_____You were spanked on a bare bottom or spanked while lying nude on a bed.

187

_____ You were massaged by a parent or adult in or around your genital area and/or breasts.

_____ You were requested to sit on a parent or adult's lap with them rubbing against or touching your breasts or genitals and feeling them get an erection or seeing them stimulate themselves.

_____ You were permitted to watch parents bathe and/or were allowed to see them stimulate themselves or each other sexually.

_____ You were forced to have oral, anal or vaginal intercourse.

How Do You Know If You Were Sexually Abused?
(Weinhold and Weinhold, 1989)

The following is a short inventory of adult behaviors that can help you discover the symptoms of childhood sexual abuse, even if you don't have any memories of such abuse. Read each question and answer each one "yes" or "no."

_____Do you have a fear of going "crazy"?

_____Do you have large time gaps of memory loss about your childhood?

_____Are you more than 50 lbs. overweight?

_____Were you physically abused as a child?

_____Have you ever sexually abused someone else?

_____Does sex turn you off?

_____Do you have trouble maintaining an intimate relationship?

_____Are you ashamed of your body?

_____Do you sexualize relationships even when you don't want to?

_____Do you regularly experience migraines, gastro-intestinal disturbances or genitourinary disturbances?

_____Do you have a general sense of depression that you can't shake?

_____Do you "freeze" in certain situations, such as when you encounter an authority figure or in certain sexual situations?

_____Are you afraid of having children or afraid of being around them?

_____Are you accident prone?

If you answered "yes" to _two or more_ of these questions, you may have experienced sexual abuse as a child. If you have these symptoms but no memory you can (1) read accounts of how others remembered, (2) talk to other people who experienced sexual abuse as a child, or (3) enter psychotherapy to help you remember.

CASE EXAMPLE

Sharon called for an individual appointment with Janae to work on a problem of frigidity that she was experiencing in her relationship with Gary. They had not had sex for almost six months when she came to therapy. Gary was very impatient with Sharon's problem in the bedroom and wanted her to "get fixed." Rather than moving directly into working with the sexual dysfunction, Janae decided to find out more about Sharon's childhood.

Her alcoholic parents separated when she was about nine-years-old and she spent the next four years shifting back and forth between them. She remembered going along to the bar with her father when he went drinking and when he entertained his cronies playing poker at his house. In both situations her father would invite his drinking buddies to notice how pretty Sharon was and would encourage them to "get friendly" with her. As she matured, their friendliness turned into seductiveness. By the time she was twelve or thirteen her father was offering her sexually as a favor to his friends.

Shortly after her fourteenth birthday, Sharon's father died and she went to live with her father's brother and his wife. They had two younger children and expected Sharon to help with the housework and the child care. Her aunt related mostly to her as hired help, while her uncle alternately criticized her and teased her in sexual ways. By the time she was fifteen and well-developed physically, her uncle began accosting her in secluded areas of the house. He would rub up against her breasts, pat her buttocks and make suggestive remarks about how sexually appealing she looked to him. That was followed by attempts to get her to undress and to touch his erect penis. His insistent pursuits began to frighten her so much that she started staying out with her friends. Sharon found places where she could stay overnight and failed to return home two or three nights a week. Sometimes she took drugs and drank beer with her friends. When the boys in the group began to make sexual advances toward her, she would return to her aunt and uncle's house for several days.

One night when Sharon was sixteen, she was out dancing at a western bar and she met Gary. He was big and strong-looking, though kind of quiet. He bought her a drink and they sat and talked. She liked Gary's quiet strength and began spending more time with him. Eventually she began to stay overnight with him, with the understanding that they were just friends.

189

Sharon spent less and less time at her uncle's house by splitting her time between Gary's place and hanging out with her friends. Her prolonged absences began to irritate her uncle. One evening he followed her to one of her friends' house. After watching for a while outside, he burst in. He was furious when he found several of her friends using drugs; and he exploded in a fit of anger at her. He called her names and accused her of being a "doper" and gave her one day to get her belongings out of his house.

At the age of seventeen Sharon had few options about where to move. She told Gary about her eviction and asked if she could stay with him for a few days while she decided what to do. Gary said it would be fine with him if she wanted to move her things there for a while. Her stay turned into weeks, then months.

During this time she slept on the sofa in Gary's living room and continued to be his friend. One night after they had gone out dancing and drinking at a bar, Gary got drunk. Sharon had to help him into the house. He passed out on the sofa and fell asleep, so she decided to sleep in his bed. Near morning he woke up and came into his bedroom and got into bed. He curled up with her and held her for a while. After a while their closeness turned into sex.

During the next few weeks their relationship became very sexual and intense. Gary, a few years older than Sharon, decided he wanted to get married. Sharon, thrilled that someone finally wanted her, accepted his offer and they were married when Sharon turned eighteen.

Sharon had managed to finish high school with good secretarial skills and found a job soon after marrying Gary. The first year or two they had a wonderful time being together, especially Sharon. For her it was her first experience of having permanence and stability with a person who cared about her. She reported to me that her sexual relationship with Gary was great, up until about the end of the second year of their marriage.

At that time she began to notice things about Gary that she had not seen before. He tended to be messy at home and not look very attractive. He also lost his full-time job and began working temporary positions. The time between his temporary positions grew longer and longer. He would stay at home drinking, watching television or playing on his computer. Sharon began providing most of their financial support as Gary worked less and less. She even came home and cooked and cleaned, even though he had been home all day not working.

After a period of this discontentment, Sharon began to feel herself growing repulsed by Gary's behavior and appearance. She started pulling away when he made sexual overtures and often avoided sex if she could. Her distancing behavior provoked Gary into drinking more, either at home or at a bar. During drunken episodes, he would pursue her and try to force her to have sex. After several months of this, Gary finally exploded and told her that if she wasn't willing to have sex with him she was to get out of his house.

This frightened Sharon, for it reminded her of her uncle throwing her out of his home. In desperation, Sharon began to talk to her friends at work about her problems with Gary. It was through them that she found counseling with Janae.

Once Janae heard her story, she suggested that Sharon's background of sexual abuse might be the source of her sexual dysfunction. She also suggested that Sharon ask Gary to come with her to counseling, so that he could learn how to support her while she healed the wounds of the abuse from her father and uncle. Gary was very reluctant to come for therapy and insisted that he was not sick and that the problems were all Sharon's. However, he did agree to come for one session with the agreement that the therapy would focus on Sharon.

When they arrived Janae spent some time discussing with the two of them how childhood sexual abuse will create difficulties in adult sexual relationships. She also described the approach she used in treating couples where one of the partners has been sexually abused and gave them both support for seeing their problem as treatable. Once Gary had this overview, he agreed to come with Sharon to a series of six sessions over three months. During that time he would try out this approach and see if it helped.

We work together when we see couples, for we have found that each person often needs an ally during conflicts. We began by helping Gary see that Sharon had never developed a sense of ownership about her body and that she had been routinely invaded by both her uncle and father. They also affirmed the positive aspects of their relationship by acknowledging that it was now safe enough for her issues of abuse to surface. We also helped them both see that Sharon's unmet developmental need was to learn to set appropriate boundaries about her body. She could learn to do this by being in charge of their sex life during the next three months. She was to say when, where and how she wanted

191

sex. Gary groaned at the idea. We reminded him that he couldn't be much worse off than he was, since he had been without sex for nearly six months. Finally he agreed to cooperate.

They were sent home with the Sexual Communication Exercise at the end of this chapter and encouraged to not have sex for a week. They could only cuddle and hold each other. After the second session, sex was permitted at Sharon's initiation. For another two weeks Sharon made absolutely no sexual advances toward Gary. In therapy he complained that she wasn't learning much and said he felt she would never want to have sex again. He was encouraged to stick with the contract and keep allowing Sharon to be in charge. With the support Sharon got in therapy, she began to grow stronger and act more assertive. When she finally did approach Gary for sex, they both were excited. Gary liked being pursued and Sharon liked being the initiator.

Toward the end of their six sessions, the tension between the two of them began to decrease. Each time they came for a session, they appeared happier and more playful, like the young people they were. By the end of the three months, Gary decided the experiment was working and wanted to stay married to Sharon. At their termination session, they created a new three-month contract around their sex life. During this period they could approach each other for sex and either of them had the right to say no. If Sharon didn't feel sexual, Gary was to surrender to her need for boundaries and safety. Gary hardly ever said no to Sharon so that was not really a problem. They were warned that healing sexual abuse requires a lot of patience and caring and that they should give themselves at least a year to get beyond the awkwardness of the rigid boundaries that Sharon had set. Barry also helped Gary see how his invasive, self-serving attitude of wanting Sharon to be sexual at his demand was not supporting intimacy between them. Janae continued to encourage them to keep talking about their feelings toward each other and about sex.

AWARENESS ACTIVITY: Self-Inventory on Barriers to Sexual Intimacy

Directions: Place a number from 1 to 4 in the blank before each statement to best indicate the degree to which this statement is true for you.

1 = Never 2 = Occasionally 3 = Frequently 4 = Almost always

_____ I have difficulty asking for what I want sexually from my partner.
_____ I am afraid to feel my sexual feelings fully and completely.
_____ I am afraid to let my partner know what I enjoy about sex.
_____ I find my enjoyment of sex largely depends on my partner's enjoyment.
_____ I am afraid that my body will not be attractive to my partner.
_____ I am afraid that my partner might be overwhelmed by my sexual feelings.
_____ I secretly wish my partner would pay more attention to me while we are making love.
_____ I experience sex as mainly a physical release.
_____ I am afraid I won't be able to satisfy my partner.
_____ I find sex to be very hard work.
_____ I feel sad and lonely after having sex.
_____ I use sex to try to smooth over arguments with my partner.
_____ I am jealous when my partner pays attention to other men/ women.
_____ I get scared when my partner initiates sex with me.
_____ I am afraid to initiate sex with my partner.
_____ I am afraid that I will lose control while making love.
_____ I am afraid that my partner will disapprove of what I am doing or feeling sexually.
_____ I don't find masturbation enjoyable and satisfying.
_____ I am afraid to explore my body and what gives it pleasure.
_____ I am afraid to be myself when I am making love.
_____ TOTAL

Scoring: Add up the column of numbers and get a total score. Use the following guidelines to interpret your score.

20 - 40 Very Few Barriers to Sexual Intimacy
(No effect on sexual functioning)
41 - 60 Some Barriers to Sexual Intimacy
(Possible effects on sexual functioning)
61 - 80 Many Barriers to Sexual Intimacy
(Major effect on sexual functioning)

SKILL BUILDING EXERCISE:
Communication Exercises for the Bedroom
(Weinhold and Andresen, 1981)

Introduction:
Communicating about sex in a *healthy* way involves clear, direct communication so both partners can get closer to each other and get their wants and needs met from an "everybody wins" position. It is from this position that total intimacy develops and people feel totally free to share sexual enjoyment and pleasure. This helps the couple develop an interdependent sexual relationship like the one described in the chart earlier in the chapter.

Directions:
A. Take turns reading each communication rule to the other person. The discussion of each rule proceeds as follows:
1. Each person, in turn, explains the rule in his or her own words, e.g., "I think this rule means _____."
2. Each person, in turn, gives an example of his or her use or misuse of the rule, e.g., "This morning, I said _____ instead of _____."
3. If you agree or disagree or want to add a comment, state your point of view, e.g., "I will agree with only part of that rule and my questions is _____."
4. Follow these directions for each of the rules.
B. Apply the ideas from each rule when discussing other rules. Also, if your partner misuses any rule during the discussion, point it out: "I think you just misused Rule 2. Will you go back and reread that rule?"

Rules:

1. When you are expressing your thoughts and feelings, use "I" instead of "one," "they," "you," or "people." Say, "I am afraid to get close to you," instead of "People are often afraid to get close to each other."
2. Use eye contact and talk directly to your partner. This demonstrates genuine interest in your partner. Also, maintain eye contact while your partner is talking to you. Avoiding eye contact is a way of avoiding intimacy.
3. Avoid interrupting your partner while he or she is speaking. This is an indication that you are not listening and may be already planning your response instead of listening.

194

4. When sharing your thoughts and feelings, be specific and provide the necessary information as well as asking for what you want so your partner can respond to your thoughts and feelings, e.g., "I'm angry because you seem to rush through having sex and I want to take more time. Will you agree to spend more time while making love?" A common error is to omit the request for what you want, which then pressures your partner to guess at what you want.

5. In order to make sure that your verbal and nonverbal communication is clear, ask your partner to restate in his or her own words the essence of your message. For example, "Will you repeat what I just said?" or "What I heard you say was that you like your breasts touched softly. Did I hear you right?"

6. Avoid asking questions unless you really need information. Many times questions are statements in disguise: "Don't you think we ought to turn off the lights?" or "Don't you feel afraid that we are making too much noise?" Your communication will be much clearer if you make a statement about your own thoughts and feelings: "I would like to turn off the lights. Is that all right with you?"

    a. "Why" questions are often meant to interrogate and as a result can contribute to defensiveness. For example, "Why do you always have to be in such a hurry?"

    b. "How" questions are generally more appropriate: "How are you feeling?" or "How long do you want to take tonight when we make love?" Though these "how" questions are better than "why" questions, even some "how" questions can be critical in nature and may create a defensive reaction or negative situation.

7. Comparative and competitive thinking can lead to power struggles. One person may act as if his or her thoughts or feelings are more important than the other person's. Or that person may put him or herself down and act as if the other's thoughts and feelings were more important. For example, "You have had more sexual experience than I have had."

    a. Assert yourself by saying, "No, I won't," or "I don't want to," instead of "I can't," or by saying "Yes," when you really want to.

    b. If your partner asks a question, respond with a direct, clear answer, or say, "I am not willing to answer that question." People often avoid answering questions they don't want to answer. Also avoid saying, "I don't know," when you do know. "I don't know" really means "I won't tell myself" and/or "I won't tell you."

    c. Consider your partner's needs and the situation when making requests. For example, when wanting a lengthy lovemaking experience, don't wait until a late hour when you or your partner may be too tired.

8. Being unassertive with your partner is an ineffective way of solving problems and indicates an unwillingness to take responsibility for your own thoughts, feelings and behavior. For example, you may not let your partner know what you like and dislike in sex and expect him or her to be able to guess or figure out what you want. Assertiveness means you are willing to take responsibility for getting your needs and wants met, without ignoring the stated needs and wants of your partner.

    a. The best way to get your wants and needs met is to ask directly: "What I want is for you to tell me what you like about me while we are making love. Are you willing to do that?" ("If not, what are you willing to do about my request?") If you are afraid to ask for what you want, admit it.

    b. If you agree to do something that your partner asks you to do, be sure it is something you want to do and/or are willing to do. For example, "Whatever you say, dear!" as a response to something you don't want to do is being unassertive and misleads your partner. It is fine to say "no" without losing your partner's love and respect. If you don't want to do what's requested, be clear about what you do want and are willing to do.

    c. When you are quiet, be sure it is because you choose to be quiet and not because you are afraid to speak. If you are afraid, you can say, "I'm afraid to ask you for want I want because my fantasy is that you might get angry and/or reject me." Then ask for reassurance: "Will you tell me that it is fine for me to ask you for what I want and that you will not reject me for asking for it?"

    d. If your partner is quiet and does not communicate his or her needs or wants to you, ask about them. If you partner says, "I don't know," it generally means "I don't want to think about it," or "I won't tell you or tell myself." You can ask your partner to think about what he or she wants and tell you later.

    e. Avoid blaming your partner for causing your feelings. Don't say, "You make me angry," or "You make me happy." Both statements are inaccurate. It is important that you take ownership for your feelings: "I am angry that you ignored my request to have sex tonight," or "I am happy with the way we make love."

    f. Avoid using the words "I'll try," or "I'll work at that" when you agree to do something. "I'll try" usually means "I won't do the best I can because I don't really want to do it anyway." Saying "I will do it" communicates that you are committed to follow through to the best of your ability. If you don't want to do it, saying "no" is more assertive and effective in solving problems.

g. Don't say "I guess," "probably," or "maybe" when you have a definite opinion or point of view: "I guess oral sex is all right with me." If you aren't sure, admit it. "I'm not sure if I like oral sex; let me talk about my reservations." If you are sure, say so: "I really like oral sex."

9. When expressing your thoughts or feelings, avoid exaggerating or understating. This is an ineffective way of drawing attention to yourself and is a way of defending your point of view rather than a way of solving your problems.

a. Avoid exaggerations such as, "I always . . ." or "You never" Instead of saying, "You never tell me you love me anymore," be specific and speak from your own experience: "I don't remember you telling me that you love me in the past two days. Will you tell me now?"

b. Don't act helpless when you are not: "I got so excited, I couldn't wait for you to have an orgasm." The truth is that you decided not to wait.

10. Avoid rescuing your partner. Rescuing, in this context, means doing something for your partner that he or she can do for him or herself. This also applies when your partner needs or wants something from you and is not asking for it. Rescuing means taking responsibility for something that is not legitimately yours (not your territory); this leads to conflicts and confusion in the relationship.

To avoid rescuing means to be willing to ask for what you want or need 100% of the time. For example, Mary wanted more physical caressing before intercourse but she was unwilling to tell Sam. Sam wasn't sure what to do, so he assumed that Mary wanted to move directly to intercourse. As a result, he hurried through foreplay in order to please Mary which was a rescue of Mary. Mary, not wanting to hurt Sam's feelings, decided to go along when he hurried to intercourse, which also was a rescue of Sam. In this case, neither Mary nor Sam was really asking for what each wanted and each ended up with unexpressed, angry feelings.

Mary could have avoided rescuing by asking Sam to caress her more before initiating intercourse, and Sam could have decided what he wanted and asked for that. If their wants were conflict-

197

ing, they could have decided on a solution that was agreeable to both and, therefore, avoided further conflicts in that area.

11. Avoid interpreting the behavior, feelings, or motivations of your partner: "You refuse sex with me because you're mad at me!" or "What you're really thinking is . . ." or "When you say nice things to me, you really mean . . ." Sometimes, interpretations are ways of saying your own thoughts or feelings and acting as if they belonged to the other person. For example, "The reason you are frowning is because you don't like what I am doing." Instead of interpreting your partner's behavior, do the following:

a. Describe your partner's actions without analyzing them: "When you put your arm under my neck like this, it pulls my hair."

b. Describe how *you* feel without telling the other how he or she feels: "My head hurts."

c. If you have an impression of what is motivating your partner, do a perception check and ask him or her if your thoughts are accurate: "Are you angry with me?"

Part Three

BEYOND COUNTER-DEPENDENCY: PATHWAYS TO PARTNERSHIP

Chapter Thirteen

CREATING PARTNERSHIP RELATIONSHIPS

"Love does not consist in gazing at each other but in
looking together in the same direction."
Antoine DeSaint-Exupery

UNRAVELING CO-DEPENDENT/ COUNTER-DEPENDENT RELATIONSHIPS

The notion of using relationships to change co-dependent and counter-dependency behavior is in itself a radical idea. Very few professionals recommend it. In fact, most professionals discourage couples from doing this kind of work together, and say it is too difficult for people to sort out their unfinished business in an intimate relationship. It is true that it is often necessary to have outside resources to help people unravel the old patterns that get woven into current relationships, especially if either partner has a history of severe abuse or other traumas. Sometimes individuals within a relationship need to work separately for a while on their issues in therapy or even live separately for a period of time. We believe, however, that the long-term goal is to bring the breaking free process back into the relationship. It is our belief is that the counter-dependent and co-dependent behaviors were created in our childhood relationships and that they now need to be transformed in our adult relationships. A committed, conscious relationship is the most powerful tool we know of for really breaking free of these dysfunctional patterns. It provides the safety, the intensity and the sustained contact necessary to both bring up issues and to work cooperatively to transform them.

We also believe that the true purpose of relationships is to help us learn how to become whole and fully functioning human beings.

201

Relationships are the richest environment for "wholing" that we know of. We also believe that part of the wholing process for intimate relationships involves the creation of social and organizational support for new forms of partnership relationships at all levels. We need new visions, new tools and new social structures that help to support and to create a partnership society. As we each learn to reach new levels of cooperation and partnership in our primary relationships, we will no longer be satisfied with anything less in other areas of our lives, including our work, schools and churches.

IDENTIFYING COUNTER-DEPENDENT RELATIONSHIP PATTERNS

In order to get beyond the battle of the sexes and move towards partnership relationships between men and men, women and men, and women and women, people will need to identify their counter-dependent relationship patterns.

There are four common relationship patterns that people with unmet counter-dependent needs create and each is slightly different. The four most common relationship patterns are:

- a male who has counter-dependent behaviors with a female who has co-dependent patterns
- a female who has counter-dependent behaviors with a male who has co-dependent behaviors
- a male who exhibits counter-dependent traits with a female who exhibits counter-dependent traits and
- people with both counter-dependent and co-dependent behaviors where partners switch back and forth between playing the co-dependent/counter-dependent roles.

Below is a brief description of each of these relationship patterns.

• A male with counter-dependent behaviors and a female with co-dependent behaviors. This is the most common kind of relationship pattern. In this combination the male, who has counter-dependent behaviors, appears strong, secure, successful, independent and self-centered while acting to dominate and invade his partner. The female with co-dependent behaviors appears weak, helpless, insecure, unsuccessful and dependent as she invites domination and invasion from him. There is usually very little genuine intimacy in this kind of relationship. Their sexual relationship is set up primarily to meet his sexual needs. Whenever obvious or subtle one-up/one-down power arrangements are present in the relationship, such as are common in this combination, very little intimacy is possible.

• **A female with counter-dependent behaviors and a male with co-dependent behaviors.** The reverse pattern is similar in structure, but with some important differences. Usually in this type of relationship, the sexual relationship is much less prominent and may even be absent. Often, under the female counter-dependent behavior is childhood sexual abuse or severe trauma involving feelings that she wants to avoid. The best way for her to avoid these feelings is by avoiding sexual intimacy. The male with co-dependent behaviors often feels controlled, one-down and may be sexually impotent. He may be depressed and hold his feelings inside, rather than express them clearly. Instead, he may wait to "dump" them on other people.

• **A male with counter-dependent traits and a female with counter-dependent traits.** This pattern is quite popular among young, urban professionals (YUPpies). There are many two-career relationships where both people work long hours, accumulate a lot of material goods, strive to reach certain career goals and, as a result, save very little time or energy for intimacy. It is likely that they both have found legitimate, socially-sanctioned ways of avoiding intimacy. In many of these relationships, there is infrequent sexual contact, maybe only a few times a year. The overriding emphasis in this kind of relationship is usually on lots of activity and keeping busy at all costs is the unspoken goal.

The couple with counter-dependent traits may also have a compulsive need to be seen wearing the right clothes, to have the right degrees, to drive the right car, to have the right friends and to take the right vacations. The emphasis is on looking as though they have the right relationship, even if they don't feel good in it. They hope that others will be impressed and approve of their life style and choice of a mate and, therefore, approve of them. This is the way they hope to "earn" their love or self-esteem.

• **People with both counter-dependent and co-dependent behaviors who switch roles.** This pattern is also very common. The way that this pattern works is that the partner uses co-dependent behaviors to pursue the partner who is exhibiting counter-dependent behavior patterns and is always running away.

At some point the partner who is using co-dependent behavior tires of the pursuit, gives up the quest for intimacy and pulls away. This will usually trigger an abandonment fear in the partner with counter-dependent patterns who then decides to pursue the now retreating co-dependent acting partner. At this point the co-dependent person may also decide to prove that he or she doesn't need the counter-dependent partner, and they end up switching roles. We call this pattern the dance of intimacy and it usually keeps things in chaos enough of the time to prevent intimacy at either end of the dance routine. At some point in the dance, however, they may both give up and decide it is easier to create a relationship where both people act out of their counter-dependent behaviors. They may also decide to end the relationship altogether.

The other form of relationship, which is not as widespread as one would think, is between two co-dependent people. This book does not specifically address this pattern. If you want to know more about the co-dependent pattern of relationship, consult *Breaking Free of the Co-dependency Trap* written by the authors.

A NEW VISION OF RELATIONSHIP

In the history of relationships, the idea of having an emotionally, psychologically and spiritually committed relationship has occurred only within the last twenty years. This new vision of relationships is the result of our affluence, the advances in psychology and our expanded understandings of human potential. It probably also comes out of our need to heal the unmet needs from childhood.

Prior to the beginning of this century, marriage was primarily a political or material contract. In that era, when the focus was more on needs related to survival, marriage was used to support political and economic alliances. This was done not only at the national and international levels, but also in the villages and countryside. Marriages were often arranged based on some economic exchange between the two families involved.

By the turn of the century, the extended family was still the primary support system for most marital relationships. As industrialization spread, the extended family began to fragment. Children moved away to cities to work and the two World Wars turned soldiers into world travellers.

By the 1950s, the nuclear family system had replaced the extended family system. In this process, we again see the developmental model at work. The extended family system of the early 1900s functioned more as a co-dependent system where members were enmeshed. By the post-war 1950s, the nuclear family functioned more as a system that supported counter-dependent behaviors. Children growing up in families during the sixties and seventies attended college away from their home towns, married strangers and took jobs in other parts of the country.

By the 1980s, many of this culture's young people had emancipated themselves and were participating in the sexual, gender and racial revolutions and were experimenting with higher consciousness through drugs, music and alternative religions. These forays into independent lifestyles provided the baby-boom generations, who were approaching midlife, with a comfortable life style and optimal personal freedom. In addition, they were having many experiences of isolation and loneliness. Becoming a cog in the industrial machine, leaving one unsatisfactory relationship after another, losing parenting relationships because of divorce and facing the realities of an epidemic of sexually transmitted diseases like AIDS, confused and scared many men and women.

The personal growth and individual freedom movements of the seventies and eighties began changing to the "relationship movement" of the nineties, as people moved toward new levels of self-actualization. In this emerging movement, there is a desire to provide more stable and functional family life experiences for children, a desire to end the battle of the sexes, a desire to create long-term love relationships and a desire to integrate psychological, emotional and spiritual values into relationships. These are signals of a new awakening of consciousness among people in the developed countries of the world.

This consciousness is frequently expressed as a growing desire for intimacy, often described as a special kind of closeness, a communication that is deeper than what can be achieved physically, a sharing that goes beyond material partnership, a spiritual connection that touches the heart and soul of the beloveds. Such relationships are possible, from our perspective, only when there is a deep commitment between partners to help each other to break free off the wounds of their past and to use the transformation process as a springboard to a spiritual relationship. The biggest obstacle blocking this new vision of relationship is the competitive attitude (one-up, one-down) that exists in almost all relationships (Weinhold & Weinhold, 1989). We predict that when men and women are able to develop relationships based on equality, cooperation and mutuality, a whole new culture based on the values of partnership will emerge.

MOVING FROM COMPETITION TO COOPERATION AND PARTNERSHIP

The primary source of competition in relationships is the belief that there isn't enough of something. This belief in scarcity is brought into adult relationships from experiences in childhood when there wasn't enough love, nurturing, mirroring, positive support, food, clothing or parenting. Changing this scarcity belief requires several steps:

* reliving the experience(s) where the belief was formed
* releasing the unexpressed feelings from the experience(s)
* reviewing the old beliefs in the experience(s) to see if they are still valid in current relationships and
* creating a new reality of abundance.

The first three beliefs you may need to do in therapy, where you have emotional support for your inner child to emerge safely. Changing the last belief is one that only you can do. It requires creating a network of supportive people around you who are available to meet your needs, people with whom you can make contracts and ask directly for what you want. Once this network is in place, you will not need to feel competitive because you will have many resources for meeting your needs. When we work with individuals and couples, the creation of this supportive network is an important step in the journey toward independence, interdependence and abundance.

The outcome from creating this kind of network can be the creation of a new form of extended family. People who are willing to cooperatively work together on healing the unfinished business of their childhood become emotionally and spiritually bonded and are able to create partnership at its most basic level.

Much of our own ability to work as professional partners has developed from our personal partnership in helping each other break free of our wounds from childhood. The depths to which we have gone in revealing ourselves and our wounds to each other has created a base of trust and safety that allows us to risk, be spontaneous and creative. This has been our experience in

206

working with other couples as well, for what most people are seeking is an emotional and spiritual partnership. From that, the mental and physical levels of partnership often emerge. This doesn't mean that all couples should become professional partners in the way we have, but they still can be more supportive of each other in the personal aspects of their lives.

DOMINATION VS. PARTNERSHIP IN RELATIONSHIPS

The emerging partnership form of relationship is distinctly different from the dominator form of relationship. The dominator form supports co-dependent/counter-dependent relationships based on dominator/dominated, passive/aggressive and win/lose models. Partnership relationships support interdependent actions based on unity, mutuality and cooperation. A comparison of the two might look like this:

Dominator Relationships	*Partnership Relationships*
• use force or threat to enforce domination	• use the vision of higher consciousness to encourage linking for common good
• create inequalities in power and decision-making	• create equal opportunities for money and use knowledge as shared power for joint decision making
• value violence and exploitation	• value nurturing qualities such as compassion and nonviolence
• utilize rigid sex roles	• utilize fluid sex roles
• are competitive	• are cooperative
• use fear to create separation	• use hope and high ideals to create unity
• are materially oriented	• are spiritually oriented
• see women and children as property or chattel	• see women and children as equal and unique individuals
• support co-dependent and counter-dependent behaviors	• support interdependent behaviors and intimacy
• follow a path of fear and protection	• follow a path of learning and discovery

•use control, manipulation and deception in communicating	• use truth, empathy and directness in communicating
•value either the needs of the relationship or the needs of the individual more	• value both the needs of the individuals and the needs of the relationship

From this comparison we can see the basic differences in philosophy and practice of these two models of relationship. Many couples come to us for help in creating a partnership relationship with each other and with their children. They tell us how difficult it is for them to live in partnership on a daily basis. Our culture is still so dominator-based that those with partnership ideals must band together in support groups and small communities to help hold firmly to their vision.

COMMON ELEMENTS OF PARTNERSHIP RELATIONSHIPS

As we have worked on our own relationship and have helped many other couples work on theirs, we have found a number of characteristics that describe partnership relationships:
•   recognizing that the unmet developmental needs from child-hood have created dysfunctional behavior patterns that each individual has brought to the relationship
•   committing to help each other heal the childhood wounds and change the dysfunctional behavior patterns
•   committing to stay together during the conflictual periods in the healing process when projections and blaming are active
•   committing to the path of learning, to self-discovery and discovering each other
•   learning skills that support contracting, negotiating, resolving conflicts, self-awareness and reflection
•   committing to partnership principles in the relationship that support equality in power, opportunity and responsibility
•   committing to tell the truth about behavior, feelings and needs (100% of the time)
•   respecting each other's boundaries
•   defining intimacy in relationships to include the "downs" as well as the "ups"
•   using prayer, meditation, affirmations, visioning, couples re-treats and other spiritual tools such as Yoga and Tai chi chuan to support the self-actualizing aspects of the relationship.
208

While these are characteristics of many partnership-type relationships, each relationship is unique. One of the joys of being in relationship today, whether it is a love relationship, a parent/child relationship or a relationship between two friends, is the opportunity for creating something unique that really meets the needs of the individuals involved. With the old rigid roles in our society fading, it is now possible to have new forms of male/male, male/female, female/female and adult/child relationships. We have many choices that can support us in finding safe and appropriate ways of getting our mental, emotional, spiritual and physical needs met.

CREATING A PARTNERSHIP RELATIONSHIP

In the previous section we described briefly the "Common Elements of Partnership Relationships." In this section we will discuss each of the elements more completely.

• **Recognizing the Unfinished Business.** This is a key awareness in a partnership relationship. So many relationship conflicts are caused by the dysfunctional behavior patterns brought into the relationship by each person, especially those from the unmet developmental needs. Until this fact is clearly acknowledged and dealt with, the relationship cannot move to a partnership or interdependent level. When both people are willing to look at the sources of their current conflicts and to identify the unmet developmental needs they brought into the relationship, the need cannot be met nor the wounds healed. No longer do individuals in a relationship have to pretend that they have it all together. They can be truthful about their unmet developmental needs and use them as a source of bonding and intimacy in the relationship.

• **Committing to Heal Childhood Wounds.** When a couple makes a commitment to help each other heal their childhood wounds and meet their unmet developmental needs they brought to the relationship, they have made the most important shift necessary for creating a partnership relationship. This commitment shifts the relationship from competitive, scarcity base to a cooperative, abundance mode. This commitment also paves the way for a deeper level of intimacy to emerge in the relationship. The real reason (but often not known) that two people establish a relationship in the first place is to heal their wounds from childhood. When this commitment is verbalized, the unspoken dream of the relationship can become conscious and be realized.

• **Committing to Stay Together.** In order to make a relationship safe enough to do the deep healing work, there has to be a commitment to stay together and work out the old unfinished business. When people open up their childhood wounds to each other, they feel very vulnerable and scared. They are afraid they will be rejected or abandoned because of their weaknesses. In fact, this is very often exactly what happened in childhood. In the midst of our childlike innocence we were emotionally and/or physically abandoned, usually with no understanding of why it happened. We are afraid this will happen again so we hide our wounds and our needs from our partner, until we know he or she will not abandon or reject us.

When we work with couples in therapy, we ask them to make short-term contracts to stay together for three months, six months or one year while they are working on these issues. During that time, they agree to stay together no matter what happens (unless there is physical abuse). They agree to work cooperatively on their relationship using the tools they learn with us. At the same time they contract to stay together, they also contract to an agreed number of therapy sessions, workshops or support groups. The couple also agrees to evaluate their progress at certain key points during that time. They can also agree to extend the time period if they feel they need more time. The length of time a couple needs to deal with their wounds depends upon how old they are, how long they have been together and how hard they are willing to work on their issues.

Some couples make it through this period quite well and some don't. We make it clear at the beginning of couple therapy that we do not primarily focus on saving the relationship. We see our primary role as helping them get clear about why they are together. We also focus on finding out if they really want to help each other heal the wounds to their inner child. If they choose not to help each other, then we help them make their separation as clean and clear as possible so that they both leave from an "I'm OK and you're OK" position. We help them to leave with dignity and to use the divorce or separation process as an opportunity to become more aware of their own issues and patterns. With this awareness they often learn to recognize the patterns earlier in their next relationship and know what to do with them. We have worked with a number of couples whose relationship actually improved *after* they went through a divorce.

There are often good reasons why some couples decide not to stay together. Sometimes the "reservoir of ill will" that has been created is so deep that the couple cannot tolerate the hurt from the deep wounds they have experienced with each other. Some people do not seem to like each other enough to be willing to work cooperatively on their old issues, while other couples seem to be people who are convinced that they got into relationship for all the wrong reasons. This group often just wants out of the relationship when they discover the truth. They are too scared to try to work it out with each other and will have to work it out in another relationship.

• **Committing to Learn about Each Other.** It still surprises us that many people who have been together for some time actually know very little about their partner. Most adults have learned to wear masks to hide their real feelings and their real thoughts. In a partnership relationship both people are committed to removing their masks and being as authentic as they can be with each other.

This commitment and authenticity also involves taking back the projections that we put on our spouses and others who are close to us. It is only when these projections are taken back that we can see the other person the way he or she really is. For instance, we may project positive images on each other such as "perfect parent," "perfect mate," "perfect person" or we may project negative images such as "critical parent," "controlling parent" or "rejecting parent." Sometimes these projections are so strong that they keep us from any real understanding of who the other person is beyond the projection. Taking back these projections allows us to see each other the way we really are, not just the way we would like the person to be or whom the person reminds us of from our past.

In partnership relationships both people must be willing to take back these projections and to check out whether or not their perceptions are based on the projections. This takes a lot of work and awareness, but it does lead to more self-discovery and discovery of the essence of the other person behind the projections.

To identify a projection, we tell couples to watch for times when they have a reaction to what their partner said or did that is greater than what the situation called for. This is how they know they are in a projection, but they may not know the nature of the projection. In those situations, they need to use a "perception check." ("I am perceiving you as angry at me for some reason. Is that true?") We also tell them to remember that they are almost

211

never upset for the reason they think. In almost any instance of feeling upset, it is possible to uncover some old hurt or unmet need from childhood.

• **Committing to Use Win/Win Conflict Methods** It is very important that couples agree to eliminate "dirty fighting" techniques. Instead they need to develop effective, responsible win/win skills for resolving conflicts. Win/win skills help to build and maintain trust in a relationship. It has been our experience that very few adults have *ever* witnessed or been part of a win/win resolution in solving conflicts. Mostly people have been exposed to the *"Four Horsemen of Conflict Resolution"* : domination, intimidation, manipulation and exploitation. So when a conflict occurs, people will automatically assume that there has got to be a winner and a loser. Since almost no one likes to lose, the game becomes "win at all costs." It is impossible to create or maintain a partnership relationship under those conditions.

Win/win conflict tools also help deepen intimacy. Instead of seeing conflict and problems as things to be avoided, people in a partnership relationship learn to welcome conflict as an opportunity for growth.

• **Committing to an Equal Relationship.** Creating a relationship that is equal in power, equal in opportunity and equal in responsibility is easier said than done. There are many subtle ways that people use to keep equality out of their relationship. We ask couples to agree to give up using "power plays" to try to get what they want. Common power plays include threats of violence, refusing to resolve the conflict, threatening a divorce, blaming the other person or becoming verbally abusive. We also ask them to avoid rescuing, a subtle power play to try to stay one-up in a relationship. When you do something for your partner that he or she could do for himself or herself *and* you don't ask them if it is okay or they don't ask you to do it, you are *rescuing*. This sets the stage for all kinds of problems. As one male client stated it, "My wife does things for me that I don't ask her to and sometimes don't even want. Then she expects me to be grateful to her for what she did and to do something for her in return."

We also ask couples to be *willing* to ask for what they want or need 100% of the time. This prevents rescuing and requires each to take full responsibility for getting his or her needs met. In order to help couples raise their awareness of rescuing, we ask them to go "cold turkey" with each other. This means that they cannot do anything for the other person unless that person asks for it

212

directly. They also cannot expect their partner to do anything for them unless they ask. During this exercise many couples discover that they have created many situations in their relationship where they rob their partner of power or they fail to use their own power.

• **Telling the Truth.** This seems, at first glance, to be easy. We can testify that it is often not easy. We both grew up in families where there were big secrets and no one ever told the whole truth. Often they taught us that truth is taboo. Unless we are conscious of these kinds of patterns, we may still have difficulty telling our partner the truth about our thoughts, our feelings, our needs, our body or our spiritual beliefs. If we are projecting "critical parent" onto each other, it may be difficult to tell the truth. We expect each other to judge us in the way our parents might have done, so we hide who we are from each other. Many people with unmet counter-dependent needs are afraid they will be rejected if they show their partner how needy and insecure they really are feeling.

• **Respecting Each Other's Boundaries.** Many people with counter-dependent issues will invade the psychological boundaries of their partners without much thought. However, when it comes to boundaries in a partnership relationship, it is a two-way street. Both people need to identify their boundaries and take responsibility for communicating their limits to each other. In a partnership relationship both need to agree to respect these boundaries and develop an agreed upon process for handling any unintentional boundary violations. These aspects of boundary setting can help build trust or destroy trust faster than almost anything else can in a relationship.

• **Finding a New Definition of Intimacy.** The old definition of intimacy usually just involved the close, romantic, highly positive times in the relationship. A new definition of intimacy also involves developing a sense of oneness, sharing, taking risks and trust. Intimacy grows as people dare to risk greater openness, learn to to be emotionally present and display a high degree of caring for one another. While much of this seems to relate to sharing positive feelings, it can also involve "dealing with your own shit" in the relationship. Intimacy is like an instrument with many strings. The music which people make together comes from playing a full range of chords, which can include both harmony and disharmony. A flow between chords begins to create a composition with interesting movement between the ups and downs.

• **Using Spiritual Tools to Support the Relationship.** Like anything you value, you have to be willing to continually put time and energy into partnership relationships. If you want your relationships to grow and flourish, adding daily rituals and spiritual practices helps to support deeper kinds of connections. These can be simple things such as taking walks together, scheduling a block of time each day to talk with each other about important happenings and finding time to nurture each other with nonsexual touch such as foot or back rubs. You can also create daily spiritual practices together through prayer, meditation, Yoga or Tai 'chi. Such rituals or activities are important ways you can support the growth of your partnership relationship.

PUTTING IT ALL TOGETHER

The following chart shows how to put all this together. It is provided here to help you look at how to work cooperatively in committed relationships and support your partner's growth. As you look over this chart, you will begin to see how you can work together to change the counter-dependent behaviors in your relationship.

Each step is matched with suggested resources to assist you with that step and the essential skills for that step. You can identify the step you are currently involved in and then check under "Recommended Activities" to determine what activities would support your growth. Finally check in the third column for the skills needed to complete that step.

Generally, each step builds on the previous one but you may find yourself skipping a step because you had learned that step previously. The main purpose of the list is to provide a map for the Breaking Free process but we are fully aware that "the map is not the territory."

THE MAP FOR BREAKING FREE FROM COUNTER-DEPENDENCY:
Recommended Activities and Essential Skills

Steps	Recommended Activities	Essential Skills
1. Become aware of your patterns	Reading books, doing written exercises to identify intergenerational patterns Attending workshops Joining support groups Individual or group therapy	Perception checks Boundary setting skills Win/win conflict resolution skills
2. Identify the unfinished business from your life drama	Reading books Attending workshops Joining support groups Contracting for individual or group therapy	Corrective parenting skills Empathy
3. Do your "original pain" work	Contracting for individual or group therapy	
4. Complete the unfinished business of your life drama	Contracting for group therapy Creating conscious, committed relationships	Corrective parenting Boundary setting
5. Learn to become an autonomous person	Joining support groups	Natural power Conscious commitment Boundary setting
6. Learn to live in your body	Having bodywork such as massage, deep tissue work or structural realignment Getting nutritional counseling Exercising regularly	Win/win conflict resolution

215

7. Develop an inner life

Working on yourself
Taking retreats
Attending workshops
Joining support groups
Creating conscious, committed
  relationships

Boundary setting skills
Natural power skills
Sexual communication skills

8. Learn to live interdependently

Working on yourself
Attending workshops
Creating community groups
Creating conscious, committed
  relationships

Sexual communication skils
Win/win conflict resolution skills

FROM COUNTER-DEPENDENCY TO COMMITMENT AND INTIMACY

The leap to commitment and intimacy is often terrifying for people with counter-dependent symptoms, so terrifying that most never make commitments and those who do often try to retreat. What we recommend is that the move into commitment come in gradual, incremental steps that provide the protection which people with counter-dependency issues require. The stages in this gradual movement toward commitment include:

- Determine if there are primary incompatibilities, such as highly divergent spiritual or philosophical values and beliefs, that will undermine intimacy in the long-term. We often use a visioning exercise to do this.
- Create for each partner a personal plan for working on the unmet developmental needs that they bring to the relationship.
- Make a short-term contract of three to six months, during which the partners will work to help each other heal specific wounds or change specific behaviors. They also agree not to end or threaten to end the relationship. To terminate or renew the contract, they agree to return to counseling. Many couples require several short-term contracts of three to six months before they are ready for a long-term contract.
- Create a long-term contract that identifies their mutual vision for the numerous aspects of their relationship. These can include financial, spiritual, recreational, educational, parental, family and occupational components.
- Practice regular ceremonies of ending and restarting the relationship as new aspects unfold which support letting go of the old parts or phases and celebrating the new ones. Such ceremonies encourage personal transformation of the partners as well as the transformation of the relationship. This approach can replace the serial monogamy (one relationship after another) so common in the last twenty years and encourage a new form of conscious, committed, cooperative, long-term relationship.

SUMMARY

The challenge of creating committed, partnership relationships opens up new opportunities for each individual as well as for

217

the relationship between them. Once the competitive basis shifts from competition and conflict to cooperative healing, the relationship deepens. The next step of getting beyond competitive conflicts is still in the visionary stage for many couples, but it is close enough for them to see that this kind of relationship could be even more rewarding. In this more advanced stage, the energy once directed toward healing each other becomes available to serve the wounded of the world: abused or abandoned children, homeless individuals and families, the polluted environment, single-parent families, unwed mothers and many other critical global problems.

CASE EXAMPLE

Sandy had decided to leave her marriage to a highly successful physician who was also a cocaine addict. During the sixteen years of their marriage, Sandy had learned how to be the strong one, supporting her children almost single-handedly. She had worked intensely on herself for two years in individual and group therapy, before the divorce, and had learned a lot about herself and her life patterns. With the divorce behind her, she was finally able to create a stable financial base for herself and her children.

As her children grew into their teen years and began to develop interests outside the family, Sandy began to yearn for male companionship. After her divorce and her inner child work in therapy, she realized she was emotionally still a teenager herself. She wished for a male friend with whom she could just have fun. About that time Lyle appeared in her life.

Lyle was also divorced and still paying a lot of child support and alimony to his ex-wife. He felt financially encumbered and decided he needed a few years to work on himself so he wouldn't recreate another unhealthy relationship. Lyle was attracted to Sandy because of her playful attitude and girlish enthusiasm about life.

Their common experiences in individual therapy had taught them that a relationship was the best place to activate and heal old patterns and unfinished business. With their common painful experiences of divorce still so fresh, they mutually decided to create a "committed friendship" contract. Without any long-term expectations, they agreed to do recreational and religious things together on a regular basis. They hoped that as their friendship matured, they would find opportunities to work on conflicts that emerged with the assumption that their conflicts would have their old business at their source.

218

After about three months of seeing each other, they were able to identify that they were each projecting their unfinished business with their mothers on each other. They were able individually to look for what wasn't finished with their mothers and to contract to consciously role play each other's mother for short periods of time. Over a period of another two months they found themselves moving deeper into their mother projections with each other. Eventually they found themselves so deep in old pain that they had difficulty in taking their mothers' faces off each other. At that point they sought therapy with us.

We helped Sandy and Lyle identify their respective roles in the relationship. Sandy's childhood history was one of extreme physical abuse while Lyle's was one of physical and emotional neglect. Lyle had counter-dependent behaviors characteristic of most men, but had flipped into co-dependency issues as the result of the trauma of his divorce. Sandy was currently playing out the counter-dependent role in their relationship. As Lyle got more in touch with his dependency needs and began to approach Sandy with them, it brought up all of her fears of intimacy. She continued to see Lyle as a potential abuser and began to pull away from her friendship with him.

Sandy confronted Lyle in therapy about the contained violence and rage that she felt from him, saying it reminded her of how it felt to be around her mother as a child. Lyle, a rather mild acting fellow, was stunned with Sandy's feedback. He experienced a quick flash of anger, which he quickly extinguished. When we asked him where the anger came from, he responded that Sandy sounded like his mother. At this point we suggested they create a corrective parenting contract.

Lyle asked Sandy to play his mother so that he could tell her how angry he was with her criticism. As he got into his anger, we quickly put our vinyl beanbag and old tennis racquet in front of him. He picked up the racquet and began smashing the beanbag with all his fury. He cried, cussed, ranted and raved about the losses in his relationship with his mother, emptying himself of fifty years of old resentments and anger. Then he moved into feeling rage at his father for abandoning him at the age of three. For another ten minutes he alternately sobbed and raged about the losses in his relationship with his father. After about twenty minutes of raging he collapsed exhausted in a heap on the floor. In a few minutes he caught his breath and began to sob quietly. He looked tentatively at Sandy and asked if she would hold him.

219

Without words she held out her open arms. He crawled over and curled himself into a little ball as she held him.

This session helped Lyle see that he still wasn't emotionally separate from his mother, so he contracted to do a *Completion Process with Your Parents* exercise with Barry. He emerged from this session saying that he felt as though a weight had been lifted off him.

As Sandy witnessed Lyle's rage during the therapy session, it brought up old anger for her at her mother. She then decided that she needed to do some more work with her mother about the abuse she had experienced from her. Sandy decided to do this work without Lyle. She felt that he had helped her get in touch with it and was grateful to him, but that she could complete her work in therapy without his presence. This fit Sandy's need to maintain her counter-dependent behavior as a safety valve against intimacy in the relationship and also honored the fact that they were not currently on a "committed intimate" relationship track.

Sandy was able to release her rage at her mother in therapy also and then went through the *Completion Process with Your Parents Exercise.* For a couple of weeks Sandy and Lyle did not see each other, though they talked on the telephone several times. They felt a need to let things settle a little bit before they got back together. Eventually they decided that this was a "transitional" healing relationship for each of them but neither was ready to have a more permanent relationship. They decided to remain friends and support each other's growth.

Chapter Fourteen

CREATING THE PARTNERSHIP SOCIETY

"The only thing that will redeem (hu)mankind is cooperation."
Bertrand Russell

In Chapter Five we examined counter-dependent behaviors from a systems perspective. From this perspective you learned that counter-dependency is also a stage in the evolution of the human species and that counter-dependent behaviors show up in all social systems: in intimate relationships, in family relationships, in religious and political institutions and in national and international relations. Understanding counter-dependency from this broader, evolutionary perspective may have helped you gain a better understanding of your own counter-dependent issues. From this perspective you can see how it would have been impossible to have grown up in this culture without learning counter-dependent behaviors. It also helped you see how important it is for you to break free of your counter-dependent patterns, that by changing yourself you are helping change the world as well. In Chapter Five we also discussed how counter-dependent behaviors in each of these social systems are creating a world crisis that may imperil the very survival of the human race.

Crisis has often been *the* opportunity for growth. Erik Erikson (1963) writes that each stage of individual development is heralded by a crisis. For instance, in the bonding stage the infant has a crisis of trust which must be resolved to move successfully to the next stage of development. The number of crises currently facing humankind may be just the impetus needed to move us forward in our evolution. Making this evolutionary leap can look a little frightening, because up until now the few humans in history who seemed to move beyond counter-dependent behaviors and reached interdependency have been deified and then killed. Jesus, Joan of Arc, Buddha, Rumi and Mohammed are examples of individuals who were seen as deities because of their demonstrated psychological and emotional independence. In more recent times Abraham Lincoln, Gandhi, John Kennedy and Martin Luther King appear to have reached a higher level of evolution and were subsequently martyred.

When Buddha's followers asked him who he was, they were astonished by his answer. They asked him, "Are you a god or a saint or an avatar?" He replied, "No, I am awake." He was able to transcend his individual identity and lived his life out of a higher, more aware self that he described as waking up. When we achieve our psychological birth, we become more awake and aware of the larger patterns that exist in our lives. At that point we often can choose to live our lives out of broad universal principles rather than local/family/cultural norms.

This chapter is our attempt to describe the healing process that is trying to happen at all levels of the global system. We believe that the process for healing individual developmental deficits can be applied to all social systems. Applying this process to larger social systems does involve a more complex way of thinking, but we hope that you will see the many parallels.

In Chapter Three you learned specific communication guidelines to follow that support individuals in becoming emotionally and psychologically separate. In this chapter we will use these communication guidelines from the *Functional Family Triangle* to show you how to break free of dysfunctional counter-dependent behavioral patterns at all levels of the system. The guidelines from Chapter Three are summarized below.

- Make no one "bad" for wanting to be separate and autonomous
- Listen to all sides
- Support everyone's feelings
- Acknowledge everyone's experiences as valid and important
- Communicate openly with all concerned to avoid secrets that create triangulation
- Empower yourself and others
- Define change as "growth."

BREAKING FREE OF COUNTER-DEPENDENCY
ISSUES IN RELATIONSHIPS

When the desire for psychological wholeness through emotional separation occurs in an intimate relationship and one of the partners decides to explore the world through new activities or by developing auxiliary relationships, it is important to frame this decision as a positive step. If the partners understand that the need for emotional separation is a normal developmental need, the conflicts over oneness and separateness can be easier to handle. In order to be available to provide emotional support to your partner you will need to understand the dynamics of the separation process, which usually involves a replay of whatever didn't get finished during childhood.

The separation process will reappear in the form of a triangle made up of the two bonded partners and the outside "attraction." At this point the partners need to reframe the attempt to separate by looking at what is right about it and trying to see what unmet developmental needs are surfacing for each of the persons. They also need to use the communication guidelines summarized above from Chapter Three to help them to work through the separation process. If one partner uses destructive methods as a way of trying to achieve separation, such as having affairs, complaining or using some form of addiction, it is important that this person be seen as using "unskilled behaviors" and doing the best he or she can. It is also important for both partners to have a vision of the relationship as a sacred place where their unfinished business can be healed without shame or blame. By working cooperatively to heal counter-dependency, the relationship becomes an opportunity for intimacy rather than something to flee from.

If one or both of the partners get afraid and the separation process breaks down, they may need to get an impartial third party to help them get through it successfully. This third party, who may be a skilled friend or a therapist, needs to follow the guidelines listed above. By using an outside resource to help resolve separation in intimate relationships, you can create the the *Functional Family Triangle* in your relationship.

BREAKING FREE OF COUNTER-DEPENDENCY
ISSUES IN FAMILIES

Up to this point in human history, most families have not dealt very effectively with the separation issues brought on by counter-dependency. Because most parents have not completed their own psychological birth, they often become frightened when their children or their spouse wants to be more emotionally separate. The children's desire to separate may bring up the parents' own anxieties about failure, abandonment and rejection. They may give indirect messages to their children that it is not okay for them to become too independent. They may cling to the children or become critical of them. When this happens, the child's drive to separate will often intensify, causing him or her to become more rebellious.

Rebelliousness is much more difficult to deal with when children reach adolescence. They will have taken the two-year-old separation process and upgraded it in complexity. At this age they are bright, articulate and somewhat experienced at playing adult games and will try your patience to its limits. And limits are exactly what adolescents need.

It is important to co-create contracts with them that clearly identify what is permissible and what is not. When children help set their own limits they are often harder on themselves than you would be. Giving them input about setting limits also allows children to have personal power and prevents them from resorting to oppositional behavior in order to rebel against your authority. At the time any agreements are jointly created, the children should be asked to define the explicit consequences for not keeping the terms of the agreements.

Family meetings are appropriate places for members to vent feelings, validate experiences, resolve conflicts, make agreements and create consequences. It is here where children learn first-hand about participatory democracy, where they see appropriate communication skills modeled effectively and where they can learn cooperation and take progressive steps toward autonomy and collaboration.

It is the parents' responsibility to see that the child takes as much responsibility as possible to enacting consequences when an agreement is broken. This supports the child in developing personal integrity and helps him or her see that the agreement is with himself or herself. Putting the child in charge of tracking on the terms of the agreement and enacting the consequences takes the parents out of the role of "policeman." This diffuses many situations which can become power struggles over "who is in charge." Giving children a sense of personal power, inner integrity and individual responsibility are critical parenting tasks for moving children into independence and interdependence.

224

By framing family conflicts and disagreements in a developmental context, all family members can be seen as attempting to grow in the best way they know how. Parents need to recognize that each older child will be bringing into the family separation process any unfinished business from his or her early childhood. With this awareness, the parents need to follow carefully the Guidelines for Completing the Separation Process described in Chapter Three. Children need permission statements that support them in becoming emotionally separate such as, "It's okay for you to have your own beliefs, your own feelings and your own dreams. I will still love you when you become a separate person."

Family separation will also bring up all the parents' unfinished business, which in some ways can be seen as a gift for adults who have difficulty in remembering much about their own childhood. Parents need to be able to separate their own unfinished issues from the issues of their children. One way to know if old issues are contaminating a current conflict with a child is to look at the size of the issue and to look at the adult's reaction to it. If the reaction is greater than the situation calls for, the parent's old issues are clearly present.

A family is also a system made up of several subsystems: individuals, the parents as a couple and the group. The adults, who make up the core of the system, must be committed to keeping their own relationship clear and work diligently to resolve any conflicts between them. Anything that they are unable to resolve between them will spread out into the children's level of the system and activate a family conflict. One child in a family usually plays an "agitator" role and will act out anything that is unresolved, unspoken or unaddressed in the system. This child often becomes the "identified patient" or the "problem child," and gets all the blame for things that go wrong in the family. This child is often the one who is taken for counseling or gets into trouble with authorities at school or in the community. In family systems theory, this kind of child is seen as the carrier of all the unresolved problems in the family. Treating this kind of problem requires that the whole family get therapy.

Parents often project parts of themselves that they don't like onto their children to avoid dealing with their own unfinished business. They will then abuse, neglect, punish or discriminate against a child who personifies their own despicable aspects. In such instances, parents may need psychological help in order to separate their issues from those of their children and learn to take back the projections they have on their children.   225

Resolving the separation issues growing out of the counter-dependent stage of development within the family is essential, even critical, work for parents. Parents often find they are parenting themselves at the same time they are trying to parent their children and are in need of outside help to separate their issues and the issues of the children. Parents also need "cheerleaders" who help empower them and continue to validate the importance of the work they are doing with their children. A knowledgeable therapist or parents' support group can often help play this vital role. When children are able to leave the family and both they and the parents feel "I'm okay and you're okay," then the children can begin to move into interdependence with a minimum of unfinished business. This means that their adult relationships and ultimately their relationships with their own children will be free of the kinds of dysfunction and difficulties that have plagued families for thousands of years.

When people experience functional ways of living and relating in their families, they will want to take these methods out into the community. They will want their schools and work places to be as functional as their family is. Functional individuals, couples and families will help create functional institutions and nations, and, eventually, a functional world.

BREAKING FREE OF COUNTER-DEPENDENCY ISSUES IN RELIGION

In *The Different Drum* (1987) Scott Peck identifies four stages of spiritual development and also looks at how this process breaks down in organized religions. The first stage he calls the *chaotic and anti-social stage.* This is the stage of undeveloped spirituality. It is parallel to the newborn who has yet to learn any limits or social rules.

In stage two, the *formal and institutional stage,* people make a decision to leave the chaos behind and agree to live according to some higher authority or to submit to the rules of a church institution. In our model, this stage parallels the co-dependent stage of individual development.

Stage three, the *skeptic and individual stage,* begins when a person starts to question some of the rules of the church or voices doubts about some of its institutional precepts. He or she may become actively skeptical, ask truth-seeking questions or rebel against the church's authority in some way. This stage parallels the counter-dependent stage of individual development where the child is trying to understand the truth about his or her world. People often leave the church at this stage and pretend to no longer need it. These people usually will become spiritually arrested. This is similar to the behaviors of a person with counter-dependent issues who hides his or her needs from others, but is unable to grow psychologically.

According to Peck, people will go back and forth between stage two and stage three as they seek to become autonomous and integrate the church's beliefs with their own experience. This vacillation is similar to the child who ventures back and forth between oneness and separateness.

Stage four, the *mystical and communal stage,* looks at religion as a mystery. People in this stage are able to empty themselves of preconceived notions and prejudices. From this empty place they seek the larger patterns of life where everything is connected. These people create their own set of principles to guide their lives and do not rely on external rules or institutional dogma to direct their spiritual thinking. This stage is comparable to the independent and interdependent stages of individual development. If a person has developed some degree of emotional and psychological independence, he or she can begin to live out of this mystical place for a very long time.

Where the process usually breaks down is in the third stage, when a devout church member begins to doubt and question the "party line." When this happens the church leaders need to support and encourage the questioning process, rather than try to dissuade the person from questioning or try to criticize them. The church officials need to listen to the skeptic and treat his or her concerns seriously. The message should be, "It's great that you are searching for a personal religion and questioning the beliefs of the church. How can we support you in finding the answers you are searching for?"

If people entering Peck's third stage of spiritual development were greeted with that kind of support, they probably would not have to leave the church in order to take the next steps in their spiritual growth. Many times organized religions drive people away at this third stage of development by not supporting the skeptic's quest.

Religious institutions are failing to meet the spiritual growth needs of many of their parishioners, keeping many people stuck in stage two co-dependent behaviors. The viability of many of these institutions is in jeopardy. Their survival depends on the church leaders recognizing that their members are involved in a process of psychological development that gets replayed with the church and support that process in ways that help both the individual and the institution.

BREAKING FREE OF COUNTER-DEPENDENCY ISSUES IN POLITICS

The democratic political system in America is designed for people who largely operate at an interdependent level of development. Unfortunately, most Americans still function largely with a combination of co-dependent or counter-dependent behaviors. Americans, like co-dependent children working on trust issues, want security and safety through government programs which will take care of their basic needs for jobs, money, medical care and retirement benefits. Like counter-dependent adolescents working on issues of separation and autonomy, they also rebel against rules or laws that they believe interfere with their freedom.

Many Americans still define freedom as "freedom from outside authority" or "freedom from freedom." Both of these definitions keep people from being responsible for taking care of their own needs and for looking at how their behavior is part of a larger problem. The current political system has become more authoritarian because most Americans do not exercise their political power by voting and participating in the democratic system. Until our individuals and our leaders recognize that the problem lies in stunted individual development, this country will limp along not serving its constituents effectively.

What is also needed from American leaders is the kind of wisdom and foresight Thomas Jefferson had when he wrote:

"Some (humans) look at constitutions with sanctimonious reverence and deem them like the ark of the covenant, too sacred to be touched. They ascribe to the (humans) of the preceding age a wisdom more than human, and suppose what they did to be beyond amendment... I am certainly not an advocate for frequent and untried changes in laws and constitutions.... But I also know that laws and institutions must go hand in hand with the progress of the human mind. As new discoveries are made, new truths disclosed, and manners and opinions change with the change of circumstances, institutions must advance also, and keep pace with the times "(Padov, 1939: 32, 67).

If Jefferson were alive today he would probably be a family therapist rather than a politician. He would call for a family meeting in the form of a "constitutional convention" where the "children" (senators, representatives and citizen activists) could come to air their grievances, be listened to, have their feelings supported, have their experiences validated and hear their "parents" (government leaders) tell the truth. Skilled "therapists" (planetary psychologists) would assist the process by making sure that communication followed the model of the *Functional Family Triangle*. After the grievances were all aired, the group would work together cooperatively to problem solve the next steps in governing the country. In this step many ideas could be discussed, refined and then brought to all the American people for adoption. Through such a "family meeting" convention the American people might begin to learn how to effectively cooperate and create a political system that empowers and preserves the rights of each individual while it supports the collective welfare.

BREAKING FREE OF COUNTER-DEPENDENCY ISSUES IN INTERNATIONAL RELATIONS

On our first trip to the Former Soviet Union (FSU), we had many opportunities to meet with Soviet men, women and families to discuss the similarities and differences between our two countries. We also met with Soviet psychologists and discussed the psychological differences that seem to exist between us. Frequently we were struck by the "chemistry" that exists between our two peoples. Our societies mirror each other in so many ways that we seem to fill some void in each other that is both individual and cultural. The interaction produces a personal alchemical reaction that everyone recognizes, but has difficulty in articulating.

Some of it is sparked by natural curiosity between two countries that have been separated because of political ideologies. It seems to go much deeper, however. The Soviet system was a very co-dependent system, which has tried to maintain central control of all aspects of daily life. The manner in which the Communist Party ruled the country parallels the characteristics of an authoritarian, enmeshed family. The system provided jobs, medical care, subsidized food and housing and a monthly salary for everyone. It also did not provide consequences for those who failed to appear for work to earn their benefits and salaries. It also failed to provide incentives to support individual initiative.

What we saw happening in the FSU, after the introduction of peristroika (restructuring) and glastnost (openness), is that the people and the culture are individually and collectively moving into the counter-dependent stage of development. Much of the attraction of Soviets for Americans may be that they are looking to us as models for becoming more separate. They see our life style is driven by individual initiative, achievement, self-actualization and reward.

Americans, on the other hand, are attracted to the collective and cooperative nature of the Soviet people. Their ability to maintain their sense of self in a totalitarian system has developed a deep sense of "soul" that seems missing in Americans.

Below are listed some of the polar characteristics that we observed between these two cultures:

USA/FSU Opposites

USA	FSU
masculine orientation (Uncle Sam)	feminine orientation (Mother Russia)
counter-dependent	co-dependent
materialistic	nonmaterialistic
de-centralized government	centralized government
wedding ring on the left hand	wedding ring on the right hand
hot water faucet on the left side	hot water faucet on the right side
individual initiative	collective initiative
a transcendent search for paradise in nature	a search for paradise in the depths
men perform manual labor	women perform manual labor
extroverted	introverted
self-reflective	nonreflective
rigid	adaptive
controlling, direct use of power	manipulative, indirect use of power
verbal	nonverbal
visually oriented	auditorily oriented
cognitive	feeling
optimistic	pessimistic

After the fall of Communism, the drive for separation and autonomy in the FSU was happening so fast that it began turning into what looked like "sibling rivalry" between Russia and some of the smaller republics. The long history of oppression and domination by the central government of the Communist regime has bred a reservoir of anger, rage, resentment and suppressed violence about the loss of individual freedom and the opportunity for self-expression. Because there is no identified person alive at whom they can direct their feelings, they project these feelings onto Russians or other racial, religious or ethnic minorities.

ADDRESSING THE GLOBAL COUNTER-DEPENDENCY CRISIS

The implication of a whole planet full of people working concurrently to resolve the challenges of counter-dependent behaviors is both frightening and exciting. On one hand, we could blow ourselves up and destroy the human race. On the other hand, we could leap into global cooperation and work collaboratively to solve the many crises facing us.

It has been our experience in traveling in the former Soviet Union (particularly Russia and Ukraine) that a part of the path to our personal enlightenment and evolution lies in nurturing the tendrils of friendship and love that these people are extending to us so trustingly. We see the potential of each "parent" (Mother Russia and Uncle Sam) being able to create a functional family system in their own country and to then bring the process into a relationship between the two countries. We can then begin to teach each other. From them we can learn more about collective initiative and cooperation. We can learn about how to create effective bonding experiences in the families. From us they can learn about individual initiative. Hopefully we can teach them how to help their children learn to separate from their families in healthy ways. In the alchemy between these two great nations somehow lies both the hope and the manifestation of a functional global family.

Chapter Fifteen

HOW WE CREATED A
PARTNERSHIP RELATIONSHIP

"I don't know what your destiny will be, but one thing I know:
the only ones among you who will really be happy are those
who will have sought and found how to serve."

Albert Schweitzer

OUR MEETING (Janae)

Part of my personal transformation was to get back out into
the world again after nineteen years of feeling isolated. Another
part was finding some meaning for my existence. After playing
out my "mousewife" script and finding myself anticipating death,
I knew the last half of my life had to have some spiritual
significance. It was the urges from both of these parts that drew
me to attend the first Mystery School led by Dr. Jean Houston in
1984.

My thirst for freedom and my yearning for spiritual meaning
in my life forced me to take new risks: driving into Chicago, flying
to New York alone, finding my way to a conference center in
upstate New York, mixing with 140 strangers for a year in a new
training program on esoteric topics. The year of 1984 was exciting
for me as I burst out of my cocoon to become a butterfly.

It was half way through the Mystery School that my friend,
Jane, introduced me to Barry. It was three months before we
would meet again, this time on the dance floor as we were doing
free movement during a Mystery School weekend. He accidentally hit me in the chest as we danced past each other. This
"accident" opened up a conversation between us that led to letter
writing and an eventual invitation to visit him in Colorado.

A series of synchronistic events made me sure that indeed I
should take him up on his invitation. Within the space of one day
I had three opportunities (including Barry's invitation) to visit

233

Colorado, convincing me that there must be something important about going to Colorado. When I arrived there for a ten day visit, I found him teaching a class at the university called *The Possible Human* based on Jean Houston's work. I went with him to the class, intending to visit quietly and observe. Part way through the class, however, he pulled up a chair beside himself and motioned for me to join him. I went into shock. I couldn't imagine him wanting a recovering mousewife as a teaching companion, but I took the risk and moved to sit beside him. This vignette became a metaphor for our relationship as it matured. From the very beginning, I felt his strong desire for a partner.

After only four days together with Barry in Colorado, I knew. My heart and soul and mind and spirit spilled over with a deep kind of harmony that I had never known before, but only dreamed of. At that point I was faced with a dilemma. I knew that entering a new relationship so quickly would be a great challenge for me. Moving from Illinois to Colorado meant that I had to leave my support system behind and begin again in a strange place. Those were things that my head said when I thought about my options. When I let my heart speak, however, there was no dilemma. I packed my belongings and headed for Colorado, pulling my U-Haul and my unfinished business behind me.

(Barry)

During the year and a half after Barbara's death and before meeting Janae, I gradually rebuilt my life. Several seemingly unrelated events led me to finally meet Janae.

In the fall of 1983, I attended a week long seminar in Chicago led by Jean Houston. One of the main themes of the seminar was finding the beloved within, which helped me complete another part of my sacred marriage (the marriage of my inner masculine and feminine aspects). Although Janae was at the same work-shop, we did not meet. I did, however, meet one of her friends, Jane.

When I signed up for Jean Houston's Mystery School in New York starting in February, 1984, I did not know that Janae also had signed up. From February until September, 1984, one weekend per month, we both traveled to New York. There seemed to be a veil between us and we only spoke briefly at the June meeting when we were introduced by Jane. When we finally connected, it was so powerful we both acknowledged later we could not have handled it had it occurred any earlier.

On Friday evening of the September weekend, I was doing free-form dancing when I spun around and my arm hit someone (Janae) in the chest. I offered an apology and continued my dancing. The next morning, I saw Janae and apologized again. We hardly spoke to each other again all weekend, but I felt a strong attraction to her. So, on Sunday afternoon as we were preparing to leave, I walked up to Janae and gave her a hug and told her I was attracted to her. I said, "I would like to get to know you better and since these weekends are so full of activity is there any chance you might be coming to Colorado any time soon?" She responded cautiously, "No, but you never know about these things."

On the plane trip back to Colorado that evening, I reflected on my uncharacteristic boldness. I decided to write Janae a letter telling her that since Barbara's death, I was in a "go for it" mode and I was willing to take more risks and say what was on my mind. Fortunately, I received a reply to my letter in a week, telling me she was coming to Colorado the next month to do a vision quest and wanted to spend some time with me.

She had planned to spend ten days in Colorado in October, and after four days together we decided to get married. What I experienced was an unbelievable connection between our physical, emotional, intellectual and spiritual bodies that was undeniable. We made plans for Janae to move to Colorado in November and planned to get married at Thanksgiving. In retrospect, we realize how shocked our families and friends were, but to us there was no doubt in our minds and our hearts. This is how we began our incredible journey together.

IDENTIFYING OUR UNFINISHED BUSINESS

(Janae)

Had I known when we met about my unfinished business, unmet developmental needs and life drama, our early days together would have been much easier. So we started from where we were with the tools we had and moved toward our mutual dream of partnership. We didn't know that we would use our journey to create a map for other individuals and couples on their journeys to wholeness and partnership.

235

Much of the first year we spent bonding with each other. Sometimes this was easy for me and sometimes it was difficult. When intimacy involved peak experiences, I did fine. When intimacy involved getting in touch with old feelings, I didn't do so well. With my history of my mother and first husband's emotionally unavailability, I had difficulty in believing that Barry was really present for me and for our relationship. Many times when I got into the old feelings, I felt an overwhelming urge to run away. Sometimes my counter-dependent urges would win out. Several times I got out of bed in the middle of some conflict to go sleep in another room. In these instances I felt tremendous confusion about my conflicting needs for getting through the old feelings and my fear of going deeper into them. I really wanted to heal my pattern of loss and abandonment and get my bonding needs met. Struggling with this conflict has been some of the most difficult work I have ever done.

Barry's earlier reparenting therapy became a guide for helping me heal my early bonding breaks. The fact that he had repaired so much of his own early childhood traumas made it possible for him to be more available for me. He held me a lot and was sensitive to my fears when I wanted to escape. He served as a solid base that I came to count on, helping me to develop trust and a sense of safety. Gradually I surrendered more and more of my inner self to the relationship, risking that I might be hurt again. And sometimes I was. This time, however, I had someone with whom I could work through the hurt.

We had been married five months when I began my first separation process with Barry. I entered a doctoral program that required a ten-day residency in Virginia. While those were some of the longest days of my life, I also found myself stretching out into the world again. I loved mixing with the diverse group of people who appeared as fellow new learners from all over the country and the world. I could feel myself stepping into an identity that allowed for an expansion of vision, of experience, of possibilities.

I found myself going back and forth between Barry and my newly found world and, like a two-year-old, having a love affair with both. This became a pattern of growth for me. The more bonded I became to Barry, the easier it became to go out and explore the world. As a result of this process, I gradually began to develop both personal and professional object constancy. I felt more secure in my relationship with Barry and I felt more confident in my growth as a therapist and teacher.

Many times Barry played the "good parent" that I never had. This required that we keep the transforming work we did between us in a context separate from our love relationship. I didn't want to become another "daddy's girl" and he didn't want a child as a wife. Keeping these two dimensions of our relationship separate helped us both define more clearly who we were and what we wanted. The vision between us was always "partnership." By the time we had been married a year, we had established a strong foundation of safety and security between us. Little did I know how this foundation would be tested in the years to ahead.

(Barry)

When we got married, I knew I still had lots of unfinished grieving to do over Barbara's death. I felt a bit ashamed about this at first, but Janae gave me permission to talk openly about my loss and was willing to hold me and comfort me as long as I needed it. This provided me with an important opportunity for bonding with Janae, as I allowed myself to openly grieve with her. Barbara's death had also brought aspects of my early traumas to the surface. I felt abandonment and loss from my early bonding break at six weeks. Janae was helping me break free of both the adult grief and the childhood grief that I had never expressed fully.

Our relationship grew very close during our first three months together. I found out that the letting go and surrendering I had learned to do near the end of my relationship with Barbara had stayed with me. I found it relatively easy to take back my projections and to receive Janae without resistance.

We have had our share of fights, but we knew how to get through them very quickly, usually in an hour or less. We made a commitment to resolve all conflicts that occurred between us from a win-win place. We don't put conflicts aside even if they occur at an inconvenient time.

We also made a strong commitment to help each other heal our wounds and complete the unfinished business we each brought to the relationship. This commitment has helped us experience more intimacy than I ever thought possible.

We both agreed that we wanted a partnership relationship and a partnership lifestyle. We agreed to live, work and play together and are with each other sometimes for days at a time,

237

although we also enjoy taking time by ourselves or with others. We feel free to act (consciously) co-dependent, counter-dependent, independent and interdependent with each other. When we seem to want different things or have different needs, we are secure enough as individuals to resolve any conflicts and get what we want or need.

HEALING OUR LIFE DRAMAS

(Janae)

During the winter semester of 1986 Barry took a sabbatical leave from his teaching at the university. We had decided to go to Switzerland for six months to live and study. The plan was that Barry would write a book, I would write part of my dissertation and together we would study with a Jungian analyst there. We both were attracted to this analyst and to his innovative approach to therapy. The foundation of his theory seemed quite similar to the self-directed, process-oriented approach of my doctoral program at the Union Graduate School, so I anticipated the two blending quite well.

During the six months of intermittent training and therapy with this analyst and his group, we attended many classes and workshops. Our last training activity was a six-week-long training intensive in his approach. I anticipated that during this intensive I would be able to learn this approach in a self-directed way. My research in learning styles told me that everyone learns in his or her own unique way. By this time I knew quite a bit about my own learning style and saw this training as a place where I could learn naturally.

By the time we were halfway through the intensive, it was clear that I seemed to be the only one who valued my way of learning. At that time the classes were taught in a highly traditional European manner, with the teachers lecturing and structuring the classes in very traditional ways. This did not work for me, for I needed more personal involvement in my learning. I preferred more discussion, experimentation, and activity-oriented methods that supported my way of learning. The more that I tried to bring in my needs and learn in my own way, the more that I met resistance, especially from the male teachers. The more I spoke out in class to get my needs met, the more *resistance* I met. I eventually found myself engaged in a power struggle which I would not win.

238

One morning I went into class and asked for time to talk with the group. I told them that I was leaving the class to go and study on my own because I could not get my needs met in this class. I received a lot of judgments from the teacher about my leaving, as he made the problem seem all mine. I also proceeded to drop out of all other classes where I was not permitted to follow my own process as a learner. The ensuing free time I used for independent study and a tutorial with one of the advanced female students, who taught in a way that was compatible with my learning style.

While this action on my part took care of meeting my learning needs, it also triggered off something deep and dark inside of me. I began to feel the ostracism of the other students who seemed to have no trouble learning in this traditional atmosphere. None of them seemed to want to examine the learning environment to see if it really served them. Mostly they seemed to identify me as the only thing wrong in the system. I felt as though I had been shot down by them. My killer pattern had returned.

I began to feel intense pain, grief, sadness, despair and death move over me. Little by little I fell into an intense state of depression in which there seemed to be no bottom. I just kept falling, falling. Deeper and deeper I went inside. Barry got frightened when I would say that I felt like I was dying, as it stirred up his old feelings about Barbara's death. Several times I lay down on our bed and closed my eyes and surrendered myself to death. Each time I descended into a deep state where I had only my own inner resources.

Here in isolation, I was forced to feel the pain of my early abandonments that were at the core of my trauma drama, along with all the layers that surrounded it. My suffering, now substantial, required that I experience the truth of these events. I could no longer just act counter-dependent, deny my feelings and armor myself to look good. I felt like an uncooked egg that had been dropped on the floor, scattering my insides in a puddle.

At this point the pain was so intense that I looked for another way of dealing with it. I had already surrendered myself to death and found myself still alive. The only other option I could find was to "go crazy." I remember the day when the pain became unbearable and I decided I would find a place deep inside myself where the pain couldn't follow. My body began to feel more and more stiff. My eyes started glazing over and I stopped responding to people. I had decided to become catatonic.

At the end of that day's classes, Barry and I headed to our car. He led me gently, seeing my pain and catatonia and not knowing what to do. Just as he opened the car door to help me in, I looked down the road. There I saw our good friend, Adam, from Hawaii, whistling his way towards us. In that moment, he appeared as an angel to me. He was the only person I knew who was not involved in our intensive training and not coping with these challenges.

When Adam saw my pain and got brief input from Barry about what I was experiencing there, he quickly responded as an ally. He went back to our apartment with us and spent the evening just sitting with us. In his quiet way he supported our feelings and helped validate our experience. He helped me reach out again. After a couple of days, I began to regain my equilibrium.

In the next weeks I began piecing myself together again. I felt quite fragile and sometimes disoriented. I still have some of the dyslexia that appeared at that time. After we returned from Switzerland I completed my doctoral dissertation, we built a new home and created our institute. These external creations helped me to restructure my inner world as well. After this breakdown I found that my brain worked much better, my thinking capacities increased markedly and my sense of personal power surged.

It took me several years to identify this experience as an "Inner Child Breakdown" and to understand how the group in Switzerland had helped me replay my family of origin trauma. As I healed this old trauma, I began to draw clients who had similar processes. With my own experience as a resource and reference, I found I was able to present their experiences in a supportive way that helped them not feel so frightened or crazy. I found descriptions of experiences similar to mine in Native American writings on the shamanic experience, particularly the Death Walk of Don Juan in the Castenada books. I also began to correlate this kind of breakdown with traumatic breaks in early childhood bonding. With a larger frame of reference about such breakdowns and my own experience in helping both myself and clients through them, I began to understand how important this process was for me.

In retrospect, I can see this experience took me into a place of my own depths that I now recognize as a place of strength. In this void I have learned to access some deeper part of myself that provides wisdom, guidance and grounding, a place where I can shed old, used-up parts of myself. I know this place of "inner death" now as a source of renewal and transformation. It is a place where I can find my own deepest nature and give it voice, as I
240

continually weave and reweave myself. This experience was my first real knowing of myself, of my own deep feminine.

My experience in Switzerland also really helped me understand how the universe operates as a large, interactive system. I was able to understand even in the middle of my breakdown how my experience with the group was bringing up an unresolved family conflict. Using a systems approach really supported my gaining an understanding of how the inner world and the outer world are always in relationship, helping to create each other. When the reactor at Chernobyl exploded and Americans flew in the night to bomb Libya, I began to see the world as a dysfunctional family. Barry and I decided we must become part of the solution to global conflict when we returned to Colorado.

(Barry)

As we got closer to each other, I found myself dealing with new and unexpected issues related to my life drama. After getting married in late November, we went to Greece and Egypt on our honeymoon in January with a group of our Mystery School friends led by Jean Houston. This was an intense experience for both of us that seemed to bring us even closer together on spiritual levels. When we returned, we also participated in a five-day Native American dance ritual that opened us up even more spiritually.

Late that spring, I began to feel ill. I experienced low energy and pain in my left side. I finally went to the doctor and found out I had the early stage of colon cancer. I was totally shocked and terrified. To me, cancer meant death, a slow horrible death.

As I began to recover from the shock and looked at my treatment options, I was determined to get to the source of the problem using a body-mind approach. With Janae's support, I selected to start with the most noninvasive physical treatment I could locate. This meant drastic changes in diet and nutritional balancing were first. Next, I began to work on the unfinished business related to the cancer. Because cancer was on the left side, at the top of the descending colon, I looked at the feminine side of my unfinished business. (The left side of the body is often associated with the feminine and the right side with the masculine.) Several contributing factors were immediately apparent.

I was under tremendous stress at the university because I was appointed as the faculty advocate for a female junior colleague who was applying for reappointment. What I encountered in the

241

process of meeting with various personnel committees and administrators was that they were "killing" the feminine aspects of faculty members. The only things they wanted to focus on were the number of publications this female colleague had published, the quality of her publications and what line of research she had developed in the less than three years she had been at the university. No one was interested in the fact that she was a single parent who had to spend lots of time with two very sick children during her first two years at the university. Also, no one was interested in the fact that she was hired at a salary below most male assistant professors and she had to teach extra classes to provide for her family. No one was interested in knowing that she received almost no mentoring from any senior colleagues about what she needed to do to prepare for her personnel review. When all my attempts to present a balanced perspective fell on the deaf ears of my colleagues, who were sitting in judgment on this case, I finally began to understand. The university system that I am a part of is designed to kill the feminine aspects of its faculty members. It was killing me as much as it would try to kill anyone who attempted to be a whole person.

I immediately resigned as chairperson of my department and put off resigning from the university, until after my upcoming sabbatical leave in Switzerland. I knew if I didn't get to the bottom of this problem that my resignation was inevitable.

I worked further with the theme of the "killer of the feminine" to see where else that was true for me as I was growing up. Certainly I never felt any support for my feminine qualities. They were either killed or put down. I loved to read, to write poetry, to listen to classical music, and none of that seemed of value in my culture. In order to be "one of the boys" in junior high school, I pretended not to study or be interested in reading books. Instead, I became a jock and played basketball and baseball in high school so I could "belong." All my adult life I had been fighting to recover my feminine side. After Barbara's death I worked very hard to reclaim it, only to find people trying to kill it again.

I had seen that Barbara's death symbolized the killing of my feminine ideal that I had projected on her. At this point I began to wonder if I had really taken that back completely. Finally, I did some more therapeutic work to uncover the source of this illness and what I found blew my mind.

In my daily meditations, I began to get images of being killed by someone stabbing me with a long spear in my left side. The

242

more I worked with these images, the more I realized that they were not from this lifetime. They were Egyptian in nature and eventually, in a waking dream, the whole story came to me.

Janae and I were part of an Egyptian Mystery School and I had threatened the power structure of this school because I wanted to integrate the feminine and masculine aspects of the teachings. Specifically, I wanted to have more attention placed on the earth and its shadow aspects, while those in power wanted the school to focus on the transcendent qualities of the light and away from the dark side of human beings. I wanted a balance between these two and apparently they decided I was dangerous and had to be killed. Janae (a man in that lifetime) was selected to be my killer. What to do with this awareness would soon become apparent.

In early July, 1985, we went to California to attend a week-long therapy workshop with the Jungian analyst that we were planning to study with in Switzerland that following January. By the end of the second day, I decided to work on this issue in the group and asked this therapist to help. He suggested a psycho-drama so I could reenact the death scene and learn what wasn't finished that I still might be trying to finish with the cancer.

I reenacted the whole scene with Janae stabbing me in slow motion with a fireplace poker. When she pressed the poker against my side where the colon cancer was, I fell to the floor and screamed in agony. I reexperienced the physical and emotional pain of being betrayed and abandoned by my friends and loved ones. The pain subsided after awhile, only to be replaced by intense anger and rage. I raged on the floor while eight or ten people held me down to protect me from hurting myself or others.

When this subsided, I got up and faced Janae. I knew there was something else to finish with her. I grabbed her and we began to wrestle. I felt as if I were fighting for every man that had every been betrayed and abandoned by a woman, and later Janae confided that she felt she was fighting for every woman who had been attacked by a man. It was an intense struggle between two strong opponents. Finally, I wrestled her to the ground and ended up sitting on top of her. She looked up at me and said, "Aren't you getting lonely up there?" Obviously I was, because all the energy immediately went out of the fight for me. I rolled off of her and I knew what I really wanted was full partnership with Janae. We ended our battle of the sexes that July day in California.

I still wasn't out of the woods with the cancer. With additional psychological and nutritional work, however, my cancer went into

243

remission and I was symptom-free by August, 1985. In the seven years since then I have continued a vegetarian diet and taken various nutritional supplements and kept myself from being overstressed.

In July, 1989, after one of my periodic checkups, my nutritionist said to me, "I have some good news and some bad news for you." I said, "Give me the good news first." She said, "The good news is that your body is perfectly balanced nutritionally and the bad news is that you will have to devote almost two hours a day of spiritual work to keep it balanced." What she was referring to was prayer, meditation, yoga and just taking time to be with myself and do unto myself. She said that she believed my next challenge was that I would need to focus on taking care of myself for a minimum of two hours a day.

My first thoughts were on how easy and nice that would be for me. What I found out in the ensuing months was that this was the most difficult prescription I ever had to fill. It brought me up against my deepest beliefs about not being worthy of two hours a day devoted to myself. Now, after three years of dealing with these issues, I still can only report success about sixty to seventy percent of the time. My oldest program of taking care of others first really is hard to shake. I am confident that I will soon reach and maintain my two-hour goal on a consistent basis.

INTEGRATING OUR NEW LEARNINGS (Barry and Janae)

Our time in Switzerland brought profound changes for us. Besides having our world view expanded greatly, we were "nuked" while walking the streets of Zurich after Chernobyl's explosion. We were also assaulted by Europeans' anti-American pronouncements after the bombing of Libya.

We returned from Switzerland even more convinced that we needed to become more a part of the solution than a part of the problem. We built an ecologically sound, passive solar, earth sheltered home and turned our efforts to finding new and active tools for resolving conflicts at all levels. We founded a nonprofit, tax exempt institute called the Colorado Institute for Conflict Resolution and Creative Leadership (CICRCL) and organized two international conferences devoted to the premise, "What would happen if peace broke out?" The events of the past year in Eastern Europe and the Soviet Union are but the first wave of the outbreak of peace on earth.

244

We began to make plans to expand our institute and develop extensive programs when we were again faced with another important lesson. Because of our energy and some old needs to caretake others, we inadvertently created a co-dependent organization that was doomed to failure. It was after the collapse of our co-dependent organization that we saw how our own unfinished business from our families of origin helped create a dysfunctional organization. The unfinished business was now in an organization and outside of us, and it was so big that we could finally see it. That was when we decided to write a book about our personal and professional experiences of treating co-dependent behavior. This book, *Breaking Free of the Co-dependency Trap*, examined the personal and cultural roots of co-dependent behaviors.

While we learned a lot from our experience in co-dependent relationships with CICRCL, we were not through. We had yet another similar experience to encounter. After our co-dependency lesson, we were very cautious about getting into similar situations. However, one began to develop right under our noses. In our local conflict resolution workshops and our training groups, the theme of "family" began to emerge. A number of people began to create a family support system which eventually became the Family Training Center and a related support network. Again, we ventured out by working to create a joint therapy practice with a group of these people. Again, a very similar result occurred. Some people in the group began to want us to behave co-dependently . They wanted us to set up the Center and to refer clients to them. When we saw what was happening and refused to allow this, they became angry at us and left.

This brought up lots of counter-dependant reactions for everybody and before very long the whole project had to be tabled. We saw in retrospect that we were being seen as "good mother" and "good father" as long as they thought we were providing everything to get the Center started. When they found out about the partnership aspects of the business arrangements, they withdrew and we became "bad mother" and "bad father."

We invited each person to come and talk with us about his or her feelings in order to resolve anything that was unfinished. At this time we still had not identified the concepts of trauma drama and we did not have all the tools we now have. Several people in the group chose to resolve the conflict from a win-win place. Several others decided to remain angry at us and refused our invitation to work things out. Since the invitation was open-ended, perhaps they still will decide to do this. We understood people's attempts to complete their emotional separation, but we were unable to help them get through it in some cases.

Perhaps the real purpose of trying to create the Center was to help everyone move closer to emotional separateness. Some of those involved took big steps toward completing their separation process. We learned how difficult it is to help facilitate this separation process with a group of people when we are in the middle of it. I learned more about how I might provide positive emotional support to a group people who are trying to change their co-dependent and counter-dependent patterns.

THE RETURN TO PARADISE

(Janae)

In the winter of 1990 a friend brought me a wonderful book, *Memories and Visions of Paradise* (Heinberg, 1989). As I read Heinberg's cross-cultural review of paradise myths, the whole concept of paradise began to fascinate me. At one point I began to see that earth did not change when I felt paradise slipping away from me at the point of my early traumas and the ensuing life drama. Only my internal reality changed. This flash of awareness helped me see that the way back to paradise was to again change my inner reality.

I began to see each day as a new day in paradise. I began to trust the flow of life and the cycles of death as part of the larger process. I began to tap into deeper realities of my beingness by spending more time in nature. I also began to really believe my relationship with Barry was real and long-lasting. I noticed how my fears of intimacy had been replaced with a joyous attitude of discovery about his unknownness. The frequent sparks of conflict from unfinished business began to quiet down into a deep glow of warmth and relatedness that feels so good in my body that I know I really have returned to paradise.

It is wonderful to find a partner who is always right there with me, challenging me to new heights and depths that require us to live in a constant state of renewal in our relationship. Sometimes we find we have to reintroduce ourselves to each other, reassemble the relationship and begin again. This now happens in such a natural and spontaneous way that it provides a nice even flow, without the extreme peaks and valleys of earlier days. My biggest challenge these days is in being able to receive paradise.

(Barry)

Over the past six months or more I have had an increasing awareness of returning to paradise again. Finally, I feel that Janae and I are equal partners in all the important areas of our lives. We have a deepening spiritual connection that we feel on a daily basis. I can experience long periods of intimacy with Janae now, without being afraid I will lose myself or be consumed by her. My boundaries are clear and I can set limits with her if I need to and I know she will respect them. I no longer feel I have to take care of her in any way. I know she is fully capable of taking care of herself and, most importantly, my worth as a person does not depend on taking care of anyone except myself.

I feel a tremendous sense of personal freedom to be who I want to be and do what I want to do. Through my spiritual practices of prayer, meditation and yoga, I keep in daily contact with the flow of my inner life. I use reflective thinking, perception checks, visioning, asking for what I want and need, setting my boundaries and conflict resolution skills to help me stay in daily contact with the flow of my inner life.

Being in relationship with Janae brings me another dimension of paradise. There is such a flow of creative energy between us that it seems like making love almost all of the time. We inspire each other and support each other in our separate endeavors and we embrace each other when we are working together. In spite of this wonderful flow between us, there is still a sense of mystery and discovery in our relationship. We use the relationship to continue to open up new and unknown aspects of ourselves and share them with each other. In that sense, our relationship serves as a holy garden made of fertile ground where we can nurture new and emerging aspects of ourselves. We are constantly surprised by the newness and freshness we feel. Just when we think we are becoming "old married folks" we find a new and unexplored dimension of ourselves to explore in relationship with each other. This may not be everybody's vision of paradise, but it sure is mine and I am certainly enjoying it.

BIBLIOGRAPHY

Alsop, R. 1988. "Drug and Alcohol Clinics for Patients, " *New York Times.* November 14, B1.

Andresen, Gail, and Barry Weinhold. 1981. *Connective Bargaining: Communicating about Sex.* Englewood Cliffs, NJ: Prentice-Hall.

Armstrong, Louise. 1983. *The Home Front.* St. Louis: McGraw-Hall Book Company.

Bateson, Gregory. 1972. *Steps to an Ecology of Mind.* New York: Ballantine Books.

Berne, Eric. 1961. *Games People Play.* New York: Grove Press.

Bly, Robert. 1989. "Your Spiritual Shadow," *Magical Blend.* July, 23:10-23; 96.

Bolton, Robert. 1979. *People Skills.* New York: Simon & Schuster, Inc.

Bowlby, John. 1969 and 1973. *Attachments and Loss,* Vols. I & II. New York: Basic Books.

Bradshaw, John. 1988. *Healing the Shame That Binds You.* Deerfield Beach, FL: Health Communications, Inc.

_____ 1990. *Homecoming: Reclaiming and Championing Your Inner Child.* New York: Bantam Books.

Brown, Lester, et al. 1988. *State of the World.* New York: W. W. Norton and Co.

Carnes, Patrick. 1989. *Contrary to Love.* Minneapolis: CompCare Publishers.

Clarke, Jean. 1989. *Growing Up Again: Parenting Ourselves, Parenting Our Children.* Center City, MN: Hazelden.

Eisler, Riane. 1987. *The Chalice & The Blade.* San Francisco: Harper and Row.

Erikson, Erik. 1963. *Childhood and Society.* New York: W. W. Norton.

Forward, Susan, and Craig Buck. 1978. *Betrayal of Innocence.* New York: Penguin Books.

Grinspoon, L., and J. B. Bakalar. 1985. *Cocaine: A Drug and Its Social Evolution.* New York: Basic Books.

Grof, Stanislav. 1976. *Realms of the Human Unconsciousness.* New York: E. P. Dutton.

Havinghurst, Robert. 1972. *Developmental Tasks and Education*. New York: David McKay.

Heinberg, Richard. 1989. *Memories and Visions of Paradise*. Los Angeles: Jeremy P. Tarcher, Inc.

Hoeller, Stephan A. 1982. *The Gnostic Jung*. Wheaton, IL: Quest Books.

Johnson, Stephen. 1985. *Characterological Transformation*. New York: W. W. Norton & Company.

_____. 1987. *Humanizing the Narcissistic Style*. New York: W. W. Norton & Company.

Kaplan, Louise. 1978. *Oneness and Separateness*. New York: Simon and Schuster.

Karpman, Steven. 1968. "Fairytales and Script Drama Analysis," *Transactional Analysis Bulletin*, 7:39-43.

Kreisman, Jerold, and Hal Straus. 1989. *I Hate You - Don't Leave Me*. Los Angeles, CA: The Body Press.

Maeder, Thomas. 1989. "Wounded Healers," *Atlantic Monthly*. January, 37-47.

Mahler, Margaret. 1968. *On Human Symbiosis and the Vicissitudes of Individuation*. New York: International University Press.

Masterson, James. 1988. *The Search for the Real Self*. New York: The Free Press.

Miller, Alice. 1981. *Prisoners of Childhood*. New York: Basic Books, Inc.

_____. 1984. *For Your Own Good*. New York: Farrar, Straus & Giroux.

_____. 1986. *Thou Shalt Not Be Aware*. New York: Meridian Books.

_____. 1991. *Breaking Down the Walls of Silence*. New York: Dutton.

Mindell, Arnold. 1985. *River's Way*. Boston: Rutledge & Kegan Paul.

Padov, Saul K., ed. 1939. *Thomas Jefferson on Democracy*. New York: New American Library.

Paul, Jordon, and Margaret Paul. 1989. *From Conflict to Caring*. Minneapolis: CompCare Publishers.

Peck, M. Scott. 1987. *The Different Drum*. New York: Simon and Schuster.

Peele, Stanton. 1989. *Diseasing of America*. Lexington, MA: Lexington Books.

Piaget, Jean. 1951. *The Child's Conception of the World*. New York: Humanities Press.

Rogers, Carl. 1961. *On Becoming a Person*. Boston: Houghton Mifflin Co.

Rosenberg, Jack. 1985. *Body, Self and Soul*. Atlanta: Humanics Limited.

Satir, Virginia M. 1972. *Peoplemaking*. Palo Alto, CA: Science & Behavior Books.

Schaef, Ann Wilson. 1987. *When Society Becomes An Addict*. New York: Harper & Row.

Strau, Murray, et al. 1980. *Behind Closed Doors: Violence in the American Family*. New York: Anchor Press.

Vailiant, G.E. 1983. *The Natural History of Alcoholism*. Cambridge, MA: Harvard University Press.

Verny, Thomas. 1981. *The Secret Life of the Unborn Child*. New York: Delta Books.

Verny, Thomas, and Pamela Weintraub. 1991. *Nurturing the Unborn Child*. New York: Delacorte Press.

Weinhold, Barry. 1988. *Playing Grown-up Is Serious Business: Breaking Free of Addictive Family Patterns*. Walpole, NH: Stillpoint Publishing.

Weinhold, Barry, and Janae Weinhold. 1989. *Breaking Free of the Co-dependency Trap*. Walpole, NH: Stillpoint Publishing.

Weinhold, Barry. 1991. *Breaking Free of Addictive Family Relationships*. Walpole, NH: Stillpoint Publishing.

Weinhold, Barry, and Gay Hendricks. 1992. *Counseling and Psychotherapy: A Transpersonal Approach*. Denver: Love Publishing.

Weisner, C.M., and R. Room. 1984. " Financing and Ideology in Alcohol Treatment," *Social Problems*. 32: 167-84.

Wills-Brandon, Carla. 1989. *Eat Like a Lady: Guide for Overcoming Bulimia*. Deerfield Beach, FL: Health Communications.

_____. 1989. *Is It Love or Is It Sex?* Deerfield Beach, FL: Health Communications, Inc.

Woodman, Marion. 1982. *Addiction to Perfection*. Toronto: Inner City Books.